REPRODUCING THE WOMB

REPRODUCING THE WOMB

Images of Childbirth in
Science, Feminist Theory, and Literature

ALICE E. ADAMS

CORNELL UNIVERSITY PRESS   ITHACA & LONDON

First published 1994 by Cornell University Press.

Excerpts from "The Birth" by William Carlos Williams from *The Doctor Stories*.
Copyright © 1962 by William Carlos Williams. Reprinted by permission of New
Directions Publishing Corp., New York, and Carcanet Press Ltd., Manchester,
England.

Printed in the United States of America

⊗ The paper in this book meets the minimum requirements of the American
National Standard for Information Sciences–Permanence of Paper for Printed
Library Materials, ANSI Z39.48-1984.

Library of Congress Cataloging-in-Publication Data

Adams, Alice E. (Alice Elaine), 1957–
    Reproducing the womb : images of childbirth in science, feminist theory, and
literature / Alice E. Adams.
        p.   cm.
    Includes bibliographical references and index.
    ISBN 0-8014-2945-5 (alk. paper). — ISBN 0-8014-8161-9 (paper: alk. paper)
    1. Childbirth in literature.   2. Feminism and literature.   I. Title.
PN56.C49A23   1994
809'.93352042—dc20   93-46282

FOR NICOLE
who made it all possible

Contents

Preface

We are in the middle of a revolution in reproductive technologies. There is no moment in women's reproductive lives that cannot be affected by medical intervention. Every decision we make about contraception, conception, pregnancy, birth, and its aftermath is potentially subject to medical and legal control, but that control is not leading us into a more deterministic reproductive universe. Technologies intended to monitor and direct events in our reproductive lives can bring about changes—in our bodies and in the medical and judicial systems—that reproductive researchers cannot predict. Technologies that merge with our bodies proliferate more quickly than our ability to reconcile ourselves, emotionally, intellectually, and ethically, to our own cybernetically transformed bodies and minds. As we rush toward (or are dragged into) a future of ever-increasing indeterminacy, we can gain a degree of power only by making concerted efforts to resist exploitative reproductive practices and philosophies. But equally important, we must learn how to use reproductive technologies to help create a livable future. My strongest hope for this book is that it will contribute to a wide-ranging, energetic debate about the construction of that future. With that purpose in mind, I explore diverse areas of cultural expression, including literary and psychoanalytic theory, women's poetry and fiction, medical writings, feminist theories of mothering, and feminist speculative fiction.

I begin by reconsidering psychoanalytic models of the processes of identity formation and transformation and their relation to women's writings about birth. In Part I, "The Mirror of Birth," I examine Jacques Lacan's male-centered account of the origins of language and develop an alternative "story" about the problems and potential benefits of constructing the self as internally fragmented and contingent on social processes. In Part II, "The Mother-State," I examine stories about the revolutionary potential of a reconstructed maternal self, elaborating one implication of Adrienne Rich's vision, that women's reclamation of their bodies, and, by extension, of their bodily and emotional connections to other women, might produce a new world. "Wholeness" in this vision is no longer restricted to the individual woman; it is a state shared among women. But although the idea of a maternal collective holds out a utopian promise to some, it represents an unthinkable nightmare to others. In this section, I demonstrate that "matrophobia"—fear of the mother—informs representations of the voracious maternal collective. Matrophobia influences literary visions of communist dystopias, but it also affects other discourses, including psychoanalysis and medicine.

In Part III, "Framing the Fetal Portrait," I interpret permutations of (and defenses against) the monstrous all-consuming mother in obstetrics and fetology. Images of whole, fragmented, and collective selves permeate visual and textual representations of the mother-fetus relationship: many representations insistently portray the fetus as fully separated and autonomous, with the fragmented image of the maternal body functioning as environment, and yet the excluded third term, the mother-child collective, continues to haunt obstetric representations. In Part IV, "Reproducing Postpatriarchal History," I examine the intimate connections and conflicts between the individual and the collective, the fetus and the mother, expressed in women's speculative fiction and in feminist theory. Feminist writers of speculative fiction were hard at work in the 1970s imagining what kind of society might result if women changed the balance of power and seized the means of reproduction. Writers such as Joanna Russ and Suzy McKee Charnas envisioned utopias that would foster a sense of shared history and solidarity among women, but they avoided reproducing sentimental expressions of maternal sacrifice or mother-daughter unity.

Throughout *Reproducing the Womb*, I've included my own experience and family history wherever I thought these stories would clarify my perspective or illuminate a point of theory. These stories were told to me so often when I was a child that they became the gospel on what it meant to be a woman. Many years ago I began to question the stories my mother and grandmother had told me, but they are the root of my fascination with women's experiences and representations of their bodies and minds. I do not, however, believe that these stories embrace a more authentic truth than the fictions I examine. No story, even an autobiographical account, captures the "real" experience of childbirth. Women's writings about birth do not reveal a common or universal experience, but they often demonstrate a dazzling ability to interweave memory, fantasy, theory, myth, ideology, and science, and they may show us a way to turn the reproductive revolution to women's advantage.

Throughout the early stages of my work on this project, I benefited from Kate Hayles's intellectual acuity, encouragement, and humor. Brooks Landon, Mary Lou Emery, and Tom Lutz offered me incisive comments. My thanks to Susan Johnson, M.D., and Susan Sipes, M.D., both at the University of Iowa Hospitals and Clinics, for sharing their expertise in obstetric medicine. Over the years, Florence Boos offered an incomparable model of intellectual and personal integrity. Many others contributed. Friends and colleagues, including Yvonne Rauch, Ruth Smalley, Tsuey Fen Lee, Pamela Bourjaily, and Debra Hartley shared the work, exasperation, and laughter of the writing process. Fran Dolan, Laura Mandel, and Kate McCullough offered their editorial prowess and encouragement at crucial moments. I thank dear friends and family members, my parents Ken and Dorothy Smith, Paul Mandelbaum, and Rachelle Selzer, for listening and for believing in me. My daughter, Nicole Daya, deserves my greatest thanks, for teaching me how to mother, for enduring with grace and humor life with an academic, and for helping me to remember that there is more to life than writing.

I am grateful for the support I received from the University of Iowa in the form of the Ada Louise Ballard Dissertation Fellowship, and from the Rockefeller Foundation in the form of a Rockefeller Post-Doctoral Fellowship. Colleagues and staff at the Center for Advanced Feminist Studies at the University of Minnesota have been extremely generous with their support. I thank in particular Shirley Garner for her advice and Carol Mason for her boundless energy and patience with the practical matters of producing the manuscript. Finally, for a grant to cover the cost of index preparation, I thank Miami University.

Portions of several chapters were originally published as "Out of the Womb" in *Feminist Studies* 19 (Summer 1993) and are reprinted here, in revised versions, by permission of the publisher, *Feminist Studies*, Inc., c/o Women's Studies Program, University of Maryland, College Park, Md. 20742.

ALICE E. ADAMS

Oxford, Ohio

I The Mirror of Birth

I lie here now as I once lay
in the crook of her arm, her creature,
and I feel her looking down into me the way the
maker of a sword gazes at his face in the
steel of the blade.

—Sharon Olds, "Why My Mother Made Me"

Origin Stories

Most of us don't remember our births. But according to Arthur Janov, father of the primal scream, we hold those memories whole and pure in our unconscious: "The miracle of it all is that the exact picture of the original, traumatic birth scene is held in storage. It is the exact birth scene which, when repressed, results in all the ailments, fears and illnesses." The birth scene has to be "decoded," but it loses nothing in the translation. Only by precisely retracing, in reverse, the "birth trauma" can one undo the "Pain" it caused. Janov stakes his claim for the authenticity of "birthing primals" on the assumption that "memories are concrete realities."[1] These realities cannot be conveyed in words. They are sensations "imprinted" on the brain and body. As "imprints," birth sensations are not subject to the transformations that conscious memories undergo as time passes. In Janov's argument, the perinatal infant's aphasia and the adult's amnesia testify to the credibility of primal birth therapy. It is precisely because we can never recall birth memories through language that those memories do not deteriorate or alter in any way as we grow up.

1. Arthur Janov, *Imprints: The Lifelong Effects of the Birth Experience* (New York: Coward-McCann, 1983), pp. 237, 239.

Janov's insistence on the purity of preverbal memory is more than a way of establishing credibility for a controversial therapy. It is also an expression of one of the most important themes in writing about fetal and infant development. Advice books to mothers urge them to identify with their infants; Frederick Leboyer, for instance, wants mothers to "become this new person."[2] The fetus in the discourses of obstetrics and fetology is often a quintessential human being whose raw, unfiltered experience inspires awe. I have no faith that an "authentic" identification with the fetus or the newly born infant is possible. My adult body and mind, and the thirty-five years that have passed since my birth, intervene between me and the fetus I once was. My "memories" of birth are built from stories I heard as a child. They are constructions, not replications, of my origins. Though an original experience, precisely recalled, appeals to the empiricist code, a constructed memory has no such authority. If the event didn't "actually" happen as I feel it or tell it now, my remembering has produced fiction, a lie.

When I was seven or eight my grandmother told me that my mother had almost died of an infection within a few days of my birth. I was shocked. Grandmother talked on about my mother's high fever, her initial refusal to leave me, the rush to the hospital, her body being packed in ice, and the operation that followed. The images Grandmother called up were almost beyond my power to envision. A storm of terror and guilt blew through me. The thought that I had made my mother suffer, that I had, without even knowing it, almost killed the one person I most needed, made my stomach churn and, later, gave me recurring nightmares. But the story proved to be a gift as well as a burden. I saw my mother as a hero who had risked her own life to get me started. This impression deepened when I asked her about the story and, rather than waxing dramatic as my grandmother had, Mom brushed the whole thing aside as a minor event.

The story my grandmother told does not replicate "the actual birth experience," as Janov puts it, but it has another kind of authority. I knew, hearing that story, how thoroughly my life was tied to

2. Frederick Leboyer, *Birth Without Violence* (New York: Alfred A. Knopf, 1975), p. 42.

my mother's. I learned (and have since tried to unlearn) that becoming a woman meant being always ready to sacrifice. My memories and interpretations of this story evolve constantly. Whatever "imprints" my first days left on my body and brain have long since become braided into the sensations and impressions of my life since then.

Much American feminist writing in the last decade has asserted that women's experiences of their bodies are always *mediated* by their interactions with institutions and discourses. Often, however, the idea of a culturally mediated body is undermined by the parallel suggestion that the material body has, or could have, an existence independent of culture and society. Barbara Katz Rothman, for instance, says that when a pregnant woman feels contractions and goes to the hospital, she is likely to agree with hospital personnel that her labor begins when she is officially admitted. The definition of "real" labor is determined during these negotiations between mother and institution, but the negotiated reality is unrelated to the physical experience: "The *physical* sensations in both cases are precisely the same. It is the *social* definitions—calling it labor or not—that make the difference."[3] The physical in this argument is a constant around which woman and institution build a social, consensual reality. Not only in giving birth but in other physical events as well, such as menstruation, sexual pleasure, and menopause, the material experience is filtered through a screen of social influences.

Emily Martin, in *The Woman in the Body*, assesses differences in how middle-class and working-class women relate to medical models of menstruation. She concludes that middle-class women "appear much more 'mystified' by general cultural models than working-class women."[4] Martin's analysis implies that the more a woman is exposed to various institutions and their discourses, the more dense the mediating screen becomes (the woman becomes "mystified"). The screen between the body-as-biology and the body-as-social-reality thickens with a woman's exposure to the stories mothers and grandmothers tell, the discourses of medicine and psy-

3. Barbara Katz Rothman, *In Labor: Women and Power in the Birthplace* (New York: W. W. Norton, 1982), p. 167.
4. Emily Martin, *The Woman in the Body: A Cultural Analysis of Reproduction* (Boston: Beacon Press, 1987), p. 111.

chology, self-help culture, feminism and antifeminism, and the conflicting rhetorics of maternal responsibility, fetal rights, and choice.

Thinking about women's bodies in this way opens the door to analyses that, like Martin's, take into account how a woman's class, race, age, sexual orientation, and health affect her attitudes about her body. But the idea that cultural knowledge intervenes between a woman and her body still retains the notion of a basic biological body. If the screening function of culture could be attenuated, then the natural, material reality of the body would dictate social realities. If women could set aside cultural influences and just listen to their bodies, debates about vaginal orgasms or premenstrual syndrome would never be taken seriously. A woman trying to determine when her labor started would attend to her body's sensations rather than the opinions of hospital personnel.

Adrienne Rich, in her landmark book *Of Woman Born* (1976), suggests the possibility of a congruence of physical and social realities when she advocates the "repossession by women of our bodies" as a revolutionary act that "will bring far more essential change to human society than the seizing of the means of production by workers."[5] Rich's revolutionary vision implies that women will find solidarity in their common need to reclaim their bodies. But women differ widely in their ideas about whether they have been dispossessed of their bodies and, if so, how they should reclaim them. At least in part because of this difficulty, the issues Rich brings up are still very much alive, and they are still constructed in terms of alienation and dispossession versus holism and ownership. Emily Martin wonders "why women's general images of their selves are chronically fragmented." She contends that perhaps by including both phenomenological (experiential) and medical (abstract) explanations in educating girls about menstruation, "we could restore a feeling of wholeness about the process."[6] Since Martin found that working-class women more often express a phenomenological paradigm and middle-class women a medical one, the "wholeness" she

5. Adrienne Rich, *Of Woman Born: Motherhood as Experience and Institution* (New York: W. W. Norton, 1976), p. 285.
6. Martin, *The Woman in the Body*, pp. 194, 111.

advocates would amount to a unifying of disparate class consciousnesses as well as a unifying of body image. The division she perceives between fragmented and holistic body images is important not only in feminist theory but also in medical and psychoanalytic theories about women's sexuality and mothering and in women's memoirs, fiction, and poetry about giving birth. The "individual" woman's body and "collective" bodies as well—family, community, and nation—are often considered in terms of fragmentation and holism. The danger in favoring holism is that it can be used to validate generalizations about how women experience their bodies and their lives, individually and across cultural and racial groups. Thinking in terms of restoring a lost wholeness suggests, too, that the "real" sensation of labor or other bodily experience is accessible through narrative or analysis.

The idea that bodily unity once existed and might be restored has much in common with the notion of original memory which guides primal birth therapy. Both involve complex interweavings of bodily experience and social influence, but both retain the concept of an ideal body, a fetal or maternal body unmarred by the traumas of being born or giving birth. The problem lies in separating out sensations that are purely of the body and those that have been distorted by their passage through the screen of social influences. I do not think that unadulterated preverbal memories or purely material experiences are possible. There is nothing constant or essential about material bodies. We change, but not just in response to reproductive cycles and maturational processes, and not just in dialogue with changing social influences. Instead, as Rich says, we embody social change. The most interesting questions have to do with who directs those changes. For instance, various reproductive technologies and practices, including *in vitro* fertilization, sterilization, fetal monitoring, and cesarean section, have been used to enforce class and race differences among women. Social service agencies, public hospitals, and private clinics have policies that ensure that certain inequities, such as white pronatalism and black antinatalism, find embodiment in women. For that reason, I think that the project of "getting in touch with"—or "writing through"—the body is more likely to confirm the inseparability of culture and biology than it is to help us rediscover an essential and constant woman's body.

The story of my mother's approach to death is a living part of my history. I construct my own origins by seeing myself reflected in her stories. There is no "real" story, separable from its retellings. Efforts in psychology to remember the womb or, in obstetrics, to imagine how it feels to be a fetus suggest the urgency of the desire to reclaim that essential fragment of personal history. Our amnesia for our own origins continues to trouble and fascinate me, and it has remained a puzzle as I explore it from the other side, through mothering my own daughter. But I am convinced that the closest we can come to reconstructing our origins is to ask our mothers to tell us their stories.

CHAPTER 1

Remembering

At the end of *The Girl*, Meridel Le Sueur's novel of the 1930s, the birth of a baby girl is an occasion for celebration for the homeless women who have gathered in a warehouse to watch her birth. Moments before the birth, the laboring woman (the Girl of the title) had been envisioning giving birth to her dead lover: "This is your face, Butch, coming down the great river, the great dark." But with the baby's birth, his image vanishes in the cries of the women hailing the child as a newborn woman, "a sister a daughter. No dingle dangle, no rod of satan, no sword no third arm, a girl a woman a mother." Celebrated as much for what she lacks as for what she is and will become, the new girl is swept up into the arms of the "Great Mothers" who attend her birth. Her mother looks around and sees the image of her own mother reflected in the faces of the women. When the cord is cut, she looks for the first time into the face of her newborn. "Now I could cup her tiny bright head. I cried out. She had the tiny face of my mother. Like in a mirror."[1]

In giving birth, the Girl undergoes a crisis in subjectivity, the lifelong process of becoming a speaker and an active creator of her

1. Meridel Le Sueur, *The Girl* (Minneapolis: West End Press, 1978), pp. 147–48.

9

own life. She produces a "mirror" in which she sees the image of her mother in her newborn daughter's face and identifies the merged image as herself. Jacques Lacan's account of the mirror stage in infants describes the potential subject's initial construction of an illusory sense of the self as whole, and predicts the "alienating destination" this illusion anticipates. Although basic aspects of the early mirror phase are worked through in Le Sueur's narrative of the Girl's process of (re)birth, the experience of the woman in labor represents a new phase in which the terms of her subjectivity must be renegotiated. Lacan's analysis of the infant's mirror phase provides a theoretical basis for this discussion; but viewing the issues involved from the mother's perspective, through a reading of Le Sueur, leads us in a significantly different direction. In Lacan's early mirror phase the infant confronts his (Lacan's infant is always male) image in the mirror, or comprehends his mother's image as his own, identifying the reflection—the other—as "I." Through this identification he experiences some relief from the "turbulent movements that the subject feels are animating him." These "turbulent movements" are the result of his physical immaturity, which prevents him from having control over his body. The infant discovers in the image a comforting wholeness, "by which the subject anticipates in a mirage the maturation of his power."[2] It is a mirage because the infant will never become the totalized image he perceives. It remains external to him; he identifies with an object from which he is perpetually alienated.

The subjective crisis of the Girl in labor cannot be satisfactorily resolved in the spirit of Lacan's account of the infant's mirror phase; the Girl's encounter with the mirror image of herself as her mother in her daughter's face complicates the original configuration. It is no longer a question of working out the contradictions inherent in identifying with an exterior image, no longer a question of an impossible reconciliation with an "other," but one of negotiating a shared subjectivity. In Chapter 4, I explore the implications of Le Sueur's vision of the Girl's renegotiated subjectivity for social and political change. For the purposes of the present discussion, the

2. Jacques Lacan, *Écrits: A Selection*, trans. Alan Sheridan (New York: W. W. Norton, 1977), p. 2; subsequent references in this chapter are cited in the text.

moment of the Girl's first glimpse of her baby girl's face suggests processes in which aspects of the mirror stage might be reexperienced—and profoundly revised—in giving birth. As other narratives of birth which I discuss will show, a woman's experience of these events is influenced by the physical process of giving birth, but is most deeply determined by social contexts. Rather than a universal process, in which each woman in labor simply relearns the lessons of the mirror stage, narratives of birth suggest diverse elaborations on basic themes of alienation, identification, and the construction of subjectivity through contradiction.

Viewing the Lacanian account from the mother's perspective presents considerable difficulty, as she is progressively and inexorably erased from the scene of the child's inauguration into language. Taking the development of the child as a starting point, Lacan constructs an understanding of the entire process of signification. The child has existed in a symbiotic relationship with its mother, his world composed of unarticulated images and unmediated communication.[3] His entry into language begins with his identification with his mirror image, approximating the connection between the signifier and signified in Saussurean linguistics.[4]

The relationship of child and image and signifier and signified is, however, also one of alienation. The child is removed from the image; the signifier is detached from the signified. As Terry Eagleton puts it: "In gaining access to language, the small child unconsciously learns that a sign has meaning only by dint of its difference from other signs, and learns also that a sign presupposes the *absence* of the object it signifies."[5] The mother, who once existed in symbiotic unity with the child and then constituted his first "mir-

---

3. Margaret Homans develops this conceptualization of the infant's earliest symbiotic relationship with his mother in her discussion of Lacan in *Bearing the Word* (Chicago: University of Chicago Press, 1986), p. 6.

4. Lacan's conception of this process emphasizes that there is no one-to-one correspondence between signifier and signified, no stable meaning, but rather "an incessant sliding of the signified under the signifier," so that meaning inheres in a sequence of signifiers, each referring to the next. Lacan describes this sequence as "rings of a necklace that is a ring in another necklace made of rings" (*Écrits*, pp. 153–54).

5. Terry Eagleton, *Literary Theory: An Introduction* (Minneapolis: University of Minnesota Press, 1983), p. 166.

ror image," also provides his first significant experience of absence. Their inevitable separation produces the symbolic death of the mother as the child learns to use language to represent his loss of her. John Muller and William Richardson, who make it their task in *Lacan and Language* to locate some firm footholds in Lacan by providing "a mapping of [*Écrits*] that strives to follow, step by step, Lacan's own tortuous path through the underbrush," point out that this death is an essential element of Lacan's account of the child's introduction to language: "The replacement of the mother by a symbol may be considered equivalent to the 'death' of the mother."[6] In developing her argument for viewing Lacan's theories as one expression of a culturewide "myth of language," Margaret Homans stresses the hostility inherent in this concept: "The symbolic order is founded, not merely on the regrettable loss of the mother, but rather on her active and overt murder."[7]

Up to this last point the whole process can be conceptualized without the father's entering into it: the child could find his mirror image in his mother, experience the alienating aspects of his discovery, and begin to experience absence and hence the necessity of language, all without reference to the father. The father, however, turns out to be the key to the whole process. Lacan pinpoints his entry at the moment of the "intrusion of the signifier" (p. 285), which is also the moment when sexual difference is introduced. The phallus, as the ultimate signifier, determines all meaning. In doing so it takes over the space of the signified. In the symbolic murder of the mother as Homans describes it, the phallus is the murder weapon.

Everything up to the point of the intrusion of the father takes place before language. Any "story" about a presymbolic, symbiotic union between mother and child is plotted out in a region where language has not yet intruded. But when I try to follow that part of the narrative to get back to my own infant experience, I find that there is nothing to say, no story to tell. I have only the stories that have been

6. John P. Muller and William J. Richardson, *Lacan and Language* (New York: International Universities Press, 1982), p. 94.
7. Homans, *Bearing the Word*, p. 11.

told to me by those who were conscious at the time. Once when my mother came to visit me, I asked her again about her illness after my birth. I asked her why she had refused to go to the hospital until she was almost dying. She answered, shaking her head, "That was really stupid of me. I just didn't want to leave you."

At the time of her illness, according to the Lacanian account, I was deep in a pre-Oedipal, presymbolic, symbiotic union with my mother. Her determination not to leave me had nothing to do with concerns for my physical well-being. She did not doubt that I would be diapered and fed while she was away, so this was not the aspect of our union that was threatened by our parting. But without her— according to the theory of presymbolic life—I was nothing: a half-jelled, spastic mind. I needed a mother to give me shape, to think for me. And she needed me, her mirror image, to redefine herself as a mother.

I was not an original player in this drama, but I have since become one. From the time I was old enough to hear the stories, in my imagination I occupied the living room where my mother almost died on my behalf. It has become a memory that belongs to my history, as much as it belongs to my mother's. It is an origin I could not have claimed at the time. And that is what a presymbolic, pre-Oedipal, symbiotic union is: it is always after the fact, a story about what happened before language, but which is always embedded in language. The mother-child union supplies a historical lack. Lacan's account of the mirror phase—a story about how the amnesia of infancy comes to an end—says nothing about what an eighteen-month-old baby experiences. But it says volumes about how an adult intellect makes up for, fills in for, the amnesia of infancy. It is a story about how an adult constructs a retrospective symbiotic union with a mother who is, of course, absent. He then reasons his way out of that union by "killing the mother."

We are to understand the mirror phase not as a literal account but as metaphor. The child's body does not really come apart. He need not encounter a literal mirror nor view the father's penis. The mother need not really die. Nevertheless, the mirror phase as Lacan tells it refers to the child's imaginative experience, and each metaphoric event is essential to his symbolic initiation. In this account, the mother and father are functionaries in the child's developing world. Although the child's experience has profound implications for the adult's, Lacan's account does not have much to say about how—or if—the mother could manage to construct her subjectivity while occupying her designated position in this drama. The mother's position in the drama is a paradox. She is at once a subject whose access to language depends on the death of the mother *and* the mother whose death permits that access. If the essential foundation of language (read humanity) is the death of the mother, how does a mother herself sustain an illusion of bodily and psychic unity while negotiating a deeply ambiguous identity?

In Anaïs Nin's 1938 story "Birth," the birth of a dead child means the death of a part of the mother herself. The story begins with the doctor's pronouncement: "The child . . . is dead." The mother has been trying to deliver a six-month fetus, and her doctor is livid with impatience. She is taking too long to birth "this dead fragment of myself." He exhorts, she pushes, but there is a part of her that is not ready to give up the fetus. She recalls:

> All in me which chose to keep, to lull, to embrace, to love, all in me which carried, preserved, and protected, all in me which imprisoned the whole world in its passionate tenderness, this part of me would not thrust out the child, even though it had died in me. Even though it threatened my life, I could not break, tear out, separate, surrender, open and dilate and yield up a fragment of a life like a fragment of the past. . . . And I was angry with a black anger at this part of me which refused to push, to separate, to lose.[8]

In this scene, though in much evolved form, the events of the mirror stage and the discovery of sexual difference are still perceptible. Through her connection with her child, the laboring woman reexperiences a form of the unity which precedes the child's introduction to language. According to Lacan's account of pre-Oedipal unity, "The infant has been engaged with the mother in a quasi-symbiotic tie that psychologically prolongs the physical symbiosis

8. Anaïs Nin, "Birth," in *Under a Glass Bell* (Chicago: Swallow Press, 1948), pp. 96–97; subsequent references in this chapter are cited in the text.

in the womb, in terms of which the mother is the infant's ALL."[9] It is the "ALL" in the mother in Nin's story that chooses "to keep, to lull, to embrace, to love" the fetus that is a part of herself. In Lacan's account, the rupture of this unity produces a gap which the subject will seek (but unsuccessfully) to rebridge through the agency of language. The death of the child in Nin's story reinforces the finality and the tragedy of the rupture. What has been called the "symbolic death of the mother" finds, in Nin's story, an (almost) literal expression, as the mother experiences the death of a part of herself.

Her doctor urges her "to push, to separate, to lose"; but it is not only the dead baby that she must separate from. She must also, under the terms of the symbolic order, separate from that part of her that chose to give life and resists giving it up; she must separate from the mother in her. At this point her internal negotiations reach a tortuous standstill. For while the mother in her struggles to "embrace" the child, the child in her struggles to separate from the mother. Meanwhile, her body is shattered by hard labor, the violence of which reflects in intensified form the "turbulent movements" and sense of fragmentation that mark the child's premirror existence. Lacan describes the images of the "fragmented body" that seem to be reflected in the play of children and the aggressive fantasies of adults: "These are the images of castration, mutilation, dismemberment, dislocation, evisceration, devouring, bursting open of the body" (p. 11). The infant's experience of bodily fragmentation resolves itself in "the integration of an original organic disarray," but this integration "must be conceived in the dimension of a vital dehiscence that is constitutive of man" (p. 121).

Nin's story suggests that the original organic disarray that later presents itself in fantasy images of the "bursting open of the body" is renewed literally in the mother's experience of labor. Struggling to deliver the child, the mother says, "I pushed with anger, with despair, with frenzy, with the feeling that I would die pushing, as one exhales the last breath, that I would push out everything inside of me, and my soul with all the blood around it, and the sinews with my heart inside of them, choked, and that my body itself would

9. Muller and Richardson, *Lacan and Language*, p. 21.

open and smoke would rise, and I would feel the ultimate incision of death" (p. 97). Again, the imaginative experience of bodily fragmentation, which seems in Lacan to be associated with the death instinct, as man "at every moment . . . constitutes his world by his suicide" (p. 28), is actually undergone by the laboring woman as she struggles moment by moment with the splintering agony of her labor, trying to "remember all the time why I should want to live" (p. 97).

Not until she ceases to condemn that part of her that paradoxically desires "to keep and to lose, to live and to die" does she begin to make progress. She drums her stomach gently with her fingers, calling the child forth. She has resolved to separate, and the decision brings with it a sense of serenity. She pushes the child out at last, and immediately insists on seeing it, though the nurses urge the doctor not to show it. "It looks dark and small, like a diminutive man. But it is a little girl. It has long eyelashes on its closed eyes, it is perfectly made, and all glistening with the waters of the womb" (p. 101). In these final moments of the story, Nin presents us with a scene evocative of Lacan's image of the child before the mirror. For the woman sees a version of herself reflected in the dead child, who presents an image "perfectly made." In Lacan's account of the mirror stage, the child's reflected image first becomes, in Lacan's term, the "Ideal-I." The Ideal-I precedes language and "is precipitated in a primordial form, before it is objectified in the dialectic of identification with the other" (p. 2). At this stage the reflected image is not identified as external to the child. The perception of the image as an external object which marks the child's first experience of subjectivity and becomes the foundation of language has not yet occurred. This moment takes place before language and memory in the child, but the woman in Nin's story captures it in the fleeting image of the "perfectly made" child.

In Lacan's account of the child's inauguration, the image of the Ideal-I provides a sense of relief from the turbulent movements and fragmentation of the premirror stage. In "Birth," the delivery of the child relieves the mother of the experience of fragmentation she undergoes in labor. She is immediately presented with an ideal image in the form of her child. But the child is a corpse, literalizing Lacan's conception of the symbol as the death of the object: "Thus the symbol manifests itself first of all as the murder of the thing, and this death constitutes in the subject the eternalization of his desire" (p. 104). Applied to Nin's story, then, the child, as the literal embodiment of the finitude of death, represents also the woman's recommitment to the symbolic. Her position as subject, challenged so profoundly by her experience of giving birth, is reconfirmed, even as her desire—the desire for a unity that can never be obtained—becomes "eternalized" through its expression as literature.

As in Lacan's account of the mirror stage, up until the moment of the "murder of the thing," the necessity for the father's role in the drama is not apparent. But "Birth" begins with the doctor's pronouncement "The child is dead," and with these words he assumes the symbolic role accorded him as the weapon-wielding interloper who severs the unity of mother and child. The woman perceives in him her absolute enemy, ascribing to him deep, even murderous hostility. The doctor, with his needles and knives, represents the phallic signifier par excellence. Lacan thinks of the intrusion of the signifying phallus as a salutary event, representing the discovery of sexual difference with all its erotic possibilities as well as the initiation into language. Although the "facts" reveal "a relation of the subject to the phallus that is established without regard to the anatomical difference of the sexes" (p. 282), his account of the phallus depends at times on its similarity to the penis: "It can be said that this signifier [the phallus] is chosen because it is the most tangible element in the real of sexual copulation, and also the most symbolic in the literal (typographical) sense of the term, since it is equivalent there to the (logical) copula. It might also be said that, by virtue of its turgidity, it is the image of the vital flow as it is transmitted in generation" (p. 287).

The linguistic and sexual functions of the phallus/penis here culminate in an orgasm (another fragmenting experience) that generates life and language. But if, for Lacan, the phallus represents all that is good, its image in "Birth" is destructive. From the beginning, the doctor is angry that the woman resists delivering her child. When his exhortations have no effect, he takes hold of "a long instrument" and rams it into her vagina, paralyzing her with pain. "That will make her push, he says to the nurse." When this does not work, he gives her an injection to intensify her contractions, but this too fails to have any effect. Burning with fury, the doctor can only wait, watching from the outside while she contends with herself: "He looks baffled, as before a savage mystery, baffled by this struggle. He wants to interfere with his instruments, while I struggle with nature, with myself, with my child and with the meaning I put into it all, with my desire to give and to hold, to keep and to lose, to live and to die" (p. 99). In Lacanian terms, the doctor's use of surgical instruments represents the work of the phallic signifier in severing the mother-child union. Here it fails to have any effect: he cannot break their unity with his "phallus," whether in the form of words or of instruments. She discounts him, leaves him on the sidelines "holding a long instrument" while she does the labor of producing meaning, a meaning that encompasses the giving and taking of life, her unity with the fetus, and her need to separate from it. The father's role is doubly discounted in this story, for the child's father, who in Lacan would represent the generative faculty of the phallus, is never mentioned, and the doctor, who represents the phallus's destructive action, is impotent. The conception and death of the mother's child remain occult phenomena, out of reach of the phallus.

As this mother's labor to produce meaning from the experience of childbirth and death suggests, there remains a region that the signifying phallus cannot penetrate, a space that may provide material for analysis but is separate from the symbolic. Lacan designates this region the "imaginary." "Imaginary reminiscence" consists of "the echo of feeling or instinctual imprint" which is resistant to inquiry. "The imaginary shaping of the subject by desires more or less fixed or regressed in their relation to the object is too inadequate and partial to provide the key to it." The key to the subject resides instead in the "symbolic," whose laws, "different in essence and manifestation" from those of the imaginary, form the basis for effective analysis. The tendency in psychoanalysis, Lacan complains, is to focus on "the subject's affective frustration, instinctual deprivation, and imaginary dependence." This shift from the symbolic to the imaginary leads to a "general infantilization." Lacan testifies that we need to acknowledge our "symbolic debt," or risk opening the door to "the forfeits and vain oaths, lapses in speech and unconsidered words, the constellation of which presided at the putting into the world of a man, that is moulded the stone guest who comes, in symptoms, to disturb the banquet of one's desires" (pp. 141–43).

The mother is not mentioned here. She is already, even at the moment of birth, an allusive absence, and birth is passively rendered as the "putting into the world of a man." Here, and in his reevocation of the mother as the bearer of "words of false hope with which [she] has baited [the child] in feeding him with the milk of her true despair" (p. 143), Lacan calls on torturous images of birth and nursing to describe the imaginary realm. The imaginary is a dangerous, even hellish region. Only ravings and despair accompany "the putting into the world of a man." Reading "Birth" from this perspective, we find that it is from the imaginary, with all its chaos and incoherence, that the woman produces a stillborn child, who will never take part in the symbolic. And yet, in Lacan's account of the mirror stage, the living child also emerges as a subject from this space at the moment when his symbiotic union with his mother is interrupted. The imaginary has its generative as well as its destructive facilities, as does the symbolic. If the symbolic realm is represented by the phallus, its counterpart, the imaginary, might in turn be represented by the womb, although Lacan does not make this connection explicit. Nin's story respects the sexual difference implied in the imaginary/symbolic model but values these respective regions differently, offering images of an ineffectual phallus and a self-generating mother/subject. Although the doctor is the voice of the symbolic, announcing death and urging the woman to "separate, to lose," the real labor of producing meaning goes on within the woman, within a conceptual space that baffles him and to which he has no access.

Toi Derricotte's poem "Delivery" recalls the struggle to produce meaning in the mute reflection of a woman who has just given birth: "i lay back, speechless, looking / for something / to say to myself."[10] With the final push, a woman giving birth, like the child being born, emerges from a space beyond symbolic language, from

10. Toi Derricotte, *Natural Birth* (Trumansburg, N.Y.: Crossing Press, 1983), p. 48.

where she is not supposed to speak. A woman in labor may produce vagrant sounds, moans and grunts, uttered from a place so far away she may not recognize her own voice. Or she maintains stern silence, or begs for release, or cries "Mother!" or "Shit!" In Margaret Atwood's novel *The Handmaid's Tale*, Janine, on the verge of giving birth, produces irrelevant and irrational statements: "I want to go outside. . . . I want to go for a walk. I feel fine." She screams, "Oh no, oh no, oh no," rhythmic negations that communicate only the inadequacy of language to convey her sensation. And she will never be able to express it, even to herself: "Who can remember pain, once it's over? All that remains of it is a shadow, not in the mind even, in the flesh. Pain marks you, but too deep to see. Out of sight, out of mind."[11] Labor and birth appear to be a journey outside memory and rational thought, to a place that supplies material for the production of meaning but remains forever out of reach of the symbolic. The expressions of women in labor bear a close resemblance to the "lapses in speech and unconsidered words" (p. 143) that greet man as he emerges from Lacan's imaginary realm.

As Anaïs Nin's story suggests, however, it is possible, with shifts in perspective, to reapportion the relative value of the imaginary and symbolic, constructing in the process a quite different understanding of their functions and relationship. This is what Julia Kristeva undertakes in *Revolution in Poetic Language*, in which the imaginary has been replaced by the semiotic.[12] Kristeva's conception of the semiotic assigns it greater power in the signifying process than Lacan assigns the imaginary, and she explores its relationship with the symbolic in greater complexity. Although the semiotic and the symbolic remain distinct and disparate regions, Kristeva emphasizes their interdependence.

The relationship between the semiotic and the symbolic is represented graphically in "Stabat Mater," Kristeva's essay on the Virgin Mother. The main text is interrupted at irregular intervals with columns of another text running in parallel. The musical rhythms

11. Margaret Atwood, *The Handmaid's Tale* (New York: Random House, 1986), pp. 160–61.
12. Julia Kristeva, *Revolution in Poetic Language*, trans. Margaret Waller (New York: Columbia University Press, 1984); subsequent references in this chapter are cited in the text.

and lyricism of this text provide a counterpoint to the rational line of the argument developed in the main text. The separated text is that of the mother, Kristeva-as-mother, reflecting on her own experience of giving birth and mothering: "Flash—an instant of time or a timeless dream; atoms swollen beyond measure, atoms of a bond, a vision, a shiver, a still shapeless embryo, unnameable. Epiphanies. Photos of what is not yet visible and which language necessarily surveys from a very high altitude, allusively. Words always too remote, too abstract to capture the subterranean swarm of seconds, insinuating themselves into unimaginable places."[13] The text of the mother both surrounds and is surrounded by the main text, and yet—to complete the paradox—it is isolated from it. Its position and its character mark it as a text that varies from the standard, that is more closely allied to the semiotic than the main text.

In *Revolution in Poetic Language,* Kristeva develops the model she later illustrates in "Stabat Mater." The semiotic is composed of the pre-Oedipal, prelinguistic, presymbolic forces that can be found within language; it is associated with the feminine because it suggests the intimate, nonsymbolic contact between mother and child: "The semiotic is articulated by flows and marks: facilitation, energy transfers, the cutting up of the corporeal and social continuum as well as that of signifying material, the establishment of a distinctiveness and its ordering in a pulsating *chora,* in a rhythmic but nonexpressive totality" (p. 40). The *chora,* a term Kristeva derives from Plato, denotes a receptacle or maternal space that underlies the symbolic. The semiotic chora evades all but the most oblique description. Its only order is created by pulsions, patterns of nonspecific drives, so that, although it is like symbolic language in that it is regulated by syntax, it remains "nonexpressive," prior to meaning. It "precedes evidence, verisimilitude, spatiality, and temporality" (p. 26). Although the chora is essential to symbolic discourse, it is also potentially destructive. It is the place where the speaking subject "is both generated and negated, the place where his unity succumbs before the process of charges and stases that produce him" (p. 28). These supreme moments—of generation and negation,

13. Julia Kristeva, "Stabat Mater," in *The Kristeva Reader,* ed. Toril Moi (Oxford: Basil Blackwell, 1986), p. 162.

birth and death—are located within the maternal space of the chora. The maternal body is the gateway between the semiotic and the symbolic; it is "what mediates the symbolic law organizing social relations and becomes the ordering principle of the semiotic *chora*, which is the path of destruction, aggressivity, and death" (pp. 27–28). If the chora is a place of generation, it is also a place of disorder and death. To remain within the chora means the destruction of the subject, a descent into psychosis, for it is a place where symbolic language is impossible. In Kristeva, as in Lacan, the symbolic saves the subject from the annihilation of unity with the maternal body.

It is significant that the chora is associated with the "maternal body." *Chora* is derived from the Greek word for womb. Although the chora is in no way reducible to the womb, the two possess certain similarities that are worth exploring. The womb, like the chora, appears to create something (body or meaning) from nothing. Even our most sophisticated understanding of the processes of reproduction has not completely resolved the mystery of how the human body is generated from its genetic origins. The womb, like the chora, is organized by rhythms—the monthly rhythms of the menstrual cycle, the accelerated rhythms of labor. The womb is the place we came from, where we took shape before we had consciousness or a position in the symbolic system. The experience of the maternal body is universal, and it is through the maternal body that we all have access to the semiotic chora. But the womb is also a place of absence—the absence of social structures and language—and always, retrospectively, of loss: the loss of the peaceful, asocial unity with the mother. If origins are lost to us, so is our end. Death presents the same uncertainty as birth, and so the womb, like the semiotic chora, is a place of "destruction, aggressivity, and death."

My memories of how I felt as a child, when I learned I had almost lost my mother at birth, validate Kristeva's interpretation in a personal way. Twenty years after my mother almost died after giving birth to me, I gave birth to my daughter, Nicole. I did not almost die, but my labor was an occasion for intense desire and fear. I longed for release from the physical force of labor, a force I had never imagined could erupt within my body. At the same time I struggled to embrace this monster womb. I did not succeed. I could not hold it in my overloaded consciousness. In the signifying process Kristeva and Lacan describe, women's bodies, as maternal bodies, represent a component of the signifying process, a place of absence and loss, with which—as speaking subjects—we cannot identify. I cannot remember my own infancy, and I cannot reexperience the labor that brought Nicole into the world. The monster womb that took over my body and mind during four hours of "hard labor" has long since shrunk to a manageable size. I recall the sensation of being caught in an infinitude, in which time and space lost their stability. I understand that many women, like me, reach a moment during labor when they are certain that they exist in a place of unremitting pain that is all they have ever known and from which there is no escape. But, however long that moment lasts, it is not forever. My mother told me, the day after I birthed Nicole, that a woman never remembers the pain of labor when it has passed. Like the infant's symbiotic unity with the mother, another state that cannot conceive of its own end, labor is finite. And its end signals a (re)emergence into the symbolic, where representation will only serve to accentuate its loss.

CHAPTER 2

Natural Birth/Transitions

In her poem "Transition," Toi Derricotte evokes what is often considered the most trying phase of labor, reaching back to the extreme verge of this experience in order to explore the relationship between giving birth and creating meaning:

> this muscle of a lady, this crazy ocean in my teacup.
> she moves the pillars of the sky. i am stretched into
> fragments, tissue paper thin. the light shines through
> to her goatness, her blood-thick heart that thuds like
> one drum in the universe emptying its stars.[1]

In Derricotte's poem sensations so intense they cannot be described are diffused and transformed through a series of disconnected metaphors. The laboring woman is "this crazy ocean in my teacup"; she is the "i" that is "stretched into fragments," recalling the turbulence and bodily fragmentation of the infant in the premirror phase.

---

1. Derricotte, *Natural Birth*, p. 30; subsequent references in this chapter are cited in the text.

But already she conceives of this fragmentation as a division between self and other, splitting her perceptual space between "she"
and "i." The laboring woman divides herself, becoming a muscle, a
teacup, a tissue. Her inward alienation precipitates the search for a
symbolic representation of the loss. It is at this point that Kristeva's
model of the semiotic and symbolic relationship becomes important. Transformed into words, the inconceivable, the overwhelming becomes manageable. The "pulsions," "flows," and "nonexpressive totality" of labor are reordered and become expressible. Derricotte describes her pain as "absolute as air"; time is meaningless,
"the clock is stuck on pain, stuck on forever" (p. 27), but even so
encompassing a description limits the sensation to a conceptual
level that one can tolerate.

The Lacanian account of the signifying process purports to describe a universal narrative but takes the male infant as the generic
protagonist. Kristeva's account, by contrast, allows us to consider
the mother's perspective. In the Kristevan account, the loss of the
original represented by its transformation into language is not peculiar to giving birth. The semiotic chora is accessible to all, not only
to parturient women. But only a woman can reexperience the entire
process, the original physical unity with another body, the rupture
of that unity and the (re)birth into language, from the perspective of
one who has already been put into process as a subject. From this
perspective the mother establishes a strong connection with the
semiotic chora in giving birth, simultaneously making possible and
posing a threat to the symbolic order as she claims the position of
speaking subject. The power—and the threat—of the mother's perspective can be perceived most immediately in the scene of birth. In
representing this experience, which is inaccessible to men, a woman may achieve an understanding of the self that is quite different
from a man's.

In both Nin's and Derricotte's representations, labor and birth are
transformative events through which women radically reorganize
their subjectivity. In this sense a woman's experience of birth ac-
complishes more than a renewal of the lessons of the mirror stage. It
may represent a stage of mental evolution that takes her beyond the
developmental limits of what Lacan fittingly calls "man's mental
genesis," a genesis that culminates in the rigidification of the ego, a

final adoption of "defensive armour."[2] Nancy Chodorow's approach
to women's development suggests that women are less likely to
adopt such rigid defenses. As Chodorow puts it, women's "experience of self contains more flexible or permeable ego boundaries" in
comparison with men's relatively rigid sense of self.[3] A woman's
lack of definitive individuation is not necessarily an indication of
psychic vulnerability or pathology. Instead, her more flexible sense
of personal boundaries, which in Chodorôw's analysis is produced
primarily through her relationship with her own mother, prepares
her to meet the challenges to subjectivity that motherhood represents. Nevertheless Chodorow's description supports the view that
women in pregnancy and labor, and in the early days of their children's infancy, may reexperience the symbiotic union they had
with their own mothers. This view infantilizes the mother with its
notion of "regression," suggesting that new mothers undo their own
development to adulthood and become infants again in order to
empathize with their own infant.

Women's poetry and narratives about giving birth offer a very
different view. They suggest that the birth process may be read not
as regression but as an evolution in which a woman's understanding
of herself becomes more complex and expansive. Derricotte's evocation of labor suggests how a woman might create a space for the
reconstruction of the self through a progression of conceptual divisions. At moments during her labor, her efforts drive her inward,
and she leaves the hospital room behind. Her consciousness dilates,
becoming its own expanding womb:

> i was
> over me
> like
> sun and i
> was under
> me
> like sky and i
> could look

2. Lacan, *Écrits*, p. 17.
3. Nancy Chodorow, *Reproduction of Mothering: Psychoanalysis and the Sociology of Gender* (Berkeley: University of California Press, 1978), p. 169.

into myself
like one
dark eye.
      (p. 42)

Entering this expansive interior space, she separates from the exterior world. No longer centered in one perceptual space, she multiplies identities. But in multiplying, she also separates, self from self. There is an "i" that she still recognizes as central. This is the "i" which she is over and under, the "i" she can look into. But even this "i" is being called into question. She is looking into herself, reexamining what it means to be "i." She is no longer fully connected to the self she was before the experience began, and she has not become the self she will be.

the meat rolls up and moans on the damp table.
my body is a piece of cotton over another
woman's body. some other woman, all muscle and nerve, is
tearing apart and opening under me.
      (p. 30)

The extreme pain of these moments marks a cusp. One part of her dies in agony as, on the verge of giving birth to a child, she gives birth to another version of herself. Her body is literally fragmented, recalling Lacan's images of the imaginary, the dislocation and "bursting open of the body" that form the basis of aggressive fantasies. The inward splitting of the self is swiftly followed by visible proof of her transformation: her son is born. As soon as his head appears, she struggles to identify him as a separate being. The inward divisions she experienced during labor culminate in a passage broken into pieces by a frenzy of slashes:

NAME PLEASE/
PLEASE / NAME / whose

head/i
don't know / some /
disconnection
      (p. 45)

At the moment of her son's birth, she is acutely aware that she is about to give him up to the symbolic order, which demands imperatively that he be given a name, "credentials . . . anything / to make him / human" (p. 47). Even as she labors to deliver him, she knows that she does not want to give him up. With the irrevocable severance of their visceral union, he is becoming someone she does not know, someone separate: "some disconnection." She associates their separation with the limitations imposed by symbolic language, limitations she is not ready to accept. Anticipating the necessity of giving him a name, a symbol of their separation, she resists. As soon as he is fully born, she finds herself "speechless, looking / for something / to say to myself" (p. 48). Her poem is the something that she eventually finds to say; it represents her entry into the symbolic as a newly (re)structured subject, separated from her son, from the self she was before she gave birth, and from the expanded identities she assumed during labor. But by disrupting the text with fragmented metaphors and rupturing the page visually with ellipses, slashes, and jarring line breaks, her account affirms its origins in the semiotic—its origins in connection.

As in Nin's "Birth," Derricotte's speaker poses the doctor and his instruments as representing the destructive action of the phallus, and then rejects it in the search for her own meaning. But Derricotte's speaker, a young African American woman giving birth without support, is coping with racial and economic as well as sexual oppression in her encounter with the doctor. His repeated examinations feel like "sticking a wooden ax handle up my cunt." He's happy to cause her pain:

> he wants me to roll and beg like a dog, *please doctor*
> *please don't hurt me any more do anything do anything you*
> *say but help me help me not to feel such pain* but i don't
> beg him. i don't beg him because I hate him. i keep
> my pain locked up inside. he'll never know how much
> he hurts, i'll never let him know.
>
> (p. 27)

The doctor has ruptured her body, assaulting her while she is paralyzed with pain and has no possibility of defending herself. She defines him as a "rapist," but, in refusing to beg for mercy, she refuses to share in the symbolic exchange that would give him control over her. She retains the privacy that derives from his inability to understand what she feels, using her opposition to him to create a free inward space for her expanding consciousness. When she begins to push and the pain drains away, she regards her attendants as if from a great distance, and wonders at their incomprehension:

> why weren't the nurses and doctors rushing toward me?
> why weren't they wrapping me in white? white for respect,
> white for triumph, white for the white light i was being
> accepted into after death?
>
> (p. 33)

The insensibility of her attendants prevents them from perceiving "the white light i was being accepted into"; they are blind to the transformation occurring before them. Her reality is defined by the magnified vigor, the heightened consciousness, of labor, and theirs by the routine demands of their narrowly defined duties. Her departure from her attendants' reality complements the inward division she undergoes as she is "accepted into . . . death," leaving behind her former self and approaching the border between the symbolic and semiotic, where meaning erupts. No one remembers her own birth, and no one knows her own death, but in Derricotte's poetry a woman approaches the extreme verge and reaches even farther, entering the dangerous realm of the semiotic. During the journey she reconstructs herself and emerges as a mother-poet.

For Kristeva, the semiotic chora is both necessary to symbolic language and threatening to it. Psychosis awaits those who, remaining too closely allied with the semiotic, fail to reenter the symbolic realm. When the signifying process corresponds too closely to the semiotic, "heterogeneity itself is lost; spread out in its place is the fantasy of identification with the female body (the mother's body), or even the mutism of the paralyzed schizophrenic."[4] In this case the subject is stillborn. Having failed to establish independence from the mother's body, subjectivity dies within her: this is "the

---

4. Kristeva, *Revolution*, p. 182.

mutism of the paralyzed schizophrenic." It is possible to read into accounts of birth such as Nin's and Derricotte's an approach to a potentially catastrophic submergence in the semiotic. At this point the essentialism with which Kristeva's philosophy flirts takes on dark tones: femininity becomes pathology, psychosis, the inability to order objects rationally. Elsewhere Kristeva suggests the possibility that each sex has "its own unconscious wherein the biological and social program of the species would be ciphered in confrontations with language, exposed to its influence, but independent from it," a notion that at least calls into doubt the assertion that her position is steadfastly antiessentialist.[5]

Toril Moi, arguing that Kristeva's philosophy *is* antiessentialist, reminds us that sexual difference has no existence in the semiotic because it is associated with the pre-Oedipal phase. But in her discussion of the development of girls, Moi describes how the little girl, once faced with the choice of identifying with the mother (representing the semiotic) or the father (representing the symbolic), is better off if she chooses to identify with the father: "Either she identifies with her mother, or raises herself to the symbolic stature of her father." Since identification with the mother leads to an inability to differentiate objects, an inherently homosexual and incestuous association with the maternal body, a regression to infancy, and possibly to schizophrenia, it seems clear that the girl's best course is to identify with the father. If she chooses the father, "the access she gains to the symbolic dominance [will] censor the pre-Oedipal phase and wipe out the last traces of dependence on the body of the mother."[6] If we look at this situation from the point of view of the developing girl, it could support an antiessentialist view: the undifferentiated little girl may choose to identify with either sex. But if we look at the positions assigned to the mother and father in correspondence with the semiotic and symbolic, the anti-

5. Julia Kristeva, "Motherhood According to Bellini," in *Desire in Language,* trans. Leon Roudiez, Thomas Gora, and Alice Jardine (New York: Columbia University Press, 1980), p. 241.

6. Toril Moi, *Sexual/Textual Politics* (New York: Methuen, 1985), p. 165, quoting Kristeva's *About Chinese Women.* Considering that language is dependent on the semiotic, it seems contradictory that a little girl—or anyone, for that matter—could "wipe out the last traces of dependence on the body of the mother." In this account the child is somehow capable of what language itself cannot accomplish.

essentialist argument weakens. The mother represents mutism and paralysis; if the little girl chooses to identify with her, she loses her voice and her mind. The father, by contrast, represents the dominant symbolic order, civilization, and signification; identifying with him, she gains some access to this power. Therefore, it seems that it is not "woman" who has the essential nature; certainly Kristeva objects strongly to totalizing uses of the term in her essay "Women's Time."[7] But the term *mother* can readily be identified with the semiotic and all its dangers, and it is from this perspective that the birth scenes of Nin and Derricotte seem to imply if not a full descent into psychosis, at least the possibility of such a catastrophic negation of the subject.

Although the model of the semiotic/symbolic need not necessarily depend on sexual essentialism, there still exists some slippage at the points where Kristeva's own account adopts the conventions of sexual differentiation. At these points the processes of signification fall neatly into familiar categories, in which the male (in his symbolic guise) is associated with rational thought and the privileges of social power, and the mother, identified with the semiotic, represents an incomprehensible place where nonspecific drives, dissociated images, and indefinable "pulsions" produce psychosis. The healthy subject (of whatever sex) is still masculine; the unhealthy or endangered subject (again of whatever sex) is still feminine.

Kristeva compares the "primal regression" of mystical and drug-induced experiences with giving birth. That moment marks

> the reunion of a woman-mother with the body of *her* mother. . . . By giving birth, the woman enters into contact with her mother; she becomes, she is her own mother; they are the same continuity differentiating itself. She thus actualizes the homosexual facet of motherhood, through which a woman is simultaneously closer to her instinctual memory, more open to her own psychosis, and consequently, more negatory of the social, symbolic bond.[8]

It is not as a woman that one enters the undifferentiated realm of the chora but as a woman-mother. In Kristeva's description, the

7. Julia Kristeva, "Women's Time," in *The Kristeva Reader*, pp. 187–213.
8. Kristeva, "Motherhood According to Bellini," p. 239.

moment of reunion is not necessarily a total loss; it suggests heightened creativity, an approach to the mystical, a fuller knowledge
of the self, and the realization of the absurdity of "communital
meaning." But it is also dangerous, shadowed by implications of
homosexuality, psychosis, a loss of symbolic language, and the dissolution of social bonds. It is a "regression" in which the woman-
mother loses access to the symbolic.

Judith Butler traces Kristeva's negative view of lesbianism back
to Kristeva's belief in the primacy of symbolic law, and insightfully
identifies a gap in Lacan's and Kristeva's theoretical construction of
the "primary relationship to the maternal body." Butler questions
whether the relationship they describe "is even a knowable experience according to either of their linguistic theories." In a critique of
Kristeva's view of the relation between motherhood, homosexuality, and psychosis, Butler says that "it designates female homosexuality as a culturally unintelligible practice, inherently psychotic;
on the other hand, it mandates maternity as a compulsory defense
against libidinal chaos."[9] Kristeva defines lesbianism as a psychotic
practice because it is incomprehensible within the "Law of the Father" in which she has so much invested. Motherhood, however, is
culturally sanctioned. But is it any more intelligible? Kristeva's
provocative statement about the relationship between lesbianism,
motherhood, and psychosis does not place motherhood and lesbianism in opposition to each other. They are, instead, joined as expressions of the relationship between the woman-mother and the body
of her mother. If Kristeva differentiates the two "practices," it is to
place motherhood at the borders of lesbianism, where it functions
as a gateway to and a container of female homosexuality. In childbirth, a woman goes through that gate; she "actualizes the homosexual facet of motherhood" by entering the mother's body. Motherhood is the only expression of that relationship sanctioned within
symbolic law because motherhood, as kinship, is regulated by symbolic law. But the experience of giving birth may position a woman,
however ephemerally, beyond the reach of that law. Her experience
is not knowable; it cannot be accounted for, and thus it is "negatory
of the social, symbolic bond," a (very close) approach to psychosis.

9. Judith Butler, *Gender Trouble: Feminism and the Subversion of Identity*
(New York: Routledge, 1990), pp. 80, 86.

The ambivalent values that surface in Kristeva's account of the semiotic chora in its relation to the experience of becoming a mother reflect a similar ambivalence coloring women's accounts of childbirth experiences. The birth scene in Sylvia Plath's novel *The Bell Jar* brings out this ambivalence especially clearly, and suggests the processes through which a woman might disassociate herself from the appalling loss of self-determination birth seems to represent. Esther, touring the hospital where her boyfriend, Buddy, is a medical student, has a chance to watch as a patient, Mrs. Tomolillo, gives birth.

"You oughtn't to see this," an intern tells Esther before she witnesses Mrs. Tomolillo's delivery. "You'll never want to have a baby if you do. They oughtn't to let women watch."[10] Esther, however, wants to see "some really interesting hospital sights," and she has been very proud of her ability to withstand exposure to cadavers and dead babies in jars. She tries to achieve a medical objectivity to match the men's, and the form of a hospital delivery encourages such detachment. The woman's inert body is hoisted onto a delivery table, where her swollen abdomen hides her face from observers and attendants. She has nothing to identify her as human, only the "enormous spider-fat stomach and two little ugly spindly legs" of an insect (p. 72). She does not speak, but utters an "unhuman whooing noise." Her stupor, shapeless body, and debased position do nothing to invite sympathy, but despite herself Esther identifies subtly with the "big white lump" moaning incoherently on the delivery table. Buddy explains that the woman has been given a drug that will make her forget the pain, and Esther reflects bitterly that "it sounded just like the sort of drug a man would invent": "Here was a woman in terrible pain, obviously feeling every bit of it or she wouldn't groan like that, and she would go straight home and start another baby, because the drug would make her forget how bad the pain had been, when all the time, in some secret part of her, that long, blind, doorless and windowless corridor of pain was waiting to open up and shut her in again" (p. 72).

From the men's perspective, Mrs. Tomolillo is simply absent, drowning in the oblivion of "twilight sleep." But Esther under-

10. Sylvia Plath, *The Bell Jar* (New York: Harper & Row, 1971), p. 71; subsequent references in this chapter are cited in the text.

stands that she possesses "some secret part" that will store the knowledge of this experience. Her groans, a voice out of the semiotic chora, announce that this secret part of her has opened up through an experience that lies outside the reach of the symbolic. When her baby is born, that secret part will close up again, but the memory of her labor will not be wiped out, just sealed up in "that long, blind, doorless and windowless corridor" her pain has created. The question implicit in this passage is: What is the motive for administering a drug that does not take the pain away but only ensures that the woman will not remember giving birth at all? It is "just like the sort of drug a man would invent," a drug that lets a woman suffer and yet prevents her from being able to remember enough to make self-determined choices in the future. The drug ensures that she will be handicapped in trying to reestablish herself as a subject. In this sense Mrs. Tomolillo's labor represents a regression in which she loses access to the symbolic; but her regression is inherent not in the experience of becoming a mother but in the doctors' successful efforts to interfere with her labor. In Plath's birth scene, as in Nin and Derricotte, the doctors and their tools represent the hostile and destructive aspect of the signifying phallus. Mrs. Tomolillo's doctors succeed where the others failed, however, because they attack the woman's ability to produce meaning: they attack her mind rather than her genitals. A significant piece of her own experience will be locked away in some forgotten corner of the semiotic chora, forever unassimilable into the symbolic.

Esther fears that "doorless and windowless corridor." Like Mrs. Tomolillo, she might possess a "secret part" that could expand and consume her. But the fear of birth is tied in with her observations of the doctors' interference; the scene she witnesses is particularly frightening because the men have turned the woman into an inert, inhuman lump, robbing her of the consciousness with which to produce meaning. Esther tries to establish her distance from the appalling scene by immediately superimposing her own imagined birth scene over its horrors. Like the speakers in Nin and Derricotte, Esther dismisses the doctors, who simply have no part in her fantasy. Instead, she envisions herself after the birth, romantically "dead white, of course, with no makeup and from the awful ordeal, but smiling and radiant, with my hair down to my waist" (p. 74).

Esther tries to accomplish what is denied to Mrs. Tomolillo by establishing an idealized mirror image of herself, an image she can identify as "I." At the same time, this image is reassuringly external: it is some other Esther, a future subject already transformed in giving birth, an image she can identify with and yet maintain distance from.

In divorcing herself from Mrs. Tomolillo's descent into forgetfulness, Esther reenacts the essential identification/separation of self-and-other (self-and-mother) of the mirror stage. At the same time, she creates an internal division that corresponds to Kristeva's model of the relationship between the semiotic and the symbolic. Kristeva describes such a division in the insertions that break up the main text in "Stabat Mater": "A mother is a continuous separation, a division of the very flesh. And consequently a division of language—and it has always been so."[11] With the division of the body in birth linked to the semiotic/symbolic division in language, it is possible to associate Esther's fear of the pain of labor, in which the womb itself figures as a "doorless and windowless corridor of pain," with a dread of the semiotic chora as a place "of destruction, aggressivity, and death." The division of language finds a similar expression: Mrs. Tomolillo's "inhuman whooing noises" erupt from a body gripped with pain and an undifferentiated self that is lost in the chora. Esther finds her comfort in opposing to this scene a symbolic representation that reaffirms her position as subject.

A similar process of inward division occurs in Doris Lessing's novel *A Proper Marriage*, as Martha Quest prepares to give birth to her daughter. A friend who has just had a baby informs Martha that "nothing would ever induce her to have another baby, and if women knew what they were in for, they'd think twice."[12] But Martha believes that one should be able to remain whole and self-possessed while giving birth. People who think of it as an ordeal, she is convinced, are "weak-minded enough to allow it to be one" (p. 197). When she arrives at the hospital, she finds that the nurses agree with her. They are vocal in their disapproval of women who lose

---

11. Kristeva, "Stabat Mater," p. 178.

12. Doris Lessing, *A Proper Marriage* (London: Women's Press Limited, 1983), p. 197; subsequent references in this chapter are cited in the text.

control, and encourage Martha to "be sensible." But Martha finds that she has to concentrate very hard to "keep that sentinel alert against the dark engulfing sea," and eventually she too loses control, giving way to pain that is her new "condition of being" (p. 205). But having entered that unknown space, having become one with the pain, she finds herself undergoing an inward division. Between contractions, her pain disappears so entirely that she cannot believe it ever possessed her: "There were two states of being, utterly disconnected, without a bridge, and Martha found herself in a condition of anxious but exasperated anger that she could *not* remember the agony fifteen seconds after it had ended" (p. 206).

Martha has divided in two, one part a "free spirit" who sweats and cries out mindlessly, giving full scope to the power of the chora, and the other a condemnatory consciousness that watches her other self with dismay. The two states between which she fluctuates correspond to both the bodily and linguistic aspects of Kristeva's semiotic/symbolic division. Her body is, as Kristeva expresses it, "a division of the very flesh," and as her body experiences a contraction, her shrieks and groans signal her descent into the semiotic. Martha struggles to "drag herself as soon as possible out of each gulf," and the "sentinel"—staunch guardian of the symbolic—takes over. The sentinel that governs Martha's conscious life condemns the "free spirit" that rushes inward to the pain, but the sentinel cannot cross over and control her other self from within. Martha remains split, each aspect of her divided self struggling vainly to establish supremacy. Finally, a black woman who is mopping the floors lays her hand on Martha's stomach, bidding her to "let the baby come, let the baby come, let the baby come." At her touch, "Martha felt the cold knot of determination loosen, she let herself go, she let her mind go dark into the pain" (p. 209). Martha's sentinel vanishes in the rhythmic crooning of the black woman, whose soft, repetitive chant is the gentler voice of the semiotic. Only when Martha ceases to fight off this part of herself can her baby be born.

In the white South Africa that forms the background of *A Proper Marriage*, the native woman scrubbing hospital floors exists on the lowest level of the social hierarchy. As such, she is not someone whom Martha wants to identify with. Yet she appears during Martha's labor to provide the mirror image, the mother image, that Martha needs in order to reestablish a sense of internal unity. Her image serves Martha as midwife, inducing her to accept the transformation, the division of the flesh, and the division of the self that motherhood represents. She provides the image through which Martha, like the infant in the mirror stage, can achieve some relief from the turbulence afflicting her body. But the woman is black, and Martha poses her as the negative image of herself. She arises like a fleeting angelic vision to perform this miraculous service, and then fades into her identity as scrubbing woman, an image of powerlessness Martha immediately dismisses, as she will repress the memory of the free spirit unleashed in her during her labor.

The power of that other self which the native woman briefly releases in Martha can be found in Derricotte's "muscle of a lady" and Nin's mysterious inner "savage." Lessing gives this inner self an explicitly external manifestation, drawing a parallel between racial and body/language divisions. As Martha's white society excludes black people, considering them incomprehensible, debased, and potentially destructive, so Martha represses the maternal, semiotic "savage" in herself for similar reasons.

CHAPTER 3

Back to the Womb:
William Carlos Williams's
"A Night in June" and
Ernest Hemingway's "Indian Camp"

If the strategy of investing an alienable image with the powers and threats of a maternal body/language allows Lessing's Martha Quest to establish an illusory sense of bodily and psychic integrity, a similar strategy is important to a masculine interpretation of birth. Lessing's South African scrubbing woman is the sister of the women William Carlos Williams and Ernest Hemingway choose for their narratives of birth: women who are as far removed from the authors' class and race as possible, and who can thus be more easily associated with an occult process that challenges conventional notions of subjectivity.

William Carlos Williams's stories about medical practice in the 1930s reflect a sometimes brutal honesty about his own professional and moral limitations. In his encounters with patients, Williams said, "I was put off guard again and again, and the result was—well, a descent into myself."[1] His collection, *The Doctor Stories*, suggests that the doctor's introversion is a defensive as well as a self-critical maneuver, serving to establish emotional distance from

1. Quoted in Robert Coles, M.D., introduction to William Carlos Williams, *The Doctor Stories* (New York: New Directions Books, 1984), p. xiii.

his patients. In dealing with patients, his fictional representative ranges from a stance of self-absorption and benevolent distraction to active and overt hostility. But always, the central focus is on the doctor's inner experience.

The occasion for "A Night in June" is the birth of an eighth child to a woman the doctor has known for almost twenty years. He delivered her first child, and remembers her as "a peasant woman who could scarcely talk a word of English, being recently come from the other side."[2] He establishes the segregation of their spirits on racial, class, and intellectual grounds, initially denying her a name, a place of origin, or a language. And yet they become, in a certain sense, allies. He calls her his friend, and expresses appreciation of her dedication "to her instincts and convictions and to me" (p. 61). Her name, we eventually learn, is Angelina, and she is Italian. But this nominal identity only reinforces her alien status. She belongs to "the other side"; thus, no insights into her mind or soul are offered.

After almost twenty years the doctor knows little more about Angelina than he knew originally. He does not believe that she understands the profundity of the gap between them: "I could scarcely understand her few broken words. Her sentences were seldom more than three or four words long. She always acted as though I must naturally know what was in her mind" (p. 61). But he doesn't, and Angelina's experience, of life and of childbirth, remains closed to him. Instead, her immediate experience is translated into an abbreviated case history: "I made the examination and found the head high but the cervix fully dilated. Oh yeah. It often happens in women who have had many children; pendulous abdomen, lack of muscular power resulting in a slight misdirection of the forces of labor and the thing may go on for days" (p. 64). While Angelina labors without progress in the bedroom of her tiny apartment, the doctor dozes in the kitchen, considers giving her hormones to speed things up, and muses on the opposing wisdoms of "science and humanity." "The pituitary extract and other simple devices represent science. Science, I dreamed, has crowded the stage more than is necessary."

2. William Carlos Williams, "A Night in June," in *The Doctor Stories*, p. 61; subsequent references in this chapter are cited in the text.

He thinks about the heightened risk of a ruptured uterus when pituitrin is used to intensify labor. "But without science, without pituitrin, I'd be here till noon or maybe—what? Some others wouldn't wait so long but rush her now" (p. 66).

Partially obscured in the abstract opposition between "science" and "humanity" is the doctor's understanding of his own internal division. The part of him that is humane wants to respect the woman and the processes of her body, in spite of their occult and unpredictable nature. But the scientist in him wants to impose his own order, his own meaning, on her experience. The pituitrin might help her or it might harm her, but he knows it is to his advantage to use it. In the end, "science" wins out over "humanity," and he administers repeated doses of pituitrin, which increase her pain but fail to help her. Angelina labors all night, but the baby is not born. Like the laboring women in Nin and Derricotte, Angelina's mind is closed to her doctor's understanding, and her body resists his control. And like his angry colleagues in the women's accounts, this doctor waits in bafflement, his need to create order out of an apparently chaotic event overwhelming him.

The struggle between "science" and "humanity" is also the struggle between an orderly or conventionally organized conception of the subject as a unified being and the image of a multiple and divided subject represented by Angelina. The laboring woman is a threat to the doctor's conception of himself as a fully separated consciousness, and his efforts to bring about a quick resolution of her ambiguous state are determined by his need to reassure himself of the stability of his own position. When his efforts with pituitrin fail, the doctor tries to maneuver the baby out, reaching up inside the womb to pull on the head while pushing on Angelina's abdomen. Her sister-in-law adds force by pulling on his arm. This maneuver requires personal and prolonged contact among all four, and Williams's account reveals the circuitous mental maneuvers he undergoes in trying to incorporate their intimate physical conjunction into his private philosophical world:

> The woman and I then got to work. Her two hands grabbed me at first a little timidly about the right wrist and forearm. Go ahead, I said. Pull hard. I welcomed the feel of her hands and the strong pull. It quieted me in the way the whole house had quieted me all night.

> This woman in her present condition would have seemed repulsive to me ten years ago—now, poor soul, I see her to be as clean as a cow that calves. The flesh of my arm lay against the flesh of her knee gratefully. It was I who was being comforted and soothed. (p. 67)

The doctor's strategy allows him to derive satisfaction from his physical contact with Angelina, her fetus, and her sister-in-law while ensuring that the experience does not threaten his self-absorption and sense of superiority. He does not call either woman by name, and confuses their identity further by referring to them both as "woman." Their significance relates only to their effect on him. He describes the touch of their bodies as quieting and soothing, but his description conveys a sense of sexual violence as well. With his hand pushed up inside the passive, compliant Angelina, her sister-in-law pulling against him with all her strength, the doctor savors his position between them, the contest between his force and their resistance. But then, as though suddenly aware of the suspect nature of his enjoyment, he distances himself further by viewing it from the perspective of the past: "This woman in her present condition would have seemed repulsive to me ten years ago." Now, if she is no longer repulsive, it is because he has learned not to identify her as human. His narrative transforms Angelina into a cow, bestial and mindless, locus of a purely maternal pleasure. Having thus disarmed her of identity, humanity, and sexuality, he finds himself free to be "comforted and soothed" by her touch.

Lacan's discussion of the murderous consequences of the production of the symbol—here, the cow—provides a compelling explanation for the doctor's determination to alienate himself from the image of Angelina: "Thus the symbol manifests itself first of all as the murder of the thing, and this death constitutes in the subject the eternalization of his desire."[3] This murder of the thing, of the mother, is the prerequisite for the doctor's establishing himself as separated subject. Angelina serves as his muse; in her image he eternalizes, or renders symbolic, his desire for the mother. He can savor his desire to merge with her, to give in to the (seductive) threat her multiplicity poses, safe in the knowledge that such a

3. Lacan, *Écrits*, p. 104.

merging is impossible: the order of symbols ensures his survival as a subject.

Whatever Angelina's experience of this birth is, whatever suffering or joys it presents, are beyond the doctor's comprehension and remain unsymbolized, outside the narrative. In refusing to ascribe human sentience to her (even her energetic defense of his skill to her skeptical husband is described as "some high pitched animalistic sound" [p. 61]), he prevents her perspective from overriding his own. He excludes the possibility of a different order of subject, systematically negating her according to her sex, her nationality, and her working-class status.

Williams's accounts of birth direct the reader to pay attention to the doctor's experience alone, making it difficult to consider the women as anything more than a catalyst for the doctor's self-analysis. Angelina's account, if she could speak, might divert our attention to her suffering and her courage. She is living in deep poverty; she already cares for seven children and an irascible husband in a tiny two-room apartment. An eighth child might seem more a burden than a boon to her, but she endures the birth without complaint. For Angelina, the kind of self-reflection to which her doctor subjects himself may be a luxury she has to deny herself in the struggle for survival. The doctor imagines that she does not cry out during labor because she feels no pain, but her sister-in-law reminds him that she is trying not to wake her other children. He translates Angelina's stoicism into bovine insensibility, assuming that because she does not give voice to suffering, she does not suffer. He is astonished when she tries to cover herself after the birth; modesty is not an attribute of a beast. Her implicit faith in him forms a poignant backdrop to his incomprehension. These two people exist in different worlds, sealed away from each other.

In a poem titled "The Birth," Williams recounts an experience reminiscent of "A Night in June." The doctor is attending a Hispanic woman who has already given birth to nine children and is having trouble pushing out the tenth. He manipulates the baby into a better position for delivery, and takes advantage of a pause in the action to reflect:

> It took its own time
> rotating.

I thought of a good joke
> about an infant
>> at that moment of its career
and smiled to myself quietly
> behind my mask.
>> I am a feminist.
After a while
> I was able to extract the shoulders
one at a time
> a tight fit.
>> Madonna!
13½ pounds!
> Not a man among us
>> can have equaled
that.[4]

"The Birth" restates the terms of the doctor's separation from and desire for the mother in "A Night In June," suggesting her role as an eternally desirable, and forever inaccessible, source of nurturance, and making explicit the sexual hostility this loss generates. His "good joke" is the Freudian adage that men spend nine months trying to get out of the womb and the rest of their lives trying to get back in. But "I am a feminist," he remembers ironically, recalling the need to keep such reflections to himself. When he discovers the reason for the woman's hard labor, a very large baby, his private joke expands along Freudian lines: this baby/penis is far larger than the inadequate penis men use in their futile struggles to regain the lost womb. The pain she experiences in birth is transformed, in his fantasy of merging with her, to the agony she would experience if he could fulfill that desire. The nightmarish implications of the fantasy are graphically described in Toni Morrison's *Sula*, after Eva kills her erring son Plum, whose birth and life overtaxed her capacity to nurture:

After all that carryin' on, just gettin' him out and keepin' him alive, he want to crawl back in my womb and well . . . I ain't got the room no more even if he could do it. I'd be laying here at night and he be downstairs in that room, but when I closed my eyes I'd see him . . . six

4. William Carlos Williams, "The Birth," in *The Doctor Stories*, p. 128.

feet tall smilin' and crawlin' up the stairs quietlike so I wouldn't hear
and opening the door soft so I wouldn't hear and he'd be creepin' to the
bed trying to spread my legs trying to get back up in my womb.[5]

From Eva's point of view, Plum is trying to accomplish what is
forbidden; his incestuous desire to reestablish their lost symbiotic
unity horrifies her, and she reasons that it is better to kill him
outright, to let him "die like a man," than to let him "suffocate" in
merging with her. But if Plum's desire threatens his subjectivity, it
also presents a profound threat to hers. She kills him to protect
herself, to prevent him from destroying her.

   The peril, and the incestuous shame, of submerging oneself in the
mother's body is the lesson the young hero learns in Ernest Hemingway's "Indian Camp."[6] Like the doctor in "A Night in June,"
Hemingway's doctor uses a laboring woman's race to create a parti-
tion between them, permitting him to disregard her pain and protect himself from the challenge to subjectivity which she represents. The doctor tells his son Nick that the screams of the laboring
"Indian lady" he has come to deliver "are not important. I don't hear
them because they are not important" (p. 16). From the safety of his
studied incomprehension, as he prepares to perform a cesarean with
his jackknife, the white doctor interprets the birth scene for his
son, trying to steady the boy's shaken confidence by negating the
woman's experience. If she feels nothing "important," it is because
what she endures is outside the men's sphere. The doctor remains
staunchly cool in the face of her affliction, but the other men suffer.
Nick is exposed to a shock his youth and naïveté have not prepared
him for, and his Uncle George is bitten by the woman while he
holds her down. Her husband, lying in the bunk above hers, slits his
throat during the operation. The doctor had joked that the men are
"the worst sufferers in these little affairs" (p. 18).

   The doctor has come without anesthetic or surgical instruments.
He finishes the job by sewing the woman up with fishing line. The
narrator provides information selectively, so that certain questions

   5. Toni Morrison, *Sula* (New York: New American Library, 1973), p. 71.
   6. Ernest Hemingway, "Indian Camp," in *In Our Time* (New York: Scribners,
1925); subsequent references in this chapter are cited in the text.

are unanswerable. Did the doctor know the woman had already been in labor for two days? Did he suspect he would have to do a cesarean section? Could he have brought the necessary supplies? The lack of information, combined with the doctor's dismissal of the woman's pain, suggest that the male focus of the text excludes precisely those questions that address the woman's experience. Her unimaginable agony is important only in that it provides the testing ground for men. The doctor's consistently jovial yet businesslike approach establishes the standard against which the other men can be judged and the model that Nick is supposed to emulate. The Indian woman's suffering is important as an initiatory experience for Nick, as he learns to remain emotionless and distanced from her experience. The Indian husband, who "couldn't stand things," fails to achieve the white man's cool indifference. He inflicts on himself a wound like the one the doctor inflicts on his wife, as though only by slitting his own throat could he silence her screams within himself. Forced by a hunting wound to stay in close proximity to his wife as she labors, he is pulled into the maternal abyss and perishes there. His wound, and his death, signal his submergence in the semiotic chora; he loses himself in this place where, according to Kristeva, the subject "is both generated and negated, the place where his unity succumbs before the process of charges and stases that produce him."[7] The fact that it is an Indian man who succumbs while the white men stand by and observe his shame suggests how racial distinctions might intersect sexual distinctions in plotting the semiotic/symbolic relationship. A man may venture close to the border, but to lose oneself in the chora is to become like an infant again, merged with and negated by the mother's body. The Indian is more vulnerable to the feminine, more likely to collapse at the sound of the mother's shrieks. And for this reason he is more like a woman. In "I Who Want Not To Be," Kristeva discusses how a woman responds to "the call of the mother," which disrupts the paternal word: "If no paternal legitimization comes along to dam up the inexhaustible non-symbolized drive, she collapses into psychosis or suicide." A man, however, responds differently. If, through homosexuality or fantasies of incest, he re-creates his pre-Oedipal

7. Kristeva, *Revolution*, p. 28.

attachment to the mother, this produces laughter: "When he flees the symbolic paternal order . . . man can laugh."[8]

In Williams and Hemingway, the doctors find laughter and satisfaction in their contact with the mother. Hemingway's doctor, "feeling exalted and talkative as football players are in the dressing room after the game," boasts, "That's one for the medical journal, George. . . . Doing a Caesarean with a jack-knife and sewing it up with nine-foot, tapered gut leader" (p. 18). Williams's "good joke," the sense of immense peace that settles over the doctor in "A Night in June," and the euphoria the doctor feels in "Indian Camp" immediately after the cesarean section suggest that their entry into the mother's body restores their vigor, reinforcing their claim to life. What kills the Indian nourishes the white man. Hemingway's young hero Nick, musing over the surgery and suicide he has just witnessed, reassures himself of his own immunity from the dangers that beset those who venture too near the semiotic: "He felt quite sure that he would never die" (p. 19).

The underside of the doctors' euphoria, however, is the fear of the destructive power the mother possesses. Only by negating the mother's power—by refusing to hear her voice—can these men preserve themselves. The laboring women in these stories are portrayed as inert, mute, or incapable of meaningful speech. They speak nothing the doctor must attend to. If the Indian is vulnerable, it is because he can hear and heed the mother's siren call. The relative identities of men and women in these stories, in which the (white) male doctor is cast as a rational thinker whose privilege is augmented by comparison to a mother identified as an incoherent alien or animal, suggest the outlines of the semiotic space as it appears from the symbolic perspective: it is an "undifferentiated" space, a place of silence and absence, in which every point of reference vanishes before detection.

As long as the mother's body is the "ordering principle of the semiotic *chora*, which is the path of destruction, aggressivity, and death," as long as her voice is thought to seduce the listener "into psychosis or suicide," it is impossible to validate her as a speaking subject. Her voice, if heard at all, erupts from an indefinable space,

8. Julia Kristeva, "I Who Want Not To Be," in *Kristeva Reader*, pp. 158, 150.

threatening the paternal order that permits us to speak and to go on living. If a woman-mother would speak, then, she must ally herself with the father and reject the mother (in herself). The impossibility of the mother's positioning is presented strikingly in Kristeva's comparison of artistic expression with the act of giving birth. Although a speaker approaches the semiotic through artistic expression, a "woman also attains it (and in our society, *especially*) through the strange form of split symbolization (threshold of language and instinctual drive, of the 'symbolic' and the 'semiotic') of which the act of giving birth consists."[9] Although Kristeva implies here that a woman is capable of both art and reproduction (a woman "also" attains the semiotic through giving birth), her discussion focuses almost entirely on male artists.[10] *Almost* like the birthing mother, the artist is positioned at the "intersection of sign and rhythm, of representations and light, of the symbolic and semiotic," but he "speaks from a place where she is not, where she knows not." The mother is positioned at the "threshold of . . . the 'symbolic' and the 'semiotic,'" and the artist is positioned at the "intersection . . . of the symbolic and semiotic," but they are not in the same place. His position is privileged, for he can speak: "Thus, before all speakers, he bears witness to what the unconscious (through the screen of the mother) records of those clashes that occur between the biological and social programs of the species."[11]

Andrea Nye, providing a metaphor for the relationship between the symbolic and the semiotic in terms of the paternal sun and maternal earth/wilderness, contrasts the processes of the male poet with those of women: "Because they are less forcibly separated from their mothers and less integrated under the patriarchal sun . . . [women] are more likely than men to remain in the maternal wilderness once their rationality has been interrupted, psychotically unable to regain the clarity of the sun."[12] Nye captures an important distinction in Kristeva's theory: the male poet will be able to use his

9. Julia Kristeva, "Motherhood," in *Desire in Language,* p. 240.

10. Terry Eagleton argues for Kristeva's antiessentialism on this basis in *Literary Theory,* p. 189.

11. Kristeva, "Motherhood," p. 242.

12. Andrea Nye, "Woman Clothed with the Sun: Julia Kristeva and the Escape from/to Language," *Signs* 12.4 (1987): 674.

connection to the symbolic as a lifeline as he makes his daring plunge into the semiotic. The woman, lacking that lifeline, will be rendered aphasic and insane. It is this aspect of Kristeva's theory that leaves commentators such as Nye, Margaret Homans, and Terry Eagleton with the impression that Kristeva's representative poets are men. Kristeva does deal with the situation of women poets in her essay "I Who Want Not To Be," where she examines their suicidal tendencies:

> For a woman, the call of the mother . . . troubles the word: it generates hallucinations, voice, "madness." After the superego, the ego founders and sinks. It is a fragile envelope, incapable of staving off the irruption of this conflict, of the love which had bound the little girl to her mother, and which then, like black lava, had lain in wait for her all along the path of her desperate attempts to identify with the symbolic paternal order.[13]

While the male poet's identification with the symbolic order is assured, the woman-poet is destined, along with Virginia Woolf, to sink "wordlessly into the river." She drowns in the "black lava" of her mother, her speech aborted. While the woman-poet is defined by her annihilation in the poetic process, the *mother*-poet cannot be accounted for in this formulation. Though a woman-poet may be a mother, it is not as a mother that she speaks. She speaks as one who has desperately, but ultimately unsuccessfully, tried to use the "symbolic paternal order" as a defense against the mother's maddening influence. The mother "calls," but her voice articulates nothing; it generates only "hallucinations . . . , 'madness.'" The mother-poet is an oxymoron.

Kristeva's denial of an *écriture féminine* once again suggests an antiessentialist position, but when coupled with her assertion that speech depends on the male principle of the symbolic and its opposition to the female principle of the semiotic, this denial loses its force.[14] What is essentially feminine, in Kristeva's view, is the inarticulate cry.

13. Kristeva, "I Who Want Not To Be," p. 157.
14. For a discussion of Kristeva's rejection of the idea of an *écriture féminine*, see Moi, *Sexual/Textual Politics*, p. 163.

The contradiction inherent in Kristeva's theory, its simultaneous assertion of antiessentialism and dependence on sexed principles, presents a gap, an unattended space which the mother-poet might occupy. Her speech would not represent an *écriture féminine*, but it would represent the special perspective of one whose position in relation to the symbolic order renders her speech illegitimate. We are free to consider the special advantages and problems of her position. The mother-poet doubles herself, existing at the "threshold" and the "intersection" of the symbolic and the semiotic.[15] To paraphrase Kristeva, she speaks from a place where she is not, where she knows not. That contradictory and occult place is represented metaphorically in the scene of childbirth. It is inaccessible from the symbolic realm, and that exteriority defines its strengths and weakness: the mother-poet occupies a position of (potentially) extreme social disruption. She is a contained chaos which might at any moment proliferate. She is at once speaker and "screen," expressing simultaneously the break between the semiotic and the symbolic and the profundity of their bond. The expressions of the mother-poet threaten to dissolve dualisms and oppositions that are essential to our symbolic order. Speech and noise, creativity and procreativity, the semiotic and symbolic threaten to merge, making unnecessary the male-female distinction that makes possible the privileged position of the male artist. This is the threat that a poet such as Derricotte or Nin poses when she takes birth as her theme. The mother-poet speaks from a position which her male counterpart cannot occupy. In representing birth, she both denies and affirms the existence of what is essentially a woman's discourse. The mother-poet produces meaning "through the strange form of split symbolization (threshold of language and symbolic drive, of the 'symbolic' and the 'semiotic') of which the act of giving birth consists." But when she speaks of this essentially female experience,

---

15. For other ways of viewing the internal division of the mother-writer, see Susan Rubin Suleiman, "Writing and Motherhood," in *The (M)other Tongue: Essays in Feminist Psychoanalytic Interpretation*, ed. Claire Kahane, Shirley Nelson Garner, and Madelon Sprengnether (Ithaca: Cornell University Press, 1985), pp. 352–77, and "On Maternal Splitting: A Propos of Mary Gordon's *Men and Angels*," in *Feminist Theory in Practice and Process*, ed. Micheline R. Malson et al. (Chicago: University of Chicago Press, 1986), pp. 183–200.

she speaks from the position of a subject within the symbolic order, a subject who has by definition lost her "imaginary identity with the mother."[16] In this way, the implied revolution is finally aborted in women's birth narratives, as the mother-poet either sustains the internal spirit—maintains the paradox—or vanishes at the threshold of integration.

16. Moi, *Sexual/Textual Politics*, p. 99.

CHAPTER 4

The Birth Machine:
Cyborg Mother

By the middle of the twentieth century, one branch of obstetrics was leaving behind the attitude of "watchful expectancy" which had dominated the profession and following a trend toward "active management of labor" for parturient women. "Active management" means regularizing the progress of labor so that the cervix dilates at a constant rate. In 1955 Emmanuel Friedman developed a "partograph," which allowed obstetricians to determine whether the progress of their patients' labor conformed to an ideal curve; labors that lagged behind the ideal could be made to follow the prescribed curve with the use of oxytocic drugs.[1] The National Maternity Hospital in Dublin, the largest maternity unit in the British Isles, has taken the lead by applying the principles of active labor management universally in its facility. Since the 1960s, when Kieran O'Driscoll and his colleagues first introduced their approach to active management, over eight thousand women per year have delivered babies at the National Maternity Hospital. O'Driscoll has developed a simple and rigidly applied system of monitoring and intervention for women in labor.

1. William Ray Arney, *Power and the Profession of Obstetrics* (Chicago: University of Chicago Press, 1982), p. 145.

The degree of dilation of the cervix is recorded on a simple graph and plotted against hours after admission. Full dilation is equated with 10 cm because this is the diameter of a baby's head. The maximum time allotted is 10 hours. It follows that the slowest rate of dilation acceptable is 1 cm per hour. . . . An unsatisfactory rate of dilation of the cervix during the early hours of labour is a clear and unequivocal expression of inefficient uterine action. This should be corrected in due time.[2]

The body O'Driscoll describes is a cyborg, or rather a cyborg-cervix. At its best, it is an organ functioning with machinelike precision. When it breaks down, it can be "corrected." And even when it does break down, it is something "clear and unequivocal," amenable to time-and-motion studies. The cervix here is not only an organ; it is a progressive series of movements.

In *Discipline and Punish*, Michel Foucault, describing how marching soldiers were regulated in the middle of the eighteenth century, uses this military example to demonstrate the uses of an "anatomo-chronological schema of behavior," in which each step is broken down into a series of precise and minute components: "The 'seriation' of successive activities makes possible a whole investment of duration by power: the possibility of a detailed control and a regular intervention . . . in each moment of time."[3] It is no longer a matter of treating the body "*en masse,* 'wholesale,' as if it were an indissociable unit"; rather it becomes an analyzable series of "movements, gestures, attitudes, rapidity."[4] The timetables, the schemata, and the partitioning of bodies in schools, prisons, barracks, and hospitals create an orderly, efficient, analyzable body. Two implications of Foucault's elaboration of disciplined and docile bodies are important for understanding the principle of active management of labor. First, the active management paradigm emphasizes physiological conformity, enforced by continuous monitoring and regulation of women's behavior and progress in labor. Active management is a practical expression of the profession's convic-

2. Kieran O'Driscoll and Declan Meagher, *Active Management of Labour,* 2d ed. (London: Baillière Tindall, 1986), p. 33.
3. Michel Foucault, *Discipline and Punish,* trans. Alan Sheridan (New York: Vintage Books, 1979), p. 160.
4. Ibid., p. 137.

tion that unregulated childbearing leads to social chaos. Second, by treating the body as a series of movements rather than as an "indissociable unit," the "active management" principle allies the material body with the linguistic subject-in-process. The body is a collection of parts in motion, contingent on internal and external forces. This is as true for those motions considered "involuntary," such as uterine contraction and cervical dilation, as it is for "voluntary" motions such as marching. The body-in-process conforms to the semiotic in that it too "is articulated by flows and marks: facilitation, energy transfers, the cutting up of the corporeal and social continuum."[5]

Active management of labor involves a reconceptualization, and ultimately a functional redesign, of mothers' bodies according to a single narrow standard. The massing and organization of bodies demands that the individual body behave in precise synchrony with other bodies of its class. This synchrony, in the active management of labor, is functional, physiological, and psychic. Each of the over eight thousand women who deliver yearly at the National Maternity Hospital is expected not only to dilate at a constant rate, but to refrain from indulging in "degrading scenes" and to keep constantly in mind her responsibilities for her own well-being, her child's, and the staff's.[6] The "Dublin Experience" is a very successful experiment in standardized health care delivery; it also attempts to standardize mothers' bodies and minds.

Elizabeth Baines's 1983 novel *The Birth Machine* is a chilling interpretation of the "active management" paradigm.[7] Zelda Harris unites with the birth machine when she gives birth in a modern hospital. Her attendants' self-serving schedule and mysterious rules perplex and enrage her. But she cannot escape, for she is literally wedded to a technological system of reproduction: her husband, Roland, is a research scientist experimenting on rats to determine the effects of oral contraceptives. Her doctor, an eminent professor, is also her husband's superior, and Roland is reluctant

5. Kristeva, *Revolution*, p. 40.
6. O'Driscoll and Meagher, *Active Management*, pp. 90–91.
7. Elizabeth Baines, *The Birth Machine* (London: Women's Press, 1983); subsequent references in this chapter are cited in the text.

to question the doctor's baffling decision to induce and regulate Zelda's labor with oxytocin a week before her due date. The unresolved mystery preoccupies her as she reports to the hospital and submits to the traditional shave and enema.

The two axes of the narrative, Zelda's perspective and the men's, repel each other. There can be no meeting of the minds between Zelda and these men. She tries to question, but she is answered in such enigmatic terms that she cannot interpret the answers. Initially Roland doubts even that she heard the doctor right: "*Induce?*" he asks, "Are you sure?" His distress shows through, increasing her anxiety, and he puts pressure on her to explain:

> "But why?"
> "That's just it, Roland, they didn't say. They said there's nothing *wrong.*"
> The words hung between them like a puzzle, a jumbled chain, upside down. Inconsistent, not making sense. She saw herself through Roland's eyes: lay person, out of touch, to whom the words of the priesthood couldn't have any meaning, would only come as an arcane jumble; pregnant woman, blown with hormones that made her flush and cry and jump in fright—a caricature of femininity, too emotionally turbulent to interpret plain English when it hit against her eardrum. (p. 44)

From Roland's point of view, Zelda's impending motherhood has cast her into an alien realm that bears the mark of the semiotic. Her position renders her inarticulate and uncomprehending; she can only flush, cry, jump. In one sense Roland's point of view reveals a truth: Zelda does not yet understand "the words of the priesthood." But his viewpoint is limited because he has already enacted her symbolic murder, reducing her to "a caricature of femininity." His understanding of birth rigidly bounded by the language and methods of science, Roland is incapable of grasping the different kind of meaning Zelda will create in retelling the story of her birth as a mother-artist. By isolating her, denying her entrance into the "priesthood" of the symbolic, Roland frees her to search out a space from which to construct her own understanding of birth. The space she will find is precisely that realm which is inaccessible to him, the "nourishing and maternal" space where the symbolic has not yet been established.[8] Nevertheless, Zelda ultimately decodes the language of the priesthood and uses her knowledge to exert a degree of control over her fate as a cyborg.

At first, Zelda's resistance to the meaning and the medicine imposed on her is passive. Her body rebels against the doctors' manipulations. Just as she has never responded to her husband's lovemaking, her body resists responding to efforts to induce her labor. While the hormones drip, Zelda's body lies inert, imprisoned by machinery. But her mind takes off, dreaming, interweaving images of hospital procedure with memories of her childhood. Like a mythic hero, Zelda must solve a riddle in order to thwart her enemies. She first attempts to create meaning out of the seemingly inexplicable events of the present by setting them against a background of patriarchal myth. She recalls Sleeping Beauty, the queen who wanted a baby more than anything, and the baby girl who grows up to be stuck by a spindle, as Zelda is stuck with the intravenous needle. Significantly, her first attempts to create meaning feature the imposition of the hostile phallic signifier, the symbolic instrument of rupture. Interwoven with the myth, however, are memories of her own past, the horrors and stolen delights of her childhood which taught her to connect forbidden sexuality, her love of women, with punishment, violence, and death. While she waits to give birth, Zelda calls up erotic memories of her earliest experience of sex with her friend Hilary, memories that mingle acute pleasure with an equally acute sense of transgression and danger, recalling Kristeva's statement that in giving birth the mother "thus actualizes the homosexual facet of motherhood, through which a woman is simultaneously closer to her instinctual memory, more open to her own psychosis, and consequently, more negatory of the social, symbolic bond." Zelda's narrative will reevaluate the meaning of being "open to her own psychosis" by calling into question the sanity of the order whose rules she has transgressed.

The two narratives, Zelda's medical case history and the compilation of memory and myth that make up her personal history, cannot be immediately reconciled. As her musings suggest, if she wants to understand what is being done to her, to reconcile somehow with

8. Kristeva, *Revolution*, p. 26.

the murderous phallus, Zelda has to deal with the symbolic on its own terms, uncovering the "facts" that will complete the medical narrative. Only fragments are available to her; as an object of the system, Zelda is denied full knowledge.

But Roland and the obstetrician are not the only ones responsible for withholding a full account from her. Zelda keeps secrets from herself, refusing at first to acknowledge what she knows. She has read her doctor's textbook description of the indications for inducing labor, and she knows that he may decide to induce her simply as a "convenience." Still, she resists believing that an important medical decision could be made for such a trivial reason. Although she feels perfectly healthy and knows that her pregnancy has been uncomplicated, she begins to believe that something must be wrong with her body. Zelda's medical knowledge and her confidence in her own health and capability are eclipsed by her need to believe in her doctor's integrity and to have her husband's respect, although both are in question from the beginning.

The cognitive gap presented by Zelda's inability to explain her circumstances satisfactorily is first bridged for the reader when the narrative shifts to the professor's morning lecture, titled "Induction of Labour." His neat, scrupulously well organized lecture marks him as a master of the paternal "word." According to the professor, the machinery of induction is utterly dependable, able to initiate labor and impose order on the otherwise unpredictable flux of contractions. The professor's lecture accurately reflects the emphasis in the active management paradigm on the "clear and unequivocal." Although they promote the use of oxytocin, proponents of active management insist on its basis in nature. The Friedman curve, for instance, is designed to help physicians keep labor advancing along a "natural" route.[9] A woman who fails to follow the natural route is considered to be having an "abnormal" labor, which can be made "normal" again with oxytocin. The professor's lecture implies a link between medical procedure and the symbolic: both seek to create order out of anarchy, to turn the chaotic and inarticulate voice/body out of its internal wilderness.

The indications for induction can be summed up by a blanket statement: "Any condition may be an indication if it is considered

9. Arney, *Power,* p. 145.

safer for the mother, or for the fetus, or both, that the pregnancy does not continue any longer" (p. 20). Zelda recalls reading about the indications for induction in the professor's textbook the night before she entered the hospital, and now begins to understand the subtext: "Her healthy body may be a condition. Their lack of faith in her healthy body may be an indication" (p. 70). But the insight comes much too late. Once caught up in the machinery of induction, Zelda cannot escape. Instead, when the machine finally overcomes her body's resistance, she is suddenly devastated by rapid and irregular contractions: "The contraction seizes her, a giant hand descending and grabbing round the middle and crushing the life out: she's like a rubber doll, helpless" (p. 68). Like the laboring women in Nin and Derricotte, Zelda discovers another self within her, now a rubber doll, now a "monster." But this is different. She does not locate the cause of her split within herself. Instead, it is induced by the machine, "a giant hand descending" from the outside, forcing her into a cybernetic alliance with the professor's machinery. Through this alliance she becomes the "Birth Machine," "their Frankenstein beauty," a collection of dissociated body parts with a detachable head, controlled by the doctor through his instruments and assistants. The machinery of induction threatens Zelda's ability to renegotiate subjectivity through labor and birth; the machine/physician has entered her by way of needles and monitors, recreating her in his image. But, like Frankenstein's monster, Zelda offends her creators. She screams and shits on them in a semiotic fury: "Her body gels, gathers, and now she's her very own monster, wolf-mouth howling, frog-legs flexing: they flinch back. . . . She laughs, wild strangled laughter, coiling helter-skelter inside the huge knot of her, she sees them looking from one to the other" (p. 72).

Although Zelda's transformation is directed by the doctor, the results are not what he would have hoped. The machinery that was to have dominated her instead becomes the medium through which she "gels" into a mass of suprahuman power, intimidating to her creators. The staff become confused and fearful, finally resorting to physical restraint and sedation to subdue her. Kieran O'Driscoll and Declan Meagher address this monstrous body as another problem amenable to correction. They have found that women's morale begins to decline in prolonged labor, making them increasingly apt to lose control or demand anesthesia. On an administrative level, lengthy labors put a strain on resources and take an emotional toll on the nursing staff. The "disruptive effect of one disorganized and frightened woman in a delivery unit extends far beyond her own comfort and safety."[10] Her disorder is infectious. The entire system, hospital and staff, are potentially vulnerable to the same disease that afflicts the maddened woman in labor.

Zelda raves, her body contorts, the machinery breaks down, and her attendants react out of fear and confusion. Meanwhile, her mind is hard at work unraveling the occult history of her re-creation. "Bad veins, bad placenta, inadequate mother who must be strapped to a machine. But that doesn't fit. A shutter clicks in her head. All along they have congratulated her on her health. A very healthy pregnancy" (p. 67). From the vantage point of the cyborg, Zelda identifies the fissures in the professor's symbolic/medical order; neither his reasoning nor his equipment works as smoothly as he professes.

At last the fetus is found to be in distress, and the medical staff decide to perform an emergency cesarean section. Zelda is injected with drugs that further dissociate her from her body: "She sits up. Unhinges her head and shoulders from the rest of her body" (p. 74). She floats away from the scene and, from this alienated vantage point, watches them remove her son from her body. He is whisked away, and she is left to struggle back to full consciousness, trying to reintegrate her head and body and piece together a cohesive narrative.

Zelda's horrific experience of technologized birth prompts her to revise her understanding of the implicit rules of the patriarchal symbolic order within which she has been trapped. She reconsiders her initial reluctance to break faith with the patriarchal myth of the handsome prince/savior. Now that she understands that the traditional myth is profoundly flawed, she revises the fairy tale that has provided the metaphoric background for her initiation into sexuality and motherhood. Zelda had once insulted Roland by having an affair with another man, an offense that correlates with her earlier and even greater crime, her erotic pleasure in her girlhood friend Hilary. Zelda associates the first beatings she received from her

10. O'Driscoll and Meagher, *Active Management,* p. 90.

father with the dawning of her lesbian sexuality. Now, like her father, Roland has arranged for revenge for her new offense: "A gouged eye for an eye. One yawning space for another. A gap in her knowledge. She had forfeited insight" (p. 111). In her story the prince has no intention of rescuing the Sleeping Beauty. After the surgery Zelda lies heavily sedated in her hospital bed surrounded by dozens of funereal lilies sent by Roland, her alienated body "a gleaming oblong. White cloth. A human shape embossed" (p. 99). Her body is the image of the dead mother, the mother murdered in the name of the symbolic order.

But when the drugs begin to wear off, Zelda resurrects herself and "steals" her own medical chart from her bedside, where it has been left in the unspoken certainty that no patient would dare claim the contents. There she finds the essential key with which she can make sense of her story: "Clinical Trial: Convenience Induction." In claiming her chart, Zelda is claiming a reintegrated subjectivity: "She names herself: Teacher, Scientist. The words taste. At last they have texture. At last, to acknowledge her own insights, to be her own author" (p. 119). The knowledge that her ordeal was unnecessary, that she has been betrayed by her husband, her doctor, and the machinery of medicine, frees her from their control. They can no longer isolate her as an inarticulate, uncomprehending "caricature of femininity," the mother symbolically murdered. By naming herself "Teacher, Scientist," Zelda lays claim to labels that carry authority within the symbolic order. But the meanings Zelda attaches to the terms are very different from those Roland and her doctor—men who bear the titles legitimately—assign to them. She has "stolen" the terms, just as she stole her medical history.

Empowered by the initial success of her transgressions, she becomes aware of her child for the first time, and finds him in the bassinet by her hospital bed, apparently waiting for her. She steals a nurse's cloak, hides her baby in its folds, and walks out of the hospital. Zelda's thievery, especially the theft of her son, rewrites the "dominant myth of language" in which a daughter seizes on the hope of having a (male) baby to substitute for the phallus/signifier she lacks.[11] Initially, it appears that Zelda lives up to the letter of the law; only through the birth of her son does she obtain access

11. Homans, *Bearing the Word*, p. 5.

to signification. But when she steals the baby/signifier, she defies those who have a "legitimate" claim to him. Under the law of the father, the mother *must* be separated from her child; he *must* be subject to the father's law. The entire symbolic order depends on their separation, which initiates the child's eternally thwarted desire for union with her. Instead, she takes the baby and runs, defiantly hoarding her plunder, robbing the symbolic order of everything it needs (the separation of the mother from the phallus/signifier/potential subject) in order to operate.

But Zelda's getaway leads out of the narrative. In *The Birth Machine*, her escape from the hospital coincides with her exit from the symbolic order. Her future and that of her son remain cached where men cannot reach—and beyond the scope of the narrative. The novel is reticent about what happens after the rebellion, how Zelda survives once she gets into a taxi and is driven away. We read that "she knows now where she'll go" (p. 120), but she doesn't reveal her destination. She leaves behind the bare implication that she will seek out her old friend and lover Hilary, a move which, in Kristeva's terms, represents the homosexual merging of the new mother with (a figure of) her own mother. If we follow Kristeva and maintain that such a maternal merging represents a plunge into the semiotic, the termination of Zelda's narrative at this point suggests the consequences of that merging. No one speaks from the semiotic realm: submergence in the semiotic is symbolic suicide, the death or stillbirth of the subject. Zelda vanishes at the threshold, an illegitimate subject already abandoning subjectivity, abducting a son she must soon either surrender to the symbolic order or commit to annihilation in the chora.

Zelda's escape illustrates some of the limitations of a Kristevan account of subjective processes. Zelda *was* a subject-in-process, constructed through struggle and contradiction, but her final destiny is fixed by her anatomy; as a mother, re-merging with her own mother, she ceases to have access to signification. Although Zelda claims to be her own author, and achieves this distinction by contradicting the patriarchal order, Kristeva's model of subjective processes denies her claim. As Toril Moi's interpretation of the little girl's development implies, Kristeva, following Lacan, preserves familiar gender distinctions and associations; her conservative philosophy cannot produce a revolutionary subject, who would not be constituted through standardized processes that are further limited by gender.

Donna Haraway, in her essay "A Manifesto for Cyborgs," delivers a new myth for mid-1980s socialist feminism, one without "claims for an organic or natural standpoint," a myth not based on claims of identity, unity, or wholeness. She finds the hero of the new myth in the figure of the cyborg:

> The cyborg is a creature in a post-gender world; it has no truck with bisexuality, pre-oedipal symbiosis, unalienated labor, or other seductions to organic wholeness through a final appropriation of all the powers of the parts into a higher unity. In a sense, the cyborg has no origin story in the Western sense—a "final" irony since the cyborg is also the awful apocalyptic *telos* of the "West's" escalated dominations of abstract individuation, an ultimate self untied at last from all dependency, a man in space.[12]

The figure of the cyborg represents the possibility of a revolutionary subject, one for whom there is no symbiotic union with Mother, no drama of separation, and no gender identifications to establish. The fusion of human and machine produces an independent being, without origin and so without a fixed destiny, perhaps without death. Thus constituted, the cyborg represents the fall of male domination. As the "illegitimate offspring of militarism and patriarchal capitalism, not to mention state socialism" (pp. 150–51), the cyborg renders its father inessential.

In a sense, Zelda becomes this being. Fused with the machinery of induction, she draws a new kind of physical and intellectual power from the connection. She is transformed into a "Frankenstein beauty" who intimidates her creators so thoroughly that they resort to physical restraint and sedation to subdue her. As a result of her transformation, she eventually breaks her ties with the patriarchal institutions of medicine and marriage. At that point she exits the narrative, taking her newborn son with her. We never learn

---

12. Donna Haraway, "A Manifesto for Cyborgs: Science, Technology, and Socialist Feminism in the 1980s," *Socialist Review* (January 1985): 150–51; subsequent references in this chapter are cited in the text.

what the rebel cyborg mother does once she has cut herself loose from the systems that produced her. The narrative cannot continue past the point of Zelda's escape because the cyborg is unimaginable outside structures of domination.

Haraway's conception of the cyborg permits a more optimistic interpretation of Zelda's fate. But Zelda's transformation into a cyborg mother is a scene of torture. Her body's resistance to the fusion is overcome only when the machine exerts extreme force. She experiences not a "disturbingly and pleasurably tight coupling" with the machine but a thoroughly unpleasurable invasion (p. 152). The machine attempts to take her over, and it is only through struggle and resistance to the machine's domination that she enacts her own transformation. It is of course inappropriate to attribute to the machine the status of an independent entity, self-generated and capable of intention. The specific machine Zelda does battle with is only an extension, a detachable arm of an entity that has already constituted itself as a cyborg, a fusion of machine and physician. This cyborg is no illegitimate offspring, but the recognized son and heir of "militarism and patriarchal capitalism," dedicated to the service of his fathers. Zelda resists merging with this entity because their coupling means her death; absorbed into the vast cybernetic network of modern medical technology, Zelda would be the prostrated object of a highly patriarchal domination.

Haraway recognizes that the dawning of the cybernetic age has not erased structures of domination. "The actual situation of women," she says, "is their integration/exploitation into a world system of production/reproduction and communication called the informatics of domination" (p. 163). Zelda's hospital experience is more reflective of women's integration into "a world system of production/reproduction" than it is of the dream—however ironic—of the cyborg as the hero of a new socialist-feminist myth. Haraway says that "cyborgs are ether, quintessence" (p. 153). And so is Zelda at the end of the novel: she is ethereal, or without body. But this cyborg, this ether, cannot occupy the same narrative space as the Zelda whose body has suffered and struggled. Whereas Haraway is calling for the end of the "border war" between the human and machine, Baines's novel warns of the danger of laying down our weapons too soon.

II The Mother-State

Childbearing could be taken over by technology, and if this proved too much against our past tradition and psychic structure (which it certainly would at first) then adequate incentives and compensations would have to be developed—other than the ego rewards of possessing the child—to reward women for their special social contribution of pregnancy and childbirth.

—Shulamith Firestone, *The Dialectic of Sex*

Revolutionary Subjects

According to Rosalind Coward and John Ellis, "Until Marxism can produce a revolutionary subject, revolutionary change will be impossible." For them the most prevalent conception of the subject in Marxism is humanistic, positing a "free" subject possessing a "human essence." This subject is alienated under the social structures of capitalism, but would be established as the center of society under communism. A genuinely revolutionary subject, by contrast, would be a subject-in-process, constructed in contradiction. Coward and Ellis believe that the Marxist analysis has failed to produce this subject because it has neglected the subject's materiality. A conception of the material subject would stress "process rather than identity, struggle rather than structure, seeing it as part of a heterogeneous (contradictory) totality rather than logical development."[1]

The material subject corresponds to Julia Kristeva's conception of a subject decentered by internal and social contradiction: "Although an externality, the contradiction within social relations de-

---

1. Rosalind Coward and John Ellis, *Language and Materialism: Developments in Semiology and the Theory of the Subject* (Boston: Routledge & Kegan Paul, 1977), pp. 91, 83.

centers and suspends the subject, and articulates him as a passage-way, a non-place, where there is a struggle between conflicting tendencies, *drives* whose stases and thetic moments (the *repre-sentamen*) are as much rooted in affective relations (parental and love relations) as they are in class conflict."[2] In arguing that such a subject, "de-centered" by both familial and class conflicts, is more consistent with dialectical materialism than is a humanistic notion of a unified subject, Coward and Ellis assent to a model in which the Kristevan subject and its world faithfully mirror each other. Only a society fractured by its contradictions could produce a subject-in-process, and only such a society could function as an authentic mirror of the subject's interior contradictions.[3]

But when "society," riddled as it is with contradictions, looks in the mirror, it would rather see a fully integrated humanist subject—Lacan's "Ideal-I"—than a subject-in-process. The subject-in-process appears to be dangerously unstable, as dire a threat to social order in general as the laboring woman is to hospital routines in particular. The practical implications of this theoretical twist become apparent only when one gives the abstract "material subject" a material manifestation, which I accomplish by reading a fragment of my own history as a "mother-in-process" through the lens of Kristeva's theory of socially contingent subjectivity.

At twenty-one I was the mother of a year-old baby. My husband was divorcing me. Although he had a well-paying job and I was unemployed, the judge awarded me $150 per month in child support. He told me sternly that I was an able-bodied young woman, and there was no reason I could not support myself. (We did not discuss how, with a high school education and no marketable skills,

2. Kristeva, *Revolution*, p. 203.
3. This conception of the relationship between the individual and his or her society is not at odds with Marx's own conception. The Marxist subject is an iso-morph who reproduces in him- or herself the larger social structure: "It is above all necessary to avoid postulating 'society' once again as an abstraction confronting the individual. The individual is the social being. The manifestation of his life—even when it does not appear directly in the form of a communal manifestation, accom-plished in association with other men—is, therefore, a manifestation and affirmation of social life. Individual human life and species-life are not different things." Karl Marx, *Economic and Philosophic Manuscripts* (New York: International Publishers, 1964), pp. 137–38.

I could find a full-time job lucrative enough to cover our expenses as well as child care costs. I could have told him, if he had been interested, that full-time child care for an infant in diapers would eat up almost half of the tiny income I could generate, and that it would be impossible to pay for housing, utilities, medical insurance, and food once the babysitter had been paid.) The judge's decision was couched in the rhetoric of personal responsibility. It depended first of all on an ideology of individualism. From the judge's perspective I was a "free" subject who had chosen to have a child. I alone was responsible for the consequences. "Society," as represented in my ex-husband, the legal system, and social service agencies, had no responsibility for my welfare as a woman, worker, or mother.

I consider this courtroom situation and its implications for my life an instance of the external "contradiction within social relations" that reflects and makes possible the subject-in-process. Standing in the courtroom, listening to the judge's decision, I felt the ground breaking up under me. I was the decentered and suspended subject Kristeva describes. This was by no means an extraordinary moment. Women are caught up in social and familial "contradictions" every day, not only in courtrooms but in welfare offices, in workplaces, in schools, and in their own homes.

It may be that such moments, when social and economic contradictions make themselves felt with special intensity within material subjects, are even now promoting a revolution in social relations of class, race, and gender. But I had long since internalized the ideology of individualism that defined my legal status. My response to the external contradictions that were breaking up my life was to attempt to achieve the subjective integrity the judge's decision implied I possessed. I did not even consider applying for welfare, although that clearly would have been the wisest course. My upbringing (white middle-class values and a working-class living) precluded it. I was deeply ashamed that financial hardship had forced me back into my parents' home for a few months. I considered this a personal failure—a failure that had forced me to reestablish a familial connection in which I was the dependent child.

At my divorce it served the judge's interest to see me as a "free subject," but that perception was also, ironically, useful to me. I dreaded being defined by a social system I experienced as hostile.

The ideology of individualism contributed to the hostility of the system, but it also provided some constructive illusions for a half-educated single mother without economic resources. I clung to the idea that I had once been and could again become a whole and autonomous person whose "essential self" was distinct from conflicted social, economic, legal, and academic systems. Fifteen years later, at a time when I am more secure financially and socially, an illusion of subjective integrity is less important to my survival. On occasion I can afford the luxury of constructing myself as a subject-in-process, but I can also quite comfortably adopt the guise of the "free" subject.

This subjective flexibility is the result of economic and social privileges I have acquired. It is not the result of any qualities inherent in my sex, although such flexibility is an advantage since I am still affected by the special social "contradictions" reserved for women. As a woman and mother, I present special problems for theories of subjectivity. The subject-in-process of whatever sex is always gendered masculine (as is the humanist subject); the feminine is whatever is excluded from signifying practices. In regard to her use of the masculine pronoun for the subject, Kristeva told her translator that "the 'subject' in this book is so abstract or universal that it concerns both sexes. We can therefore keep the 'he.' . . . In reality, feminine 'subjectivity' is a different question but it does not elude the general realm of *subjecthood* [*subjecticité*], or of subjectivation."[4] Kristeva reproduces the old problem of the generic "he" whose universality specifically excludes women (their " 'subjectivity' is a different question"), but what is excluded is not merely an abstract femininity; as Margaret Homans points out, Lacan's infamous comment that women are "excluded by the nature of things, which is the nature of words," attests to the materiality of their exclusion.[5]

But the generic (i.e., masculine) subject is also demarcated by the symbolic. He is constituted only in the process of constructing and deconstructing discursive positions. Subject to "the nature of

4. Kristeva, *Revolution*, p. 235n.
5. Lacan, quoted in Homans, *Bearing the Word*, p. 9; see also Luce Irigaray, *This Sex Which Is Not One*, trans. Catherine Porter (Ithaca: Cornell University Press, 1985), p. 87. *Seminar XX: Encore* (Paris, 1975).

words," his psychic processes are isomorphic to the production of language. For this reason, there is nothing in "generic" human nature that can change course to allow for alternative subjectivities. The revolutionary potential of the subject-in-process is limited because he is locked into the cyclic processes that construct and deconstruct him. ("At every moment . . . [man] constitutes his world by his suicide.")[6] Alternately annihilated and reconstituted in language, the Lacanian subject has no more revolutionary potential than the humanist subject.

The gendered logic that constructs the generic subject as masculine provides a theoretical loophole for the excluded feminine. If the masculine subject is incapable of a revolutionary transformation because he is bound to symbolic processes, the feminine escapes the symbolic bind. French feminist theorists exploit the feminine loophole to conceive a revolutionary subject whose multiplicitous sexual and reproductive body grounds her speech. "Her flesh speaks true," writes Hélène Cixous, because "her speech, even when 'theoretical' or political, is never simple or linear."[7] Luce Irigaray writes that women's libidinal economy "upsets the linearity of a project" and "disconcerts fidelity to a single discourse." Their exclusion from the linear—from the logical, symbolic processes that bind the masculine—frees the feminine subject to embody the revolutionary transformation. Although Irigaray warns against simply reversing the sex-based distribution of power, she sees separatism and lesbianism as "indispensable stages" in the revolution that will enable women to "escape from their proletarization on the exchange market."[8] And Cixous, recalling the "American" slogan "We are all lesbians," declares that women's "libido will produce far more radical effects of political and social change than some might like to think."[9]

My divorce proceedings have taken on the quality of a nightmare in my memory, but not because I was forced by circumstance to

6. Lacan, *Écrits*, p. 28.
7. Hélène Cixous, "Laugh of the Medusa," in *Feminisms: An Anthology of Literary Theory and Criticism*, ed. Robyn Warhol and Diane Price Herndl (New Brunswick: Rutgers University Press, 1991), p. 338.
8. Irigaray, *This Sex Which Is Not One*, p. 33.
9. Cixous, "Laugh of the Medusa," p. 339.

betray some essential truth abiding in my multiplicitous sexual-maternal body. I was not interested in negotiating a "truer" discursive position, but I was vitally concerned with negotiating more humane material terms. I had been assigned, and I accepted, a humanist subjectivity, but I did not then have access to all of the material advantages necessary to support that or any other illusion. Certainly my rebellious body "spoke true" in that I shook inwardly, accurately reflecting the crisis in which I found myself. But I struggled to hide my emotions. I thought that, if my ex-husband's lawyer and the judge saw my hatred and fear of them, they would impose even harsher terms. The symbolic was speaking my body that day, in the sense that the courtroom proceedings established the conditions under which I and my daughter would live. Asserting myself as a "revolutionary" feminine subject would not have improved my situation within the legal, medical, and financial systems that dominate our society. It is true that women represent a "special problem," in Kristeva's phrase, but not because they are women. The "problem" and the betrayal reside not in women's bodies but in the terms of their material relationship to the symbolic.

Zelda, in Elizabeth Baines's *Birth Machine*, survives her confrontation with the social contradictions within the health care system because she turns away, for a moment at least, from the lyric expressions of her multidimensional, image-heavy memory and learns to speak the linear language of medicine. I am still curious about where Zelda might have gone once she stole out of the hospital and found her old lover Hilary. It is possible that by following her, I might find a way out of the courtroom that still haunts my own memories. Despite my doubts about the material efficacy of the revolutionary subject, I am drawn to the utopian ideals implied in Cixous and Irigaray, especially as those ideals are expressed and challenged in American feminist speculative fiction. Several contemporary writers, including Alice Sheldon writing as "James Tiptree" ("Houston, Houston Do You Read?"), Joanna Russ (*The Female Man*), Marge Piercy (*Woman on the Edge of Time*), and Suzy McKee Charnas (*Motherlines*), envision utopias in which women escape from masculinist modes of production and reproduction into closed communities that valorize close familial and sexual relationships between women.

Charlotte Perkins Gilman is perhaps the most obvious fore-mother of the contemporary American feminist utopia. Gilman's mothers are "a unit, a conscious group."[10] The women of Herland achieve social cooperation by being in tune with, and having perfect control over, their reproductive bodies, a biosocial advance that women in the contemporary utopias have largely replicated. Terry, a male guest in Herland whose aggressive stupidity leads him to rape, anticipates the absurdly naive but lethal men who appear in the utopian novels of Tiptree, Russ, and Charnas. But I find another, less expected predecessor in Meridel Le Sueur's depression-era novel *The Girl*. Unlike Gilman's utopian women, Le Sueur's Great Mothers experience sexual tensions and pleasures as well as physical pain and interpersonal conflict. Le Sueur's portrayal of manipulative social institutions, and her implication that they depend on capitalism and patriarchy, prefigures Marge Piercy's account of oppressive welfare and medical institutions in the late twentieth century. Le Sueur's novel offers a model of a maternal subjectivity that, if it were dominant, would abolish these institutions and the class hierarchies they represent. Whereas Piercy produces a utopia that reflects a Marxist model of a harmonious community of social individuals, *The Girl* has more in common with contemporary French feminist theory, since its final passages surmise a utopian communal consciousness, produced by and for women out of the economic and sociopolitical crises of the depression.

The revolutionary subject in Le Sueur's dazzling vision would possess no bodily boundaries because she would be the sum total of place and history, an ever expanding universe. But a multiple feminine subjectivity that stakes its claim to authenticity on the basis of the material (i.e., biological) female body does not represent a radical departure from traditional notions of femininity and maternity. In fact, it accords well with a traditionally gendered subjectivity, where Man functions as the singular, stable humanist subject and Woman as the multiple, boundless, socially contingent subject. This standard dichotomy is as apparent in Tiptree as it is in earlier novels by Le Sueur and Gilman. Standing behind Multiple Woman

10. Charlotte Perkins Gilman, *Herland* (1915; rpt. New York: Pantheon, 1976), p. 79.

are Ahistorical Woman and Mass Woman. Utopian women in Gilman, Charnas, and Tiptree aim for social and technological stability, in which history moves not forward but in circles, in accordance with the reproductive cycles that determine every woman's life.

This model of unadulterated social and psychological femininity is as problematic as the Lacanian subject-in-process. Its subject describes a predictable and repetitive course, determined in this case not by the exigencies of language production but by the demands of the biological body. A multiple (i.e., maternal) subjectivity cannot resolve the class- and gender-based "contradictions" in social relations. Straining to define the differences between men and women, many writers overlook (at the very least) social, racial, and economic differences among women. Multiple Woman, a figure for maternal and sisterly unity, serves as an excuse for the dominant group's specious assumption of a unified "we." Nevertheless, in the feminist utopias the notion of a shared subjectivity has allowed writers to consider how women's reproductive labor might serve as a model for a separatist community designed to meet *some* women's social and economic needs better than the writer's own society.

In the chapters that follow, after considering the promise and problems of the revolutionary feminine subject in Le Sueur's fiction, I turn to the more ominous implications of the "woman is body" model. Reproductive technologies in Piercy, Tiptree, and Charnas are used to multiply the benign influence of maternal physiology throughout the social body. But similar technologies produce monstrous bodies in fictions by David Rorvik, Sven Delblanc, and Aldous Huxley. In their unhappy speculations, the mother's body is appropriated, broken down into its constituent parts, or abolished altogether to make room for the production of homunculi and clones, figures ironically designed to resurrect, à la Frankenstein's monster, the defunct autonomous masculine subject.

CHAPTER 5

Great Mothers:
The Girl as a Feminist Utopia

In Meridel Le Sueur's 1930s novel *The Girl*, first published in 1978, the extreme social and economic contradictions of the depression era produce a potentially "revolutionary subject."[1] The title suggests her lack of personal boundaries. The Girl could be any woman, and in fact her hunger and passion, even her slow-growing wisdom, reproduce the common hungers and passions of all the women who form her community. According to Le Sueur, the title character embodies the lives of at least four women who were lost or crushed or incarcerated. The Girl is constituted by their experience of crisis, by the leftover fragments of these disintegrated women. Le Sueur asks us to celebrate "those wonderful women our mothers ourselves who keep us all alive,"[2] but such a celebration is possible only if we posit, however fleetingly, a world in which these women—united as "our mothers, ourselves"—could themselves have survived.

---

1. Linda Ray Pratt calls Le Sueur the "most prominent female literary figure in the Communist Party USA," in "Women Writers in the CP: The Case of Meridel Le Sueur," *Women's Studies* 14 (1988): 247.
2. Le Sueur, *The Girl*, "Afterwords"; subsequent references in this chapter are cited in the text.

In *The Girl*, external contradictions reproduce themselves internally. The revolutionary subject cannot survive perpetually at the moment of political and social crisis that constitutes her because that moment will also, paradoxically, annihilate her. In its final moments the novel seeks to resolve the external and internal contradictions that constitute The Girl as a revolutionary subject. She resolves her internal contradictions by.bearing a child, a gesture that takes her simultaneously out of history and out of herself. The birth places her in timeless continuity with all women, effectively removing her from the material and psychological circumstances that put her in crisis.

Until the final moments of the novel, Le Sueur's portrayal of the effects of depression poverty on the Girl's interior experience is consistent with Rosalind Coward and John Ellis's assertion that a conception of the revolutionary subject should stress "process rather than identity, struggle rather than structure, seeing it as part of a heterogeneous (contradictory) totality rather than logical development."[3] My focus is on the novel's closing passages, in which the Girl gives birth and undergoes a subjective transformation in which she ceases to experience herself as alienated. When she achieves motherhood, she negates her "revolutionary" potential, as both internal and external contradictions dissolve.

I will return momentarily to Kristeva to emphasize the relationship between language and the processes of the revolutionary subject. Kristeva argues that poetic language, in which resistances to and facilitations of nonspecific semiotic drives find expression in the varying rhythms and discontinuities of language, demonstrates how the internal "unity of consciousness," the illusion of a unified subjectivity, is shattered by the processes of signification. During the 1930s, the period when she wrote many of the stories that were later incorporated into the novel, Le Sueur was at times in conflict with the Communist party over her "lyrical" writing style. In *The Girl*, Le Sueur uses the voices of working-class women as the basis of her own poetic expression. The Girl's friend Belle recounts the story of her first abortion:

3. Coward and Ellis, *Language and Materialism*, p. 38.

I was just a kid, I was keeping house for a dame and her husband got at me. She sent me to the city with a paper with an address. I felt like a worm, I walked those streets, a kid. Then they just shafted the kid and left you to bleed to death. I passed it in a restroom, wrapped it in the St. Paul *Dispatch* and threw it in the Mississippi.

And then she began to weep for all the long dead and the coming dead, all the dead in the earth, all the dead in her.

Belle was a great tomb and I moved into her fat arms and her warm great bosom. (p. 75)

The criticism leveled at Le Sueur by the Communist party—a criticism with which she concurs—was that the language of passages like this one tended to pull the reader's attention away from its political purpose. At certain points throughout *The Girl*, women's identities tend to overlap or merge. In this passage Le Sueur imposes no firm division between Belle's voice and the Girl's, and Belle, who often refers to the Girl as "kid," also names herself and her aborted fetus "kid." As her narrative flows into the Girl's, Belle expands, taking into her "great tomb"/womb the living, the dead, and the yet-to-be born—including the Girl herself. The specific social outrage that underlies Belle's narrative, the exploitation of a young working-class girl by her bourgeois employers, is less important than the expansive maternal consciousness that Belle has achieved through her grief. The Communist party encouraged—and perhaps pressured—Le Sueur to suppress the characteristic lyricism of her writing. Loyal to the party, Le Sueur worked to overcome this apparent fault: "I now question the lyricism of my early stories, as if they were covering the horror and loss, the terrible sewage of bourgeois life. . . . Before, I defended myself by saying we should not leave the beautiful, lyrical use of language to the ruling class—the workers must have, and do have, beautiful language."[4]

Others, however, have celebrated Le Sueur's unusual style, finding in *The Girl* "a pattern reflecting the underlying spirit of a truly revolutionary human culture."[5] *The Girl* exemplifies the problems of constructing a revolutionary subject for political ends; Le Sueur's

4. Quoted in Pratt, "Women Writers," p. 259.
5. Neala Schleuning, "Afterwords," in Le Sueur, *The Girl.*

style, modulated to the "basic rhythms" of the semiotic, is well suited to a narrative of a (maternal) subject-in-process, but represents a challenge to a Marxist-humanist conception of the free subject. The novel, however, also challenges the Lacanian and Kristevan conceptions of the subject, which Coward and Ellis represent as the revolutionary prototype, by positing a collective and embodied subjectivity—the definitive end of alienation—as the goal of the class struggle.

For the Girl, the occasion of her daughter's birth marks the decisive end of her sense of herself as singular and isolated. This is the climax her narrative has been working toward from the beginning. In labor, she says, "the river broke in me and poured and gave and opened" to an uninterrupted stream of relationships, of sisters, daughters and mothers, each woman flowing into the others. She finds her mother's image reflected in the women, and herself reflected as the image of her own mother in the face of her newborn daughter (p. 147).

It is this vision of collective female identity, in which the needs of the one will be felt by all and answered by all, which Le Sueur offers as an ideal prototype of a revolutionary culture, a women's commune. It is *post*revolutionary in the sense that it represents a version of the society one might expect after the class struggle has resolved itself. Such a communist society would involve the de-alienation of the self from the self, others, nature, labor, and the material products of that labor. Nancy Chodorow provides a psychological argument for ascribing to women the capacity to resolve social and economic alienation: "The care and socialization of girls by women ensure the production of feminine personalities founded on relation and connection, with flexible rather than rigid ego boundaries. . . . This is one explanation for how women's relative embeddedness is reproduced from generation to generation, and why it exists within almost every society."[6] Le Sueur's vision of a women's collective is a politicized and class-sensitive version of Chodorow's model of the feminine personality. The "relation and connection" that are reproduced cyclically and within different so-

6. Nancy Chodorow, *Feminism and Psychoanalytic Theory* (New Haven: Yale University Press, 1989), p. 57.

cieties (and hence economies) in Chodorow's model become, in Le Sueur, the occasion for a sudden break with western patriarchal-capitalist history. The break occurs at a specific historical moment when the weight of women's double oppression as productive and reproductive laborers becomes unbearable.

The exclusionary aspect of the final passages, in which men, who have played only peripheral roles throughout the novel, vanish entirely, allies *The Girl* with other separatist feminist utopias. Protected in inaccessible places on Earth, on separate planets, in other dimensions, women form a utopian matriarchy in which a vision of collective mother-rule replaces the Marxist vision of the dictatorship of the proletariat. In *The Girl*, however, the threat that men pose to mother-rule is more immediate than in the utopias. Men and their oppressive institutions press on the walls of the warehouse/womb that contains the women's commune. The women's search for a collective maternal consciousness is a struggle to transcend the harrowingly brutal exterior world produced by the wedding of capitalism and patriarchy.

On her journey toward membership in the commune of "Great Mothers," the Girl must negotiate a series of obstacles set up by (masculinist-capitalist) society. She narrowly escapes the abortion her boyfriend Butch tries to force on her, and then faces a day-to-day struggle to nourish and house herself and her unborn child. Butch is a would-be bank robber who is planning his first (and, as it turns out, last) heist. The bank robbery provides the Girl with a metaphor for her illicit pregnancy: "I had to smile. I had already robbed the bank. I had stolen the seed. I had it on deposit. It was cached. It was safe" (p. 85). The metaphor of theft highlights the "illegitimacy" of her claim to ownership of her own body and its "product" in a patriarchal society.[7] If her illicit pregnancy is a crime against society, it is also a crime against Butch. It is his seed she has stolen, and she keeps it "hidden" from him after she escapes the abortion he has arranged. He dies of gunshot wounds after his own (failed) robbery attempt. Butch, like the Girl, is ultimately a victim of mer-

7. The Girl's perception of her determination to keep her child as a kind of thievery is comparable to Zelda's self-perception in Baines's *Birth Machine*. Another similarity connects them: like Zelda, the Girl steals her file from a social worker's desk in an attempt to learn the official "story" of her life.

ciless patriarchal law. The risk of retribution the Girl takes in "robbing the bank" is as great as Butch's, but when he dies, one aspect of
the double threat dies with him. Although hard times may threaten
her, at least Butch will never again try to force her to give up her
child. Butch's death, following closely on the death of the Girl's
father, removes from the narrative any possibility of a "Great Father" to match the "Great Mothers" who survive and multiply
throughout the novel. Instead, Father is constituted by the patriarchal institutions that oppress men and women both. Men's relationship to this patriarch in *The Girl* is problematic, for although
they are victimized by it, they also reproduce it, indulging in violent
behavior, killing one another, beating their women, and deserting
their children.

The innocent victims are women and children. The Girl's friend
Clara is a prostitute consigned to a mental hospital when she seeks
government relief. She undergoes shock treatments and loses much
of her memory, her ability to speak, and eventually her life. Clara's
nightmare exemplifies Le Sueur's perception of the machinery of
capitalism and the patriarchy as joined in an infinitely brutal program of social control. The Girl, driven by hunger to apply for relief,
falls into a similar trap. A social worker recommends her for a psychiatric evaluation and sterilization, and for a while it appears that
the Girl may share Clara's fate. She ends up in the "relief maternity
home," a prison where babies are taken from their mothers as soon
as they are born and where, the Girl fears, she will be involuntarily
sterilized after giving birth. Fortunately, an underground network
of members of the Workers' Alliance puts her in communication
with Amelia, a mother of six, leader of the alliance, and a midwife.
Amelia eventually obtains her release, and shortly before giving
birth, the Girl joins a group of homeless women in a warehouse.

Her labor to give birth makes the Girl realize that although she
contains and reflects the contradictions of her society, she can transcend alienation. She strives to leave behind her "own loneliness
and death" and give birth to herself as a member of a women's
commune: "It makes you shake all over, but you've got to do it,
you've got to take the chance to do it. It takes guts to speak out of
the lonely room, after looking at yourself in a mirror, after smelling
out yourself alone, after hearing emptiness sound off. It makes the

sweat stand on you, and your blood starts up, for what is one voice alone, or what good is it to cry in a room with the door shut?" (p. 143).

In labor, the illusion of singular consciousness is shattered; this is the Girl's first step toward a revolutionized subjectivity. In the "lonely room" that is the semiotic womb of language, she uses the mode of expression natural to that space, shaking, sweating, and crying out. The Girl faces an image of unified, individual subjectivity, expressed through her confrontation with a metaphoric mirror image of herself, and discovers that the isolation and mortality represented by the image is illusory. Rejecting the illusion, she "speaks out" from her body, laboring to push her isolated inner self outward to join with "the great Mothers." The women of the alliance provide protective shelter, a womb in which the Girl can give birth, not just to her child but to herself as a mother: "I felt I would stand there and just drop my child into their hands, the great Mothers, that's what I saw and will always see as long as I draw breath. I got no words but it will be . . . inside us forever" (p. 46). The space "inside us forever" is beyond words and therefore beyond men's reach or control. Although the threat posed by capitalist patriarchy is immediate in a material sense, it cannot violate the women's unity of consciousness. The women experience her birth with her, breathing "a kind of great wind through their bodies like wind in a wood" (p. 147). The Girl achieves an inviolable solidarity with women because they too are mothers, in fact or in spirit.

At the moment the Girl achieves an ecstatic union with her companions and establishes the identification across the generations between herself, her own mother, and her daughter, the novel closes. Viewed against the background of Kristeva's account of the relationship between the semiotic and the symbolic, the Girl's identification with the Great Mothers casts her out of the symbolic. She passes beyond the reach of the symbolic and enters an unspeakable realm. The Girl's identification with the Great Mothers corresponds to Kristeva's model of a birthing mother's reunion with the body of her own mother. This reunion has both its beneficial aspects and its dangers; although she is "closer to her instinctual memory" and therefore achieves a deeper understanding of herself, she is also "more open to her own psychosis, and consequently,

more negatory of the social, symbolic bond."[8] By ecstatically cele-
brating the union of women, Le Sueur places a more positive valuation on this excursion into the semiotic than Kristeva might, suggesting that the eternal moment of union with the mother is a more
than satisfactory replacement for the "social, symbolic bond."

In *The Girl*, the revolution in culture is a revolution in subjectivity. Only women can participate, however. Le Sueur's vision of
revolutionary subjectivity excludes men. They are eclipsed by the
women and left out of the symbolic operations of the communist
Workers' Alliance, which now operates its press out of the warehouse. As the women gather around the Girl, "the men kind of hung
back," strangers in this gathering of women (p. 146). And it is not
finally Butch's face "coming back down the great river" (p. 147) that
the Girl envisions as the image of her child but the Girl's own face,
and her mother's, re-mirrored throughout the gathering of Great
Mothers.

As she overcomes her isolation to join the community of mothers, the Girl also finds herself becoming committed to the Workers'
Alliance. Within the scope of Le Sueur's vision, the merging of the
women in the context of the alliance represents the birth of a newly
politicized communal consciousness. The promise of communal
identity gives her the courage to reproduce her kind amid the violence, poverty, and rootlessness that threaten her individual life.
The notion of the individual as a basic and stable unit of consciousness is shaken by Le Sueur's portrayal of a collective entity, but the
political potency of the collectivity is compromised by its isolation.
The women of the alliance can communicate perfectly with one
another, but their communion shuts them off from the world outside, where their material circumstances are determined by hostile
forces. Le Sueur's community of women resolves itself into an isolated moment of bliss that will shatter as soon as men and the forces
of capitalism break through the walls of the warehouse/womb. Le
Sueur's poignant vision of a protected women's world is undercut
by her pithy account of the fate of the young woman whose experience inspired the Girl's story: "The getting and birthing of the child
is the story of Natalie, who has been for thirty years or more in an

8. Kristeva, *Revolution*, p. 239.

asylum and is still alive" (p. 150). The tragedy is political as well as personal. In *The Girl*, women are labeled insane and locked up whenever they offend the capitalist state. The insanity is not Natalie's but the government's, and the cure consists in removing her from the historical moment of capitalism.

Le Sueur presents certain elements of the communist ideal as essential feminine attributes. Women's fluidity of identity within the community and across the generations, their commitment to meeting the material needs of each member of the community, and their distrust of hierarchies make them the ideal founders of a communist utopia. All these women, whether they have given birth to babies or not, are mothers because together they constitute the collective Great Mother. They are her mind, voice, body. If communism is maternal, and therefore beyond history, oppression, and alienation, then capitalism is patriarchal. The oppressor is a masculinist state in which every man schemes to profit as an individual. "You don't owe your father anything," Butch concludes after his partner in the bank robbery shoots him (p. 101).

Le Sueur celebrates a communal, maternal subjectivity gestating within the body of patriarchal capitalism, but her vision does not extend far enough to imagine society after the revolution. Grounded in the grim political and economic realities of the depression, Le Sueur stops short of projecting a utopian future in which women and communism achieve hegemony. Among the writers who have attempted to envision a more definitive end to patriarchy is Alice Sheldon. Her science fiction novella "Houston, Houston Do You Read?," written under the pen name of "James Tiptree, Jr.," is based on an argument similar to Le Sueur's.[9] Women in her futuristic fiction are essentially nonviolent and nurturing, but men are driven to violence and asocial behavior. Given this distribution of qualities between the sexes, Tiptree imagines a postapocalyptic Earth inhabited only by women, for whom the repeated cloning of the original eleven thousand survivors has produced a stable society. All the members of a clone group share certain innate talents and liabilities. Everyone knows, for instance, that Judys talk too much and Wool-

9. James Tiptree, Jr. [Alice Sheldon], "Houston, Houston Do You Read?"; subsequent references in this chapter are cited in the text.

agongs are great inventors. Tiptree's postrevolutionary communal subjectivity is similar to Le Sueur's in that each woman sees her own reflection in the faces of her contemporary sisters (there may be as many as two hundred genetically identical women in each generation).

The women's reproductive revolution has slowed technological progress. According to Julia Kristeva, the sexual division of labor has retarded women's involvement in linear, or historical, time. Whereas feminists before 1968 strove to insert women into linear time, some later feminists "almost totally refused" linear temporality as masculinist.[10] What is left to them is cyclical time (the menstrual cycle, the seasons, the repetitive routines of daily life) and monumental time (the eternity subsuming both cyclical and linear time). Tiptree, like Le Sueur, situates her women on the margins of linear time, where they achieve a subjectivity that retains, in Kristeva's terms, "*repetition* and eternity." Specifically, Kristeva says, "female subjectivity" consists of "cycles, gestation, the eternal recurrences of a biological rhythm which conforms to that of nature" (p. 191). Kristeva's "female subjectivity" is essentially a maternal subjectivity, since it is determined by women's reproductive cycles and childbearing. The women of Tiptree's postrevolutionary Earth have been freed from linear time.

Their idyll is interrupted when three twentieth-century male astronauts are accidentally hurled into the women's time. Under orders from their commander, the astronauts initially resist the women's attempts to help them abandon their ship, which is low on fuel and heading out of the solar system. The women cannot understand the men's hierarchical system of command: "But don't they know they're on a bad course? I mean, could the dominant one make the others fly right out of the system?" (p. 190). The men have already flown "right out of the system," and that is what paralyzes them. When the astronauts finally allow themselves to be rescued, the women have a hard time providing a history that will satisfy the men. No one on Earth is interested in history anymore. Even the evolution of language has stopped; all children are taught to speak a

10. Julia Kristeva, "Women's Time," p. 194; subsequent references in this chapter are cited in the text.

standard, unchanging English so that no one will have trouble communicating. They have no governmental hierarchies, and capitalist enterprises have disappeared. The women have made few attempts to improve on the technology the men left behind three centuries previously, and they are only cautiously increasing Earth's tiny population of 2 million. In response to one astronaut's shocked realization that evolutionary and technological progress has ended, one woman disagrees: "No. . . . It's just slowed down. We do everything much slower than you did, I think. We like to experience things *fully*. We have time. . . . There's all the time" (p. 222).

Time on the new Earth is predicated on shared identities that surpass bodily boundaries and linear time. Sisters/mothers born several centuries before are as present to their descendants as those currently living. Women usually bear their own clones for the next generation. They have created a version of cyclical or monumental time which, within the story's purview, ensures a socially stable, nonracist, communist society.

The astronauts, however, are staggered by the failure of linear time—a failure they experience firsthand when they are catapulted out of the twentieth century and into a static future. The attitudes of the three astronauts toward the women who pick them up in space loosely parallel the attitudes exhibited by the three adventurers who stumble into Charlotte Perkins Gilman's Herland. The captain, Dave, is a deeply religious man who feels, with maniacal and finally murderous intensity, that women should be obedient and silent under a stern patriarchy. Bud, the engineer, is a lewd and selfish "man's man" who tries to rape one of the women who has rescued him. And Lorimer, the physicist, is both attracted to and bemused by the world the women have worked out for themselves. But each man in his own way reacts to the women's sharing of identities by reasserting the superiority of a masculine, singular identity. Lorimer responds to the news that the women reproduce through cloning by trying to convince them of "the horror of manipulating human identity, creating abnormal life. The threat to individuality, the fearful power it would put in a dictator's hand" (p. 218). The women don't even know what a dictator is; dictatorship is unthinkable in a world of women. They are moved to tears by the thought of a world full of "poor singletons" ignorant of who they really are. Bud, most ridiculously, identifies himself with his penis. In a parody of monomaniacal masculinity, he imagines that the grateful women will "make statues of me, my cock a mile high, all over. . . . They'll worship it" (p. 228). Dave vows to God that he personally will "lead Thy erring daughters out of the darkness. I shall be a stern but merciful father to them in Thy name. . . . *For God so loved the world that he sent his only begotten son*" (p. 232).

Tiptree's novella appeared in 1976, well after Kristeva's feminist watershed. In "Houston, Houston Do You Read?" Tiptree envisions an exclusively women's world, defining their communal sharing of property, work, and identity as uniquely female. Such a world, she implies, could never be built with men. Their aggression, competitiveness, lust, and obsessive singularity would prevent them from participating as equal partners in such a utopian venture. Tiptree seems to be advocating a radical separatist community of women. But as long as her imagined world is isolated in "women's time," it obeys gendered categories already in place. Kristeva notes cogently that "the fact that certain currents of modern feminism recognize themselves" in a female subjectivity embracing cyclical and monumental time "does not render them fundamentally incompatible with 'masculine' values" (p. 192). But Kristeva, along with Le Sueur and Tiptree, is prepared to recognize "the real *fundamental difference* between the two sexes" (p. 193) in the multiplicity of identities contained in the term *woman*.

6

The Thinking Man's
Gestation

The gendered political-economic schema that underlies *The Girl* and "Houston, Houston Do You Read?" finds its masculinist expression in David Rorvik's *In His Image: The Cloning of a Man.*[1] Rorvik, too, is interested in the economics of reproduction, though his judgments of the effects of capitalist institutions on the health and reproductive lives of the poor are less clear-eyed and critical than Le Sueur's. If Le Sueur and Tiptree invalidate the patriarchal capitalist by valorizing a maternal collectivity, Rorvik shows him alive and well. The premise of *In His Image* is that a rich capitalist wants to see himself and his values perpetuated in an heir who would be more than a mere son; he wants an exact copy of himself. Rorvik presented *In His Image* as fact, but even before the book came out, a debate about its credibility was under way.[2] More inter-

1. David Rorvik, *In His Image: The Cloning of a Man* (New York: J. B. Lippincott, 1978); subsequent references in this chapter are cited in the text.
2. Michael Crichton, in the *New York Times Book Review* for April 23, 1978, joined many other reviewers in decrying the absence of "scientific evidence" and, perhaps more tellingly in terms of Rorvik's credibility, noted that the "plot is highly unlikely" and "the characters sketchy and improbably motivated" (p. 7). As of 1980 Rorvik was still refusing to admit to fraud. He claimed to have withheld names and

esting than the question of Rorvik's veracity, however, is his (perhaps unintentionally) parodic portrait of Max, the thriving capitalist, a man so obsessed with the purity of his own genes that he has never married or had any children for fear of having a daughter or diluting a son's genes with a woman's inferior DNA.

Max, now an old man, was orphaned at birth. Few clues remain about his mother and a twin brother, and he has been unable to trace his family. But his exclusion from family life is one of the factors determining his later success. Eli Zaretsky, describing the increasing distance between the family (reproductive life) and the economy (productive life) under capitalism, finds that the family, as a female domain, has always been associated with "the agonies of birth, sickness, and death. . . . Certainly it is the association of women with this realm that has been among the earliest and most persistent sources of male supremacy and the hatred of women."[3]

Max has in effect no origins external to himself. He is his own creation, an absolute individual. His vast wealth, his education and refinement, and his perfect health are the result of his own effort and his dissociation from family life and women. His wish to reproduce himself, and only himself, is in part an ironic desire to verify his perfect autonomy. Rorvik describes Max as "one of the fittest who had survived—a sort of crypto–Social Darwinist, an adherent of the philosophy espoused by Herbert Spencer in which success in all things, including finances, is regarded as a consequence of superior heredity. But Max, I guessed, had enlarged and mystified the concept to embrace superior will, as well, since he conceived of himself as largely a creature of his own imagination" (p. 99).

But Max's need to affirm his own authenticity as an individuated subject speaks to his subjective insecurity under capitalism. It is

---

places to protect the privacy of all the participants in a highly secret project, and said that his book was important because "it raised questions about biological research that otherwise would not have been addressed" (*Newsweek*, January 14, 1980, p. 17). But in 1982 his publisher settled a defamation suit with J. Derek Bromhall, a geneticist at Oxford University whose name appears in the book. At that time Lippincott admitted the book was a hoax.

3. Eli Zaretsky, *Capitalism, the Family, and Personal Life* (New York: Harper Colophon Books, 1976), p. 28.

not enough to see himself faithfully reflected in his many enterprises. The capitalist, in common with the laborer, finds himself
alienated from the products of his labor. Seeking by force of "superior will" to resolve the worker-product division that attends his
participation in capitalism, he turns to another kind of product: the
ideal fetus, created from Max's own genetic blueprint. This fetus
would reflect him perfectly, affirming his subjective integrity and
obviating the sense of alienation that inevitably, for a man at least,
accompanies other forms of production and reproduction.

Rorvik helps Max find a researcher willing to undertake the project in total secrecy; a site is found in an unnamed third world country; equipment is gathered, and the research gets under way. The
research team begins by paying women (some of whom work at a
local plantation owned by Max) to come to the hospital for hys-
terectomies or sterilizations. There, Darwin, the chief researcher,
collects their eggs. The narrator (ostensibly Rorvik himself) has
some reservations about using poor women of color as experimental material, but he comforts himself that the project "lacked truly
sinister dimensions" because, he reasons, the women would be better off because of their encounter with the project: "On balance,
I had to concede that the women who came to Darwin's facility
seemed to benefit, not only in terms of the payments they received—and the importance of those could not be discounted, given
the poverty in which many of the women lived—but also in the
sense that they also received the best health care available in the
area" (p. 125). In a book as disingenuous as Rorvik's, it is impossible
to guess at the sincerity of this particular passage. His main intent
throughout the book, however, is not to settle questions of ethics
but to create the impression of plausibility. He wants the reader to
conclude that a project like the one he describes *could* take place.
The proposition that poor, isolated women of color seeking employ-
ment or medical care are vulnerable to exploitation by the rich
white men who control both is, perhaps, the most credible aspect of
the book.

The research team act as pimps in that Max wants not merely a
healthy woman to carry his clone but a beautiful young virgin who
might become his mistress (Rorvik reports, with characteristic un-
derstatement, that he suspects Max of possessing "a dash of the old-

fashioned double standard" [p. 150]). The girl who is ultimately chosen for this honor is characterized as a serious, even studious, orphan of sixteen, who, because her arm has been damaged in the fire that killed her family, cannot expect to do well on the local marriage market. She is impregnated with Max's clone, and carries the child to birth under round-the-clock supervision by the research team. Just before her labor begins, she is flown to the United States so that there will be no question of the child's citizenship. A perfect, white male child of privilege is born. All concerned live happily ever after.

In *In His Image* genes determine identity. Although Max protests that he expects his clone to be an individual in his own right, that new individual is patterned precisely after himself. The anonymous mother, excised when her genes were sucked out of the egg, leaves no impression. The clone is a mirror image who reflects nothing and no one but his male creator. In a way, Rorvik's portrayal of Max's relationship with his clone is reminiscent of Le Sueur's novel. Both Max and the Girl see their own image in the faces of their children. The Girl sees no trace of Butch in her daughter, and the anonymous egg "donor" leaves no impression on Max's clone. In *The Girl*, however, the birth of the daughter celebrates a continuously expanding unity of identity between generations of women, while the birth of the clone in Rorvik's novel celebrates the enduring singularity of Max. In both novels the maternal is associated with a shared identity in which the individual loses specificity. Politically the mother poses a potential threat to patriarchal capitalism and its valorization of the self-made man. Her genes dilute the male child's inheritance of his father's political, economic, and genetic privilege. The cloning project fantasized in *In His Image* obviates that threat by excising the mother even as it uses her body to reproduce a purified white male capitalist, isolated but no longer alienated from himself.

Paracelsus' formula for producing a homunculus reads:

If the sperm, enclosed in a hermetically sealed glass, is buried in horse manure for about forty days and properly "magnetized," it begins to live and move. After such a time it bears the form and resemblance of a human being, but it will be transparent and without corpus. If it is now artificially fed with the *arcanum sanguinis hominis* until it is about forty weeks old, and if allowed to remain during that time in the horse manure, in a continually even temperature, it will grow into a human child, with all its members developed like any other child, such as may have been born of woman, only it will be much smaller. We call such a being a *homunculus*, and he may be raised and educated like any other child, until he grows older and obtains reason and intellect and is able to take care of himself. This is one of the greatest secrets, and it ought to remain a secret until the days approach when all secrets will be known.[4]

If Le Sueur's and Tiptree's maternal collectives garner power by divorcing themselves from the patriarchy and holing up in a womb of their own making, Rorvik presents us with a mother who has been isolated and emptied of power, just as her eggs have been emptied of genes. From that perspective mothers are an oppressed and exploited class. The only evidence that they figure as a potential threat to a masculinist psychology and politics are the ingenious and extravagant efforts aimed at subjugating them.

The threat of maternal power only hinted at in Rorvik, however, becomes a major force in Sven Delblanc's story of a manmade man in *Homunculus: A Magic Tale.*[5] In place of the wealthy capitalist obsessed with reproducing himself, *Homunculus* features Sebastian, an alcoholic high school chemistry teacher who, following his dismissal from the faculty, undertakes the task of self-generation. The novel is a complex interweaving of commentary on cold war espionage (the United States and the USSR are in hot pursuit of Sebastian's life essence) and allusions to alchemy and magic. A central issue is the keeping of secrets, the opposition between a select inner circle of the initiated and the ignorant masses outside. Sebastian possesses the ultimate secret, the knowledge of creation, and is determined to keep his knowledge to himself. Unable to obtain his secret, the megalomaniac military superpowers prepare to drop nu-

4. Translated in Henry M. Pachter, *Paracelsus* (New York: Henry Schuman, 1951), p. 278.
5. Sven Delblanc, *Homunculus: A Magic Tale*, trans. Verne Moberg (Englewood Cliffs, N.J.: Prentice-Hall, 1969); subsequent references in this chapter are cited in the text.

clear bombs on his home country, Sweden. In the grim farce that
ensues, Sebastian the creator eludes annihilation long enough to
produce his homunculus.

Unlike Max, Sebastian plans to recreate himself without recourse
to women's bodies. His character embraces seemingly opposed
principles: he is the scientist and the magician, destroyer and creator, man and mother. An obscure figure, Nagari, seems to have
provided the "essence" Sebastian needs to create a homunculus.
Nagari, identified by various scholars as an alchemist's dragon, calls
Sebastian his "servant." Delblanc describes Nagari as "vital, powerful and destructive, an image for the power of inspiration."[6]

Sebastian's relationship with this shadowy but all-powerful in-
seminator invests the maternal aspect of his character with mas-
ochism. Struggling manfully to create the homunculus from muck
and urine in his bathtub, Sebastian produces a series of monsters he
must kill. Preparing to slit the throat of his latest creation, Sebastian prays, "Death, let this suffice. Let my time come. Open my
body and let me give birth" (p. 70). Sebastian is the battleground
where the female and the male, the power to create and the power to
destroy, meet and clash in a nuclear catastrophe.

In the scene in which Sebastian's efforts to produce the homunculus succeed at last, he sees the white body of his "son" in the
bathtub, growing in a translucent egg:

> And he saw with intense joy that this white body was a boy child,
> enclosed in the egg, a Tom Thumb, and thought he made out the boy's
> loving gaze; and he was seized by a shivering devotion when he saw
> this child, no larger than a hand, lay his finger on his smiling mouth
> as if admonishing him to silence, and with his other hand the child
> clasped his male sex member and let his water pass, smiling, looking
> with a promise and tenderness that made the creator wince with plea-
> sure. (p. 105)

The image is, of course, reminiscent of Paracelsus' formula. The
scene of creation is definitively male, occurring between a male

6. Quoted in Lisette Keustermans, "Nagari Revealed: The Genesis of Nagari in
Sven Delblanc's novel *Homunculus*," *Scandinavica: An International Journal of
Scandinavian Studies* 2.23 (November 1984): 161.

parent and his male progeny. The child clasps his penis to confirm their affinity. The male's urine is an essential element in the homunculus formula; the child's urinating establishes his origins and seems to promise future generations of homunculi. When the process is complete, and the homunculus is "born" a full-grown young man, he roots at Sebastian's chest, which suddenly sprouts breasts. This and Sebastian's constant awareness of something—a cancer or a pregnancy—growing painfully in his belly attest to his androgyny. In Sebastian's story women figure mostly as the dull-witted victims of exploitation or violence, especially Sebastian's or his monster's rapes. But the earth mother, a figure as powerful and elusive as Nagari, hovers around Sebastian and eventually serves as midwife to his death.

The act of creation has already sapped his blood and his "essence." Significantly, it is in meeting the homunculus's eyes that Sebastian experiences his enervation most acutely: "He raised his hand from his eyes and met for the first time the living gaze of his creation. (Living eyes, gentle, but so empty; for these eyes drink their life through my own; fiercely my life is drained, streaming into the wells of these pupils)" (p. 106). This is the prototypical scene of scientific creation, in which the scientist confers life through his gaze. But in giving life to the fetus, the scientist gives up his claim to disinterest. Although the homunculus takes shape in an artificial womb (here, the bathtub) rather than in the man's own body, his substance is Sebastian's. Their gaze is the umbilicus from which the homunculus draws his sustenance. The scientist cannot observe the experiment with cool, white-coated objectivity; it is his blood, his own life, that animates the homunculus. Sebastian feels death approaching, but his selflessness is ecstatic; he nurses his son and exults, "I am a creator, and a creator is both woman and man" (p. 109).

At the moment Sebastian gives life to his son, he abandons masculine sovereignty and enters a no-man's-land of maternal chaos. His confusion of self and other transforms him into an androgyne. S/he is a nothing because s/he cannot be accounted for in linear structures of thought. Sebastian as androgyne occupies the mother's indefinable space. Sebastian longs for motherhood, but it is motherhood-as-self-annihilation that he seeks—the only tolerable form of motherhood within a masculinist logic of oppositions. Trying to be all, to contain all possibilities, Sebastian loses his individual boundaries and is reduced to nothing.

In a novel in which the powers of birth and death are so completely in the hands of the (male) androgyne, I look for the mother between the lines. Once Sebastian's alchemy collapses the man/woman opposition, other essential oppositions depolarize as well. Most significant, the opposition between life and death disintegrates. Destruction follows Sebastian's appropriation of maternal power. It is only through the mounting disorder of Sebastian's narrative that the (all-powerful) mother makes herself felt. The threat of atomic annihilation that hangs over Stockholm throughout the novel is not evidence of male destructiveness but the "earth mother's" vengeance enacted through her children. Wolfgang Lederer, in *The Fear of Women*, an encyclopedic history of gynophobic thought, offers a similar logic when he maintains that our contemporary reproductive excesses "may yet again have to be redressed by the Great Mother herself in her most terrible form: as hunger, as pestilence, as the blind orgasm of the atom."[7] In *Homunculus*, the atom bomb is this raging mother seeking revenge for Sebastian's trespasses.

With the nuclear superpower on his heels, Sebastian takes his creation into hiding, but the homunculus begins to die after a few days. Sebastian imagines he hears the voice of the woman he lives with: "I am Olga. I live in the womb of life. My horizon is bound by damp red walls. Yet I am Queen of an endless domain. You can deprive me of nothing. Abuse me, and I arise refreshed from your brew. Steal my treasures and you enrich me. Suck life's milk from my breasts—it's your own downfall if you drink. You refused to be taken into my life and to let yourself be closed up inside it. And so you must die" (p. 171). Sebastian's primary offense against nature was his resolution to be independent of her. Refusing to be swallowed up in her womb, determined to create new life without recourse to woman, Sebastian claims an essential selfhood which is by definition a refusal of his origins in woman. And for this offense

7. Wolfgang Lederer, *The Fear of Women* (New York: Grune & Stratton, 1968), p. 248.

he is sentenced to mortality. Olga, later identified as the earth mother, rejoices in his failure. (Feminine) nature has opposed (masculine) science and won. The Great Mother, indestructible and omnipotent bestower of life and death, is the alchemic goddess who, Lederer claims, haunts the male imagination. As Lederer puts it, "Deep within the unknowable darkness of the womb, unconsciously purposeful, silent as the night, woman transforms food and blood into new life."[8] If she has the power to transform dead matter into living, she also has the power to undo that transformation. Sebastian cannot, finally, maintain his independence from her. When Olga tells him "You must die," she is demanding his return to the earth mother.

The homunculus dissolves, and Sebastian locks himself away in his apartment and goes into labor, determined to give birth alone to the heavy burden, mortality, he carries in his belly. Olga, the earth mother/midwife, is outside, trying to find the right key to open the lock. Sebastian's "birth" is a cesarean; he splits himself open with a knife at the moment when Olga finally locates the right key. Then "a new pain came, at last, and his body opened up like woman's in first childbirth" (p. 188). Olga has found him; his death unites him inexorably with her. At the moment when he is at last "taken into [Olga's] life and . . . closed up inside it" (p. 188), Armageddon is averted. The nuclear bombs once destined for Stockholm are detonated relatively harmlessly.

Delblanc's image of the "damp red walls" that describe the "endless domain" of the terrifying earth mother, like Lederer's "unknowable darkness," represents the womb as a negative space which is at once limitless and claustrophobic, an inescapable but unknowable point of origin. When Lederer speaks of the mother's power, he calls it *unconsciously* purposeful. If we follow the implications of this assertion, then mother/nature is found to be incapable of penetrating the secret of her own power (she does not, in fact, possess the instruments for such penetration). She cannot know herself because she does not possess personal boundaries. If science masters nature, it will be because "he" unearths the secrets

8. Ibid., p. 115.

mother/nature does not even realize "she" contains. Jean Baudrillard's analysis of certain conceptual parallels between Marxism and psychoanalysis points to their roots in the objectification of nature: "*Nature is the concept of a dominated essence* and nothing else. In this sense, it is Science and Technology that fulfill the essence of Nature by indefinitely reproducing it as separated."[9] Mother/nature can be fulfilled—that is, can become herself—only through man's labor; she is "born" in the separation of subject and object, man and woman.

I would add, however, that the earth mother, the primitive (that is, repressed) antecedent of a dominated mother/nature, remains to threaten the apparent finality of her objectification. The most vivid, and the most commonplace, image of the earth mother is the pregnant woman, whose paradoxical unity and duality denies the final separation of subject and object and calls into question the validity of such oppositional categories. The homunculus promises an ultimate solution to the nihilistic threat she poses. The victory of the individual (man) over the collective (mother) would be the victory of man over his own mortality.

Baudrillard cites two Greek myths in which a father, trimming vines or slaughtering livestock, unwittingly injures his son. "All the myths of a vengeful, bad, *castrating* nature take root here," Baudrillard claims.[10] The stories describe the moment when the concept of nature erupts: the moment when man's body is alienated from nature. One could add to Baudrillard's examples Delblanc's "magic tale" of Sebastian's failure to keep his homuncular son alive. In Lacanian psychoanalysis the infant experiences separation from the mother—a primordial castration—as death. It is essential to one's development as a mature, autonomous individual to accept this separation. The failure to separate from the mother is a fatal pathology; if science can alter the etiology of the "disease" by finally appropriating the position of the mother, erasing all traces of the primitive union of mother and fetus and applying scientific controls to fetal development, then we will have precisely what

9. Jean Baudrillard, *The Mirror of Production*, trans. Mark Poster (St. Louis: Telos Press, 1975), p. 55.

10. Ibid., p. 61.

Marx wanted: a better baby, ready from the start to accept his status as a unique, independent individual. But the clone or homunculus is also a manufactured being. The processes that produce such creatures are suited to standardization and mass production, opening up the possibility of infinite Maxes or Sebastians. By this route the monomaniac returns to his origins in the collective earth mother.

7

Community, Identity, Stasis: The Mother-State and the Postrevolutionary Subject in *Brave New World*

Aldous Huxley, in the 1947 foreword he added to his 1932 novel *Brave New World*, says that a "really revolutionary revolution is to be achieved, not in the external world, but in the souls and flesh of human beings."[1] The "really revolutionary revolution" he proposes is an experiment which demonstrates that familial and sexual relationships, as well as class structures, are contingent on the formation of the body and the mind. The body and the mind, in turn, are highly malleable to technological intervention and behavioral conditioning. Working from this premise, Huxley constructs a nightmare society in which individualism has been engineered out of the human being. Huxley identified the denial of the individual as the crucial dogma that separates communism from liberal democracy: "To the Bolshevik, there is something hideous and unseemly about the spectacle of anything so 'chaotically vital,' so 'mystically organic' as an individual with a soul, with personal tastes, with special talents. Individuals must be organized out of existence; the communist state requires, not men, but cogs and

1. Aldous Huxley, *Brave New World* (1932; rpt. New York: Perennial Library, 1989), pp. xi–xii; subsequent references in this chapter are cited in the text.

ratchets in the huge 'collective mechanism.' "[2] As Huxley develops
this nightmare in *Brave New World*, "Collective Man" is the monster born out of the body of a fascist state. In keeping with his idea
of what would constitute a "really revolutionary revolution," the
absorption of the individual within the collective results directly
from biological engineering.

Although Huxley regards communism as a clear evil, his feelings
about the Freudian nuclear family are more ambiguous. The design
of the new world has eliminated families, and especially mothers,
who are condemned as the source of emotional and sexual dysfunc-
tion. Individual mothers are outlawed, but the "maternal" still has
a stranglehold on society. The citizens of the new world never have
to undergo the painful realization of their alienation from "mother"
because "mother" has been replaced by a ubiquitous state that provides for all needs and from whom no one ever separates. Mustapha
Mond, a leader in the new world, boasts that "even the primitive
matriarchies weren't steadier than we are" (p. 234). The "steadi-
ness" that Mond values so highly, however, is the result of judi-
ciously applied science, a masculine sphere of influence, at least in
the society Huxley imagines, where all scientists and all leaders are
men.

The stable "Collective Man" in *Brave New World* is allied politically and psychologically to the postrevolutionary subject developed in *The Girl* and "Houston, Houston Do You Read?" The "really
revolutionary revolution" in these fictions occurs, as Huxley asserts, not in the external world but within the "soul and flesh" of
the human subject. In each case it is merging with a Great Mother,
the absorption of the individual into a communal consciousness,
which permits the de-alienation of the subject under communism.
Huxley, like Le Sueur and Tiptree, represents the communist state
as maternal.

But the state's assumption of the traditional maternal role does
not obliterate structures of sexual difference; instead, it fixes these
structures more rigidly. Huxley joins the name of Freud to that of
Ford, suggesting that psychoanalysis operates on the assembly-line

2. Aldous Huxley, "The New Romanticism," in *Music at Night* (London: Chatto
& Windus, 1931), p. 214.

principle, producing a subject whose psychic organization—however conflicted—is identical to that of every other subject. Because of its emphasis on a child's initiation into the symbolic order, the Lacanian model of the mother-child relationship provides a suitable model for Huxley's use of psychoanalysis. The "symbolic" death of the mother that marks the child's entry into the symbolic is taken to its logical extreme in *Brave New World*, where the word *mother* is proscribed. Nevertheless, Mustapha Mond evokes the Name-of-the-Mother during a masculine initiation rite, a boys' tour of the Central London Hatchery and Conditioning Centre: "Maniacally, the mother brooded over her children (*her* children) . . . brooded over them like a cat over its kittens; but a cat that could talk, a cat that could say, 'My baby, my baby,' over and over again. 'My baby, and oh, oh, at my breast, the little hands, the hunger, and that unspeakable agonizing pleasure!' " (p. 37). Mond evokes the mother as an empty name that reminds the boys of the power of the state, which has vanquished the biological mother-monster. But the mother's symbolic death is not what it appears to be. The death of the Name-of-the-Mother belies an irrevocable union between the citizen and the mother-state. In this eternal maternal presence, the individual subject has little value. "For I am you and you are I!" chant the twelve participants in Orgy-Porgy, a celebration of collective identity (p. 91). The obliteration of personal boundaries, in which each is expected to identify with all others, is a universalized form of the supposed unity of mother and child. It is this "motherliness" of the state, the refusal of the individual, that makes it a dystopia. Its citizens are forever children held tight in (over)protective maternal custody.[3]

If the design of the Brave New World obliterates privacy and personal boundaries, it does not, however, challenge structures of dominance based on racial and sexual difference. Social roles are patterned after Huxley's own British class structure, but biologically

3. One of the more whimsical manifestations of the state's assumption of the maternal function in *Brave New World* is the attempt to sentimentalize the gestation bottle. The bottle stands in for the literal body of the mother, as the lyrics to the dance music at the Westminster Abbey Cabaret suggest: "Bottle of mine, it's you I've always wanted! / Bottle of mine, why was I ever decanted?" Huxley, *Brave New World*, p. 77.

engineered to prevent any movement up or down the hierarchy. The mass-produced underclasses are kept down not by financial want and despair, but because they are engineered biologically to be happy in their assigned rut. The biological caste system in effect in the world Huxley imagines represents the realization of "scientific" arguments made before and during Huxley's era to the effect that class and race inequalities are biologically determined—in other words, that the working class and people of color are kept down by their own biological inferiority. In "History and the Past" Huxley expresses doubts about the "native equality and potential perfection of people" which democracy (a "bedraggled and rather whorish old slut," no more promising that communism, it seems) had once promised: "Psychology and genetics have yielded results which confirm the doubts inspired by practical experience. Nature, we have found, does rather more, nurture rather less, to make us what we are than the earlier humanitarians had supposed. We believe in Mendelian predestination; and in a society not practicing eugenics, Mendelian predestination leads . . . inevitably to pessimism about the temporal future."[4]

Although Huxley affirms the priority of genetics, his treatment in *Brave New World* of artificial gestation suggests that the class system results from the combined forces of "nature" and "nurture." The human engineers in the novel certainly believe in the power of "nurture"; their techniques profoundly affect the physical and intellectual development of fetuses. But the Director of Hatcheries and Conditioning's deadpan comments about the greater productivity of embryos taken from black women uncritically repeat contemporary stereotypes about the galloping fertility of the "lower races." Delta-Minus servants, the lowest of the lower classes, are "small, black and hideous" (p. 64). It remains uncertain whether these judgments represent the conditioning of the characters or reflect Huxley's own views, but his comments on eugenics suggest the latter. Chemistry and social conditioning are used to exaggerate certain *innate* patterns. There is a limit to the malleability of the human being, and so the best genetic material goes into the making of Alphas, the highest caste, who are also the most likely to in-

4. Aldous Huxley, "History and the Past," in *Music at Night*, p. 51.

sist on their individuality. Huxley's Alphas represents the British upper-middle class, Huxley's peers, whose advantageous heredity and education suit them for useful work as high-echelon managers. By contrast, the phenomenally fertile "negro ovary," an object of great pride to the Director of Hatcheries, has created 12,700 children destined for the Delta-Minus caste.

Huxley makes similar assumptions about sex-based differences, re-creating in the new world hierarchal patterns of sexual difference in force in Huxley's own society. Without the burden of motherhood to eat up their time and energies, women are freer to give in to men's sexual whims. Outlawing viviparous parenthood seems to contradict the values of Huxley's own society, but it results in the release of men from the responsibilities of personal fatherhood. They are free to indulge their sexual appetites without fear of consequences.[5]

But women's conditioning fails to rid them of the "maternal instinct." Fanny, a worker who feels "rather out of sorts," is instructed by her doctor to undergo an early Pregnancy Substitute, a therapy that involves taking "syrup of corpus luteum," "mammary gland extract," and "placentin." The therapy is compulsory for all women over the age of twenty-one, but Fanny needs it early because "brunettes with wide pelvises . . . ought to have their first Pregnancy Substitute at seventeen" (pp. 37–38). Huxley interweaves Fanny's discussion of her need for a Pregnancy Substitute with Mustapha Mond's derisive evocation of biological motherhood as an "unspeakable agonizing pleasure." Without proper therapy, women would revert to Freudian patterns of femininity marked primarily by the pathological pleasures of the intimate mother-child bond.

Women still bear the responsibility for tending to children, however. They are consigned to familiar feminine roles of reduced responsibility, watching over embryos on an assembly line, babies in nurseries, and children in institutions. This system, in which one

5. Women, in contrast, look upon promiscuity as a duty. Lenina, a Beta hatcheries worker who is repeatedly described as sexually "pneumatic," tends to forget that it is her duty to be promiscuous. She confesses to her friend Fanny, "I haven't been feeling very keen on promiscuity lately," but Fanny, though sympathetic, reminds her that "one's got to play the game." Huxley, *Brave New World*, p. 43.

woman tends many children, prevents personal attachments. Women carry out the orders of their superiors, having no voice in the production plan men have devised.

The replacement of mothers by institutions that manipulate children's bodies and minds is designed to shock, to make us think seriously about how our children could end up in a world of horrific depersonalization. To this, Huxley warns, we might descend: a world where no one is unique, where children become biological machines devoid of human warmth and love. But his vision fails as an elegy to the vanishing miracle of motherhood because Huxley does not provide an alternative model for a successful mother-child relationship. There is no woman in *Brave New World* worthy of motherhood.

The only "natural" mother depicted, Linda, a Brave New World woman left behind after a vacation trip, is a grotesque and ludicrous figure. Having lost the protection of the state, she has degenerated into a filthy, obese, and alcoholic outcast. Her son, John Savage, who looks to her in vain for the madonna worthy of his devotion, eventually ends his life in suicide. Although she had been thoroughly conditioned to have no emotional attachments, Linda gives in to her maternal instincts when she is removed from the care and control of her society. The result is the quintessential Freudian mother, alternatively abusive and clinging. Her emotional dependence on her son and his helplessness in the face of her instability form the core of his own pathology. Given the disaster of their relationship, a return to close mother-child bonds is no solution to the problems posed by Huxley's postrevolutionary society. Whatever its faults, no one in the Brave New World lives with the lethal despair that plagues Savage as the result of his relationship with his mother. Linda is the product of the combined evils of her nature and her conditioning. Though one might change her conditioning, training her to perform motherly functions, her basic nature, her pathological "maternal instinct," would remain to create chaos.

The Brave New World, with its bottle babies and fatuous, purposeless happiness, anesthetizes the masses not only with drugs and sex but also with a limitless stability. In contrast to this banal hell, Huxley represents in Savage the life of an *individual* who is steeped in maternal intimacy and torn apart by family passions.

Such a life is just as insane as, and much more miserable than, life in the communist dystopia. Huxley later regretted what he considered to be the novel's greatest flaw, that he offered no third society to accommodate Savage. This alternative society, hinted at in Mond's references to distant outcast islands to which freethinking Alphas are banished when they pose too great a challenge to the stability of the society, would offer a sane alternative to the dual madnesses of the "primitive" and "civilized" worlds. It would be "composed of freely cooperating individuals devoted to the pursuit of sanity." In this world "the prevailing philosophy of life would be a kind of Higher Utilitarianism, in which the Greatest Happiness principle would be secondary to the Final End principle—the first question to be asked and answered in every contingency of life being: 'How will this thought or action contribute to, or interfere with, the achievement, by me and the greatest possible number of other individuals, of man's Final End?'" (p. x).

In *The Perennial Philosophy* Huxley identifies "man's Final End" as "the direct and intuitive awareness of God."[6] This utilitarian mysticism could be considered Huxley's version of a "real" utopia. If it rejects the deeply conflicted subjectivity produced by biological mothers, it just as plainly rejects the maternal mindlessness of the Brave New World. A true utopia would offer the Buddhist Eightfold Path, leading away from "separative, ego-centred existence,"[7] although how the Eightfold Path might serve the "race of free individuals" created through "applied science" which Huxley advocates in his 1947 foreword (p. xvii) is uncertain. Given this admittedly piecemeal reconstruction of what Huxley would construe as a true utopia, it may be that its ideal subject would represent a mix of the individual and communal subjectivities that are presented as untenable opposites in *Brave New World*. The figure of the mother is crucial to Huxley's depiction of these competing subjectivities in that her roles as biological mother and communist state are equally detrimental to the development of a "race of free individuals." What would be done with her in an alternative society?

6. Aldous Huxley, *The Perennial Philosophy* (New York: Harper & Bros., 1945), p. 294.
7. Ibid., p. 202.

Brave New World does not, as Huxley believed, represent the possibility of a "really revolutionary revolution" in the souls and flesh of human beings, any more than does David Rorvik's sensational exposition of the possibilities of cloning. A real revolution would involve the overthrow of the entire ideological and psychological edifice on which Huxley's critique of the political uses of human engineering is founded. By "overthrow" I mean not that the dynamics of dominance would be reversed, that the dispossessed would, at long last, own the means of production and reproduction, but rather that the whole idea of political structures of dominance based on race and sex would collapse.

CHAPTER 8

The Handmaid's Tale:
A Banished Mother

Margaret Atwood's critical approach to the idea that motherhood is a politically powerful basis for a collective maternal subjectivity is as fitting a counterpoint to Meridel Le Sueur's valorization of motherhood as it is to the deprecation of mothers in Huxley, Delblanc, or Rorvik. In *The Handmaid's Tale*, the gathering of women, their absorption into a maternal space granted them by the patriarchy, forms the ideological core of an oppressive regime. Here in Gilead, women's authority in matters of childbearing in no sense produces a politically powerful women's community. Like *Brave New World*, *The Handmaid's Tale* depicts a world in which social stability and communal identity are associated with intensified gender and class polarization, but Atwood's novel underscores the relationship between the two. There is some possibility of upward economic and social mobility among the men, but women's positions are fixed—except for the possibility of exile.

In both novels, technology assists in bringing about a social revolution. Huxley proposes that new technologies could provide the tools for creating a stable society in which—despite its damning flaws—disease has been eradicated and natural resources, including "reproductive" resources, are managed with such extraordinary efficiency that the main problem is an excess of products. Atwood, by contrast, shows how technological expansion could amplify social and environmental instability, making us vulnerable to a government takeover by extreme right-wing religious fundamentalists. In *The Handmaid's Tale* the rule of religious fanatics suspends the spiraling technological and industrial expansion that threatens to poison our world. Although fertility (never a problem in *Brave New World*) has been severely compromised, reproductive technologies such as *in vitro* fertilization and all medical intervention in the birth process have been banned.[1] Whatever their differences, these novels present us with a common irony, for each implies that the twentieth-century technological revolution, whether it succeeds or self-destructs, will increase the polarizing effects of capitalism and patriarchy, leading to a society of even more rigid class and gender divisions.

Huxley's faith in men's ability to dominate the world without reducing it to ashes contrasts starkly with Atwood's more cynical view. In part, Huxley's and Atwood's very different assessments of the effects of technological expansion are a product of history. Huxley's confidence in technological progress is difficult for later generations to emulate. His foreword to the 1947 edition of *Brave New World* demonstrates how the years since the novel was first published in 1932 had challenged his own faith. The foreword ends with a warning that paves the way for Atwood's revised vision of the future: "All things considered it looks as though Utopia were far closer to us than anyone, only fifteen year ago, could have imagined. Then, I projected it six hundred years into the future. Today it seems quite possible that the horror may be upon us within a single century. That is, if we refrain from blowing ourselves to smithereens in the interval." Among the more ominous alternatives Huxley offers to this definitive end is a "supranational totalitarianism, called into existence by the social chaos resulting from rapid technological growth, and developing, under the need for efficiency and stability, into the welfare-tyranny of Utopia."[2] *The Handmaid's*

1. The ban does not extend to all forms of intervention, however. Some forms of technology, including methods of predicting women's fertile periods, are still allowed.
2. Huxley, *Brave New World*, p. xvii.

Tale presents a regional version of this totalitarian regime. But Huxley's faith in the doctrine of scientific progress was not completely destroyed by the military technologies developed in the Second World War. He remained hopeful that a eugenic program could be used for the creation of a "race of free individuals."

Atwood, refusing Huxley's conditional hope that science and technology might be used to engineer free people in a clean society, offers a more disturbing vision of the future. Her Gilead is frightening because it is dependent not on moderately remote technologies but on the political ascendancy of a right-wing Christianity. Given the increasing visibility of similar groups in recent years, Atwood's dystopian vision seems more immediately threatening than Huxley's.

As in *Brave New World*, the overarching goal of the masculinist society in *The Handmaid's Tale* is the appropriation of childbearing and child rearing as state-controlled functions. The aims of Gilead's Commanders remains the same as that of Brave New World's Controllers: to produce as many "desirable" individuals as possible. In Gilead, however, the measure of success of the newborn is necessarily much less precise; any viable white baby is considered desirable (although for some reason boys are still valued over girls, an inexplicable preference, given the society's need for more wombs).

The state becomes a surrogate mother in *Brave New World*, but in Atwood's Gilead the state is all Father, imposing a rigid quasibiblical law enforced by various coercive methods. According to Gileadan propaganda, Handmaids, fertile women enslaved as surrogate mothers, who do not become pregnant are negated as "unwomen" and consigned to this "no-man's-land." Exclusion from the male order means a loss of identity, but it does not place the "unwoman" beyond the scope of that order. Instead, exile is just one version of the exclusion that defines her place within the male order. If there is no way *out* for Handmaids—or for any woman— neither is there any way *in*. The communal maternal subjectivity expressed in *The Girl* and "Houston, Houston Do You Read?" becomes a hollow parody in *The Handmaid's Tale*, where the state treats women as a collective resource. Uniform but divided from one another, women cannot achieve solidarity. Handmaids and Wives, for instance, are necessarily divided over issues of class, sexuality, and childbearing, issues that unite women in Le Sueur and Tiptree. Within the Wives class, women are reproductive consumers, competing with one another for access to the scarcest commodity: children. Handmaids, as reproductive laborers, also compete among themselves to produce children for the market.

The separation of biological mothers from their children, enforced by laws that give their babies to the Commanders they serve, is another feature of Atwood's dystopian vision which touches on issues uncomfortably close to contemporary concerns, such as the intensifying battle over surrogacy, abortion, and fetal rights. The incarceration of mothers and their forced separation from their children is a feature of many writers' portrayals of masculinist rule. The Handmaid Offred's separation from her daughter and her confinement in the Commander's home is reminiscent of the Girl's incarceration in the state-controlled "relief maternity home" and her fear that the state would take her baby. Another contemporary version of this theme is found in Marge Piercy's *Woman on the Edge of Time,* when the daughter of a poor Chicana named Connie is given to a "rich white couple" when Connie is committed to a mental hospital.

Atwood views the likely dystopia through Offred's eyes. Because of the Handmaids' status in Gilead, that means that her range of vision is narrow. At the Rachel and Leah Re-Education Center, Gilead's version of Brave New World conditioning teaches Handmaids that they are powerless, empty vessels whose only purpose is to be filled by the state. Offred is among the first potential mothers conscripted after the totalitarian takeover. During re-education Offred and her peers are systematically brainwashed to erase any remaining sense of autonomy or self-worth. Although they are taught not to trust one another, they are encouraged to develop a mob consciousness based on their uniform identity; incidents such as the state-sponsored execution of a supposed rapist by a swarm of maddened Handmaids demonstrate the success of their reconditioning. But the collective consciousness that Gilead creates among its Handmaids does not effect the banal happiness evident in *Brave New World* or the exultation of the women's collective in *The Girl.* Rather, the Handmaids' new communal consciousness is a paralyzing mix of helplessness, rage, and self-blame. Certain Aunts,

Gilead's equivalent of drill sergeants, berate the Handmaids, and there is evidence that physical torture is being used on women who resist, but Aunt Lydia sympathizes with her charges:

> You are a transitional generation. . . . It is the hardest for you. We know the sacrifices you are being expected to make. It is hard when men revile you. For the ones who come after you, it will be easier. They will accept their duties with willing hearts.
>   She did not say: because they will have no memories, of any other way.
>   She said: Because they won't want things they can't have. (p. 151)

In scenes such as this one Atwood reinterprets the notion of an essential maternal subjectivity. In *The Girl*, the mothers' collectivity, and the feminine consciousness it promises, create an ecstatic unity among women, implying that by joining together for a common purpose they will be empowered to alter, or at least survive, their appalling circumstances. In Atwood's treatment of a similar theme, the collective maternal consciousness makes action impossible. "The ones who come after," the Handmaids' daughters, will never question their reproductive slavery. Nancy Chodorow's model of mothering as a force that reproduces a certain feminine personality type in each succeeding generation—a model that, in Le Sueur, expresses a dream of women's revolution—finds a more sinister expression in *The Handmaid's Tale*. The new generation of Handmaids will be born and raised by women socialized to replicate "maternal" qualities such as nurturing and self-sacrifice. In Gilead these are characteristics that render women especially vulnerable to sexual and reproductive exploitation.

The rhythms of women's reproductive physiology are potentially disruptive to the government in *The Girl* and *Brave New World*, but in *The Handmaid's Tale* the reproductive body is just another tool for oppression. Handmaids endure an existence of intense boredom, the empty routine of their days ordered by reproductive cycles. Without the distractions of public life, with its varying demands and rhythms, a Handmaid exits linear time and enters into the limbo of her own womb, her consciousness reduced to the rhythms of her body. Offred imagines Janine, heavily pregnant, eat-ing cookies from the hands of indulgent Wives and then, "up in her room, what does she do? Sits with the taste of sugar still in her mouth, licking her lips. Stares out the window. Breathes in and out. Caresses her swollen breasts. Thinks of nothing" (p. 148).

Offred occupies herself remembering her life before and imagining her husband and daughter as they might be now, after years of involuntary separation, but her static condition threatens to overcome her, as she, too, is drawn into the somnolent contemplativeness she identifies with late pregnancy. While she waits, nothing happens. All her potential worth is concentrated in her uterus, an investment awaiting maturity.

> Now the flesh arranges itself differently. I'm a cloud, congealed around a central object, the shape of a pear, which is hard and more real than I am and glows red within its translucent wrapping. Inside it is a space, huge as the sky at night. . . . Every month there is a moon, gigantic, round, heavy, an omen. It transits, pauses, continues on and passes out of sight, and I see despair coming toward me like famine. To feel that empty, again, again. (p. 95)

Offred's resistance to her conditioning begins to slip away as she allows herself to focus on her womb. It is not clear whether her desperation to become pregnant arises from her fear of being exiled, a hunger to fill the empty space within her, or a desire to justify the state's investment in her. Offred can define her position, in relation to society and in relation to herself, only with reference to the negative space of her womb. The organ becomes her mirror. That "central object . . . more real than I am" is her defining attribute or essence, and yet it exists independently of her, obeying a mandate over which Offred can exert no conscious control.

While Offred struggles between resisting and vainly hoping for fruition, society defines her as a living factory. In its rejection of birth technology in any form, as in its official reverence for motherhood, Gilead is the antithesis of the Brave New World. Matrons in the re-education center show potential mothers films of birth in the pre-Gilead world. The mother is shown hooked up to monitors and intravenous tubes, shaved, tied down, and drugged, while a masked man looks up inside her and prepares to use his scalpels. Modern hospital birth is a violation; the mother in labor is an object. The lesson implies, against all the evidence, that in Gilead no such objectification will occur.

The representative birth scene in *The Handmaid's Tale* is no less chilling than the realistically clinical film of male-designed birth. And yet at many points the methods employed correspond to a near-utopian dream of natural birth. In Gilead only women attend births. Midwives have replaced the doctors who had once usurped their place, and hospital births are unknown. No needles or knives touch Janine as she labors. She gives birth without drugs, an inspiration to the audience of Handmaids that surrounds her. Their ritual chant recalls Le Sueur's Great Mothers breathing with the Girl: "Breathe, breathe. . . . Hold, hold. Expel, expel, expel" (p. 185).

As the gathered women breathe with the laboring mother, they identify with her, their bodies sharing the sweat and pain of labor. In Le Sueur's vision the women's communal identity is a form of power; each woman gives what she can, each takes what she needs from the abundant store of shared maternal power. The child is immediately absorbed as part of the feminine collectivity. But in Gilead the collective mothers will not claim the newborn child. She, like her mother, is the property of the Father-state, and a single Wife will function as caretaker. The Gileadan propagandists have reworked a familiar communist aphorism: "*From each . . . according to her ability; to each according to his needs*" (p. 151).

During the birth, the Handmaids' shared consciousness creates a momentary sense of "impregnability." Their unity is a kind of womb, seeming to protect them from the patriarchy that has walled them in. But the sense of invulnerability their communal experience creates is illusory. Removing men and their controlling, intrusive technology from the scene of birth does not allow women to reappropriate maternal power. Atwood shows how natural childbirth methods could be integrated into a social machinery that subjugates women and severs mother-child ties. Although Atwood's birth scene is similar to Le Sueur's, her purpose is to demonstrate the futility of basing hopes for revolution on the creation of a specifically maternal subjectivity. Mothers' ability to merge in the experience of birth, their willingness to reduce their identity to their reproductive capacity, becomes a tool of the state, useful to induce obedience.

But though Atwood discredits the idea that women could create a basis for activism on a shared experience of motherhood, she does nothing to refute Le Sueur's essentialist approach. The Handmaids' exposure to the birth triggers a biological response. They lose themselves in the bodily sensations of birth, their consciousness uniformly enclosed in the womb. The chanting "envelops us like a membrane," says Offred, who, at one with her fellow Handmaids, obeys Aunt Elizabeth's command that she identify with her body (p. 159). Drugged with her own hormones, she feels her womb contract and her breasts begin to leak. As the baby is born, she says, "We can feel it like a heavy stone moving down, pulled down inside us, we think we will burst. We grip each other's hands, we are no longer single" (p. 161). The Handmaids achieve a collective consciousness during the birth, but their solidarity serves the state. The Gileadan patriarchy has accounted for the connection between women's consciousness and their biology in its plan for social stability. The Commanders effectively use the Handmaids' biologically reinforced maternal consciousness to prevent them from resisting their own enslavement or establishing coalitions across class boundaries.

The infertile Wife who will claim the baby enters and takes her place above Janine on the birth stool, but she is not part of the Handmaids' experience. They identify with Janine: "We're with her, we're the same as her" (p. 162). The Handmaids' status as potential "surrogate" mothers divides them irrevocably from their closest counterparts, the Wives, who are all potential "adoptive" mothers. The two maternal classes of women are situated in opposition, their social division predicated on a biological difference. The Wives, motivated by an overpowering desire for offspring, a maternal instinct made all the more virulent for being unsatisfied in a society that permits them no other fulfillment, envy the Handmaids' ability to reproduce. As in *Brave New World*, each class tends to identify only with its own kind, and class divisions are based on "natural" biological differences reinforced by deliberate social conditioning.

Atwood offers no solution to the problem of gender and class divisions in *The Handmaid's Tale*. Her acceptance of an essential maternal femininity precludes the possibility of a revolution among the Handmaids. Offred finally escapes not because she has resisted her conditioning or her hormones but because her lover Nick rescues her. Her escape, and her adoption of a forbidden public role when she narrates her own story, implies the possibility of some forms of resistance even under the most pernicious of patriarchal regimes, but nowhere does Atwood suggest that the basic forms of patriarchal society, and especially women's place within it, could be transformed. Even the reassuring news in the novel's epilogue that Gilead failed is undercut by evidence that the patriarchy is alive and well. The less virulent form of the post-Gilead patriarchy is attributable to improved circumstances, specifically a reduction in infertility, rather than to any substantive changes.

Joanna Russ's *We Who Are About To . . .* provides a bitter antidote to the essentialist definition of women as mothers. The novel examines an abortive plan to impose a fascist reproductive program on women after an accident lands a group of space travelers on an uncharted but marginally livable planet.[3] One woman refuses to cooperate with the program of "colonization" the men devise. She observes that the men, weakening under the stress of their traumatic and nearly hopeless circumstances, revert to the most simplistic version of patriarchal domination in an effort to achieve some control over their fate. Men automatically designate themselves as leaders and builders of a new nation, and assign the women to be workers and childbearers. The narrator, who is never named, rejects their plan to found a new nation. She believes it would be a cruel blunder to bring children into an unknown and potentially poisonous world. Finally, unable to make anyone see reason, and unable to escape, she kills the entire party one by one and awaits her own death by starvation. She is able to face their doom squarely because she has situated herself outside the ideology that values production and reproduction above all. Having divorced herself from the patriarchy, she is granted a clarity of vision denied the men, who fall back reflexively on traditional dogma which prevents them from realizing the insanity of their project.

In *We Who Are About To . . .* Russ signals the urgent need for a feminist resistance to patriarchal constructions of motherhood.

3. Joanna Russ, *We Who Are About To . . .* (London: Women's Press, 1975).

More effectively than Le Sueur or Atwood, she considers the practical forms such a resistance might take. Women can resist being consumed within an aggregate maternal subjectivity by refusing to participate in the fascist reproductive program that produces it. Nonetheless, there is a strong indication in *We Who Are About To . . .* (more fully developed in *The Female Man*, published in the same year)[4] that a redistribution of gender roles is not possible as long as men are present. Even in completely new surroundings, beyond the reach of official enforcement, patriarchy will reassert itself like a mutable (and lethal) virus. One woman, at least, rejects feminine passivity and refuses to identify herself as a sexual and reproductive vessel. But no man has the ability to transcend the worst masculine stereotypes. Men are utterly under the control of an essential masculine drive to organize people and resources around their own fears of mortality.

More troubling, however, is the women's inability to organize themselves for action. All the women, other than the one who finally puts everyone else out of his or her misery, have too much invested in the patriarchy to be willing to abandon it for a nonreproductive women's commune. Given the chance to make a new world for themselves, they see no option but to cooperate, with varying degrees of enthusiasm, with the most degrading form of sexual and reproductive organization men can devise. Even the woman who rebels exhibits a nihilistic subjectivity. Unable to live with others, and unwilling to try to survive alone, she pushes herself inexorably into death by starving herself. She poses no threat to the status quo because she remains alone, unable to gain the cooperation of other women. From her perspective, women's chances of surviving the revolution—either as sovereign individuals or as a communal entity—are grim.

The revolutionary subject does not finally materialize. No more, of course, does the more traditional postrevolutionary humanist subject. Reading our prospects through Baines, Le Sueur, Huxley, or Atwood, we find it impossible to imagine a future in which material contradictions are resolved or philosophical oppositions broken down. Both versions of the postrevolutionary subject, the sovereign

4. Joanna Russ, *The Female Man* (Boston: Gregg Press, 1975).

and the maternal-communal, are the lethal extremes, the points at which imagination balks and the narrative stops. In the opening pages of Part II, I recalled my divorce proceedings as a transformative moment when the subject-in-crisis meets, or crashes into, the humanist subject. These extremes, I thought, should not be able to coexist. Both should be annihilated at the point of contact. But I was able to pick myself up and continue on—although only limpingly for quite a while. The subjective contradiction I faced at that moment was produced by material contradictions I could not, by myself, resolve.

I learned, however, that a chameleon subjectivity had great survival value. It is possible to be a humanist subject and a subject-in-crisis at the same time. In the years since then I have come to doubt the usefulness of thinking in terms of oppositions between an essential and a socially constructed subject, or between the individual and her community. These oppositions, and attempts to break them down, have vital implications for the mother-child relationship which is at the heart of this book. Aldous Huxley wrote in his 1947 foreword to *Brave New World* that the "really revolutionary revolution is to be achieved, not in the external world, but in the souls and flesh of human beings." But an oppositional relationship between "the external world" and the "souls and flesh of human beings" is only one of many possible relationships between people and communities. None of these relationships, however intimate or de-alienated, is natural. If there is a way to construct new forms of subjectivity, it will be through new methods of reproduction, material changes in how human beings are formed and how we reconstruct our origins. Given the political and psychological opposition between the authentic, capitalistic, father-oriented individual and the amorphous, communally identified, boundaryless mother, how do we conceptualize the mother-fetus relationship? And how might we reconceptualize that relationship?

III Framing the Fetal Portrait

As for the mother, let there be no mistake about it, *she has no eyes*, or so they say, she has no gaze, no soul. No consciousness, or memory. No language. And if one were to turn back toward her, in order to re-enter, one would not have to be concerned about her point of view. The danger would rather be of losing one's bearings (or perhaps finding them?). Of falling into a dark hole where lucidity may founder.

—Luce Irigaray, *Speculum of the Other Woman*

I still would like to leave with the idea that if man can go to the moon, then a doctor should be able to go into the uterus.

—Carlo Valenti, *Intrauterine Fetal Visualization*

Conception

Months before my daughter, Nicole, was born, I recorded a dream in my journal. In the dream I was separate from my pregnant body, looking at it from above. I saw my womb opened out, my body an amorphous cloud framing it. A fetus curled up in the womb as though in a cradle. It turned its head to look back at me and smiled, capturing me with its gaze. It recognized me, *knew* me. For an instant the gap between us closed. As though satisfied, the fetus closed its eyes and nestled into my womb. In the months that followed, one image occurred to me again and again: the intelligent eye of the fetus, the illuminating moment when our eyes met.

Vision, in the dual senses of sight and imagination, is crucially important to the psychology and technology that informed my nine-months' dream. The images of the dream were freely borrowed from my limited understanding of ultrasound and Lennart Nilsson's pictures of fetuses in the 1966 edition of *A Child Is Born*.[1] The book depicts stages of fetal growth through an amazing series of photographs. In some the fetus is illuminated against a dark background flecked with white particles, like stars against a night sky. Um-

1. Mirjam Furuhjelm et al., *A Child Is Born* (New York: Delacorte Press, 1966).

bilicus and placenta intact, enveloped in a transparent caul, the body of the fetus floats as if suspended in the sky. These photographs entranced me, and I came back to the book again and again as my pregnancy advanced. The fetus's physical immaturity and unself-consciousness produced a mood of serene isolation and suspension. I felt like a voyeur. I loved the detail: blood vessels glowing just underneath transparent skin, delicate fingers wrapped around the umbilical cord. The fetus of *A Child Is Born* presents the semblance of a kindly alien in orbit, patiently awaiting its birth into human-ness. In these photographs the mother's body has disappeared, or rather it has become a vast nothingness, a universe in which the fetus is the only well-organized, complete system. Nilsson's fetuses don't look back; their eyes are unfocused or veiled by a membrane. My dream fetus not only saw me but recognized me as its mother. Our gaze was mutual, but the connection it established was founded on a foreglimpse of our separation at birth. It still disturbs me to realize that my reconception of myself as a mother was mediated at its deepest level by obstetric technology. When I entered the hospital to give birth, I felt isolated and invisible amid the machinery, terminology, and mechanical routines of my obstetrician and his support staff. But my relationship to all that machinery was not one of simple alienation. To some degree I absorbed, and was absorbed by, the obstetric machinery. The dual experience of connection and alienation I encountered while negotiating my daughter's machine-mediated birth created an enduring, and very personal, concern for how technology affects the way we think about the relationship between mothers and fetuses.

Jane Gallop, commenting on the photograph of a fetus's head emerging from its mother's vagina which appears on the cover of her book *Thinking Through the Body*, describes an "uncanny little head . . . surrounded by body for but a brief pause in an irrepressible progress."[2] The new body progresses from interior to exterior and unity to separation; moments before it was invisible, but now, captured at the moment before it has completely emerged, its image is a tribute to the life-giving power of the visual. Its first photograph,

2. Jane Gallop, *Thinking Through the Body* (New York: Columbia University Press, 1988), p. 8.

taken before its eyes have opened on the world, establishes it as a visual entity, separable from the body that labors to give it birth. In another moment the fetus will be a baby; it will have a sex; and its relationship to its mother will have changed forever.

As I argued earlier, women's writings about giving birth demonstrate that labor can be experienced as a transformative process through which a woman reformulates her subjectivity. The evolution of modern obstetrics, and more particularly the advent of technologies that permit visual access to the fetus, have profoundly influenced representations of the maternal-fetal relationship in women's writings as well as in scientific literature. In this section I show how images of the fetus, including medical illustrations, ultrasound scans, and direct photographs, become figures around which the viewer constructs narratives of self-creation. Nilsson's work in *A Child Is Born* speaks to the aesthetic, psychological, and political implications of the technologies involved in obtaining information about the fetus. The visual technologies developed in the last forty years have enabled physicians to study and even treat the bodies of living fetuses for the first time, but the images research has made possible have entered a wider cultural milieu. Images of the fetus provide material for debates about abortion, research involving fetal tissue, and the fetus's right to treatment *in utero*.[3] But at the same time, and often as an integral—though unexplored— aspect of the moral and ethical debate, these images mediate narratives of subjective transformation.

Although I explore the uses of fetal images in many different literatures, including women's personal and polemical writings and the literatures of psychology, obstetrics, fetal medicine, and biomedical ethics, it is not my intention to analyze these images in terms of simple moral or political polarities. Writers in these divergent fields, although apparently separated by professional, philosophical, political, and (in many cases) gender barriers, speak with as well as against one another. Feminist writers of fiction who take up pregnancy and birth as a theme do not always position themselves in rigid opposition to reproductive science, obstetric prac-

---

3. Ian Donald, one of those who introduced the use of ultrasound in obstetrics, used ultrasound images to convince women not to have abortions.

tice, and technologies that visualize the fetus. From their different perspectives, obstetricians and researchers in the new field of fetal medicine often also express a notion of birth as a transformative, revelatory event. My readings of physicians' professional writings show that they are not necessarily opposed to considering gestation and birth in imaginative and even mystical dimensions.

After a brief look at the general influence of technology on women's experience of labor, and the economic and machine metaphors used to represent birth in the contemporary hospital setting, I focus on the development of visual technologies in obstetrics since the beginning of modern medicine in the eighteenth century. From there I examine imaginative conceptualizations of the relationship between the fetus and womb in contemporary writing and photography, including Marge Piercy's *Woman on the Edge of Time*, Lennart Nilsson's *A Child Is Born*, and Frederick Leboyer's *Birth without Violence*. Luce Irigaray's evocation of the uterine metaphor in "Plato's Hystera" is important to my discussion of contemporary reconceptualizations of the relationship between mother and fetus. Finally, I discuss the propagation of the Platonic uterine metaphor in contemporary reproductive medicine, as scientific and popular representations of the fetus reenact the drama of the prisoner's release from the cave.

CHAPTER 9

Technology and Economy:
Metaphors for the Laboring Mother

The influence of advanced visual technologies, including ultrasound, fetoscopy (viewing the fetus directly), and NMR (nuclear magnetic resonance), is best understood by placing them in context, amid a vast array of low- and high-tech methods of observing and managing pregnancy and childbirth. In Chapter 2 I described techniques for the active management of labor which depend on a collection of technologies and interventions, including fetal monitoring, amniotic puncture, and intravenous drugs, with cesarean section as a (rarely used) backup. The obstetric clinic that practices active management is modeled on the same principle as a well-run factory, where efficient production is the primary value, and waste, in terms of time, energy, and resources, is the enemy. Robbie Davis-Floyd, reporting the results of a study of American obstetric practice, shows that ordinary hospital routines "can work to map a technological view of reality onto the birthing woman's orientation to her labor experience."[1] In any hospital labor and de-

---

1. Robbie Davis-Floyd, "The Technological Model of Birth," *Journal of American Folklore* 100 (October–December 1987): 479–95; subsequent references in this chapter are cited in the text.

livery unit, according to Davis-Floyd, rituals reinforce an assembly line pattern of birth and encourage women to conform to a "technological model of reality" which reinforces "the core values of science, technology, patriarchy, and institutions" (p. 481). Fetal monitoring, enemas, pitocin, anesthesia, and episiotomies are ordinary procedures that Davis-Floyd identifies as components of the technological birth. Davis-Floyd found that a majority of women were comfortable with technological birth, and that many discussed their birth experiences fluently in the language of medical technology. One woman reported that during her labor

> it seemed as though my uterus had suddenly tired! When the nurses in attendance noted a contraction building on the recorder, they instructed me to begin pushing, not waiting for the *urge* to push, so that by the time the urge pervaded, I invariably had no strength remaining, but was left gasping, dizzy and diaphoretic. . . . I felt suddenly depressed by the fact that labor, which had progressed so uneventfully up to this point, had now become unproductive. (p. 487)

Davis-Floyd contends that parturient women who align themselves with the technological model also accept a "basic tenet" of this model: that when something goes wrong, the mother's body is to blame. Her body is a machine that has broken down. But the metaphoric framework employed by the mother just quoted is not only technological; it is also economic. In her own representation she is the reproductive laborer as well as the means of production. When her labor becomes "unproductive," it is not only the laborer who is at fault. Her "managers," the nurses and physicians, are also at fault because they have failed to account for the particular needs of the machine that is her body. By evoking a technological metaphor, she allies herself with her attendants' perspective, and then uses that perspective to frame her grievance.

But the alliance is also important in itself; it may be necessary if she wants to receive adequate care. In her study of the training of residents in obstetrics and gynecology at two U.S. hospitals in the mid-1970s, the sociologist Diana Scully notes that the residents and nurses she observed tended to ignore or berate women who protested, refused to submit to procedures, or "lost control" during labor.[2] By viewing her body as part of the medical machinery of birth, a woman may save herself the trauma of being abandoned or rebuked during labor.[3] The economic component of her birth metaphor, especially in its Marxist implication of a struggle between worker and management, is also a way of meting out responsibility to the doctors and nurses. The metaphor allows her to establish a protective distance from her body (as machine), its processes, and her attendants.

The framework of economic and technological metaphors that structures hospital birth for women and hospital personnel also makes it possible for women to participate in obstetric constructions of the mother-fetus relationship. According to Rosalind Petchesky, women undergoing ultrasound "frequently express a sense of elation and direct participation in the imaging process."[4] She goes on to point out that women have actively campaigned for many technologies, from obstetric anesthesia to *in vitro* fertilization. (In this context it is not as workers but as consumers that women have participated in the technologization of childbearing.) Petchesky notes that many women feel that they have bonded with their baby after seeing it on an ultrasound screen. They report that it makes the fetus seem more real, "more our baby."[5] Viewing the fetus

2. The patients who encounter the greatest hostility are poor women. Diana Scully has observed residents in obstetrics and gynecology in action in labor and delivery wards. She reports: "Numerous painful pelvic examinations were done on institutional patients, sometimes four or five at a time to provide training for medical students, who were, by rule, not allowed to touch private patients. . . . During these examinations, if the woman squirmed or yelled, she was told in an angry, authoritarian voice to behave or she would not be helped. . . . Another form of punishment was the withholding of pain medication." Diana Scully, *Men Who Control Women's Health: The Miseducation of Obstetrician-Gynecologists* (Boston: Houghton Mifflin, 1980), p. 135.

3. According to the technological model of birth, the mother's body is often defective. Approximately one in five pregnancies is now considered to be "high risk"—meaning that more vigilant monitoring and specialized technology may be needed. Included in the "high risk" category, along with diabetic women and illegal drug users, are women over thirty-five for a first birth, women who have had a previous cesarean section, and women more than 10 percent overweight. Adrienne Lieberman, *Giving Birth* (New York: St. Martin's Press, 1987), p. 76.

4. Rosalind Petchesky, "Fetal Images: The Power of Visual Culture in the Politics of Reproduction," *Feminist Studies* 13.2 (Summer 1987): 297.

5. Ibid., p. 279.

through the medium of the imaging machine permits women to claim ownership of the fetus in a way unavailable to those who do not ally themselves with the values of a highly technologized obstetric medicine. If, as Petchesky maintains, any individual woman's perspective on the fetal image is influenced by culturally dominant images of pregnancy and the fetus, as well as by a vast array of circumstances, including class, race, and reproductive status, then there is room—even in the same viewer—for both collaboration with and resistance to culturally prescribed readings of fetal images.

"The Fetus" by Maxine Chernoff, quoted here in full, is one woman's expression of her simultaneous attraction to and distrust of the technological gaze. She describes a mother's dream or fantasy in which her fetus struggles to gain control of their relationship through visual technology:

> The fetus came up to me. It was a normal fetus—large, translucent head, stumpy arms and legs, a heart resembling a bird's nest visible through the chest cavity. It looked at me imploringly, pointing in its ambiguous way at something on my face. The fetus, it seemed, wanted to touch my glasses. I bent down slowly, so as not to startle it. It seemed to take hours and I realized how low I'd have to bend to accommodate my visitor. The touch of the fetus was the touch of someone groping to turn off an alarm. Inept and sleepy and furious all at once. In its small commotion the fetus knocked my glasses to the floor. I hesitated, not daring to speak, to see what it would do. The blurry fetus looked at me, turned and left abruptly as it had arrived. I wondered whether it wanted to wear my glasses for a moment or if its intention had been to touch my eye. When my daughter came home from school, I told her this story. Her eyes strained at mine; they had the same look I've detected when she's being lied to by a stranger.[6]

The fetus she encounters has already taken on a life of its own. It is a "visitor" who comes to her, not from within her body but from some other place. It has formulated its own desires and needs, and moves on its own to satisfy them. Nevertheless, it needs the mother

6. Maxine Chernoff, "The Fetus," in *Cradle and All: Women Writers on Pregnancy and Birth*, ed. Laura Chester (Boston: Faber and Faber, 1989), p. 21.

and seeks a connection with her. The point of connection it seeks is both visual (it reaches for her eyes) and technological (it grabs at her glasses). The (figurative) fetus wants to see through its mother's eyes and will be able to accomplish this only if their shared gaze is mediated technologically. But things go wrong. The mother is blind without her glasses. In order for the fetus to acquire vision, she must give up her eyes. The fetus becomes more blurry, less real once she gives up her glasses. And as soon as she is blinded, the fetus loses control. It cannot see through its mother's eyes once they have been blinded. It is still too unformed to be able to manipulate the glasses, the visual technology, for itself. The organic and technological bond between them fails, and the fetus, frustrated, wanders off. The dreamer wonders if it was really the glasses the fetus wanted, or whether it was trying to establish an unmediated visual connection by touching her eye directly.

The failure of vision implied in their encounter is redoubled in the last part of the narrative. The mother, now seemingly awake, sees her daughter's eyes "straining" at her while she tells her dream. Her daughter cannot see what she is trying to say. Paradoxically, she identifies with her daughter (seeing through her eyes) at the moment when her daughter sees her as a stranger who lies. She expresses the ambivalence in the relationship between the mother-and-child mirrors as a tension between vision as connection and vision as alienation. Mother and child struggle to establish a mutual gaze, but the result is instead a mutual blindness, represented in the figure of the blurry, dim-sighted, transparent fetal image of the dream.

At the end of the eighteenth century, coinciding with the birth of modern medicine, writes Michel Foucault,

> seeing consists in leaving to experience its greatest corporal opacity; the solidity, the obscurity, the density of things closed in upon themselves, have powers of truth that they owe not to light, but to the slowness of the gaze that passes over them, around them, and gradually into them, bringing them nothing more than its own light. . . . The gaze is no longer reductive, it is, rather, that which establishes the individual in his irreducible quantity.

Rational discourse is organized around this clinical gaze, which made it possible to "hold a scientifically structured discourse about an individual."[7] Such a truth-giving gaze is preeminently a creative power; as it establishes the individual as an "irreducible quantity," it also gives "birth" to modern medicine.

Although metaphors of conception, gestation, and birth permeate Foucault's history of the clinical gaze in *The Birth of the Clinic*, women are not present in it except occasionally as its object. Among the few examples of women as patients, all deal with pregnancy and birth. For instance, Foucault mentions an eighteenth-century maternity clinic in Copenhagen that admitted only unmarried women, who, in return for the care they received, provided educational material for doctors; in this role they "[repaid] their benefactors with interest."[8] But if women are largely absent, the idea of mother, an unanalyzed maternal metaphor, provides the referent for Foucault's analysis of the clinical gaze. The gaze he describes—penetrating and rational—is traditionally masculine. And the object of that gaze is opaque, obscure, mysterious, unable to generate its own truths, and empty of light until it is penetrated by the rational gaze. No matter what the sex of the individual under observation, such an object is aligned with the maternal.

Foucault is uninterested here in the maternal metaphor that underlies his characterization of the object of the medical gaze, but Luce Irigaray is most concerned with gendered organizations of the gaze. She addresses the maternal metaphor directly in her essay "Plato's Hystera," when she describes the womb as the "unformed 'amorphous' origin of all morphology." Under the terms of the metaphor, the mother cannot know herself but can be penetrated by a paternal light which imparts form and reason—not *to* her, but *through* her—to the individual life forming within her. "*Seeing remains the special prerogative of the Father. It is in his gaze that everything comes into being.*"[9]

If this gaze is paternal, its maternal counterpart is a shadow.

---

7. Michel Foucault, *The Birth of the Clinic: An Archeology of Medical Perception*, trans. A. M. Sheridan Smith (New York: Vintage Books, 1973), pp. xiii–xiv.

8. J. B. Demangeon, quoted ibid., p. 85.

9. Luce Irigaray, "Plato's Hystera," in *Speculum of the Other Woman*, trans. Gillian C. Gill (Ithaca: Cornell University Press, 1985), pp. 265, 323.

Though she has a character, she lacks her own authentic form. Her "opacity" and "obscurity" repel the paternal-clinical gaze, but eventually it overcomes her resistance and, inexorably, finds its way in. The paternal-clinical gaze depends on a clear differentiation between the viewing subject and the object of his gaze. The gaze that imparts, in Foucault's words, "powers of truth" as it "passes . . . into" its object is a seminal gaze, penetrating its object without risking its own subjective rationality. The viewing subject retains his clinical distance and his bodily integrity.

The mother in Chernoff's narrative challenges the validity of this gendered model of the gaze. In the context of her dream, the mother possesses a life-giving gaze. She creates the image of the fetus—who immediately demands that she give up that creative power and surrender her vision. She risks losing the rational, formative power of the gaze when she tries to endow the fetus with her own gaze. At that moment the fetus becomes blurry, its image undefined, and she simultaneously gives up her sense of *herself* as an "irreducible quantity."

It is the quality of the gaze rather than the sex of the viewer which puts her in jeopardy. The gaze that enters into its object in order to endow it with light and form carries the viewer with it, where each one, viewer and object, acts on the other. The model at work in Chernoff's narrative refutes the assumption in Foucault's description of medical vision that the viewer can enter the object through the gaze without being radically, and unavoidably, transformed in interaction with the object of his or her gaze. Although Foucault states that reason permits the subject to be the object as well, he also maintains that rational discourse is not affected by their mutability.[10] But the creative gaze does undermine rational discourse in that the bodily and psychic integrity of the viewer is broken through as a consequence of the act of viewing.

Death, Foucault says, is the "great analyst." It is a force that breaks down the individual body, cell by cell, into its constituent parts. By dissecting the dead, the medical gaze, now the "gaze of an eye that has seen death," becomes an agent of death's analysis of the

---

10. "The *object* of discourse may equally well be a *subject*, without the figures of objectivity being in any way altered." Foucault, *The Birth of the Clinic*, p. xiv.

body. The gaze no longer respects the body's opacity; it "plunges from the manifest to the hidden" as it crosses the border between life and death.[11]

This new way of seeing confuses categories that once were distinct: the surface and the interior, the intact and the analyzed, the living and the dead are not easily sorted out. Only later, long after the birth of modern medicine, does the gaze effectively enter the *living* body, enabled by new technologies—by means of X rays, for instance—to analyze the body's interior without literally breaking the body down. But its history, the long merging of the medical gaze with death, continues to influence analyses of the living body.

The issues are still more complex when we are dealing with images of the fetus *in utero*. A woman's womb is the inner frame that contextualizes the surface image of the fetus. In the remainder of this section, I trace several broad shifts in the history of visual depictions of the fetus and uterus in modern medicine, coincident with and dependent on the advent of new visual technologies. It is impossible to understand the development of new medical technologies without considering economic influences: modern obstetrics has always been a business as well as a healing profession. Representations of the mother-fetus relationship in medical illustrations must be read as channels of economic as well as informational and ideological exchange.

Before the eighteenth century, images of the fetus and womb tended to the idealized. They might, for instance, feature an outline of a round and rigid vessel, like a narrow-necked vase, containing a fetus with an erect body proportioned like an adult's. Intimate physical connections between the fetus and the mother, the umbilical cord, placenta, and the uterine walls surrounding the fetus, are elided in these images. But the figure of the fetus and its physical relationship to the scene of its development undergo a shift dating from the moment when printed anatomies directly represented the results of dissections of women in pregnancy. William Hunter's *Anatomy of the Human Gravid Uterus*, first published in 1772, exemplifies this shift.

Hunter viewed the change aesthetically as a progression from "a

11. Ibid., pp. 144, 135.

figure of fancy," or an imaginative rendering that merely describes the object, to a truthful depiction of an actual body that would convey its own truth, hardly needing textual interpretation. He tells the reader in his preface that he has chosen to represent "the object as it was actually seen" rather than as it might be "conceived in the imagination." Such an image is superior because it "carries the mark of truth, and becomes almost as infallible as the object itself."[12] Though his anatomy dates from the eighteenth century, Hunter's definition of the relationship between the anatomist's gaze and his object differs from Foucault's in that Hunter insists that the object contains its own truth; the task of the anatomist is to reveal, rather than to construct, the "mark of truth" that originates in the object. Nevertheless, Hunter's visual record of his observations in the *Anatomy* suggest that a creative, rather than a revelatory, gaze is at work.

The *Human Gravid Uterus* was very successful, proving the popular appeal of Hunter's aesthetic. Images from Hunter's atlas were circulated throughout the nineteenth century in encyclopedias and home medical handbooks.[13] The book itself went through several editions, the latest in the mid-nineteenth century. Twenty-five years in the making, *The Human Gravid Uterus* was Hunter's masterpiece, an emblem not only of his prowess as an anatomist but also of his phenomenal success as an entrepreneur. Hunter built on his contacts with the outstanding British physicians of his day and established a thriving practice, mainly in obstetrics, catering to the aristocracy and even royalty.

Hunter also founded and operated until his death a prestigious in-

12. William Hunter, *Anatomy of the Human Gravid Uterus* (n.p., 1772), p. ii. Although *The Human Gravid Uterus* was influential, the kind of realism Hunter argued for did not take precedence over more idealized anatomical representations. The historian Ludmilla Jordinova says that Samual Thomas von Soemmerring's *Icones Embryonum Humanorum* (1799), although intended to supplement Hunter's atlas, was "governed by a notion of the *ideal*, in contrast to Hunter's emphasis on the natural." Ludmilla Jordinova, "Gender, Generation, and Science: William Hunter's Obstetrical Atlas," in *William Hunter and the Eighteenth-Century Medical World*, ed. W. F. Bynum and Roy Porter (London: Cambridge University Press, 1985), p. 398. Soemmerring was looking for " 'the true norm of the organs,' " and in doing so, he felt that the artist's representation should correct flaws apparent in the specimen.

13. Marcia Pointon, "Interior Portraits: Women, Physiology, and the Male Artist," *Feminist Review* 22 (February 1986): 18.

dependent anatomy school. He succeeded in part because he promised that each student would dissect a corpse of his own, in the "Paris Manner," a practice Hunter claimed to have brought to Britain. The school needed a profuse supply of bodies in an era when cadavers were not available in great numbers.[14] Hunter's ability to provide a steady flow of bodies, combined with the reasonable fees he charged and the unusual depth and extent of his instruction, made his course a good value for medical students. Roy Porter describes Hunter's anatomy school as "an enterprise essentially self-created, self-owned and self-managed right up to his death.[15]

Hunter's claims regarding the scientific superiority of the "Paris manner" of dissection and his enthusiasm for naturalistic representation in medical art must be viewed in the context of his entrepreneurial zeal. Hunter's aesthetic, demanding as it did continual access to "the object itself"—in this case a highly perishable commodity—required considerable business acumen. He invested his substantial monetary and social capital in promoting the aesthetic and the science, which, in their turn, validated his business. Hunter tells the reader of *The Human Gravid Uterus* that "opportunities of dissecting the human pregnant uterus at leisure very rarely occur. Indeed, to most anatomists, if they have happened at all, it has been but once or twice in their whole lives." But Hunter has been more fortunate: "numerous opportunities . . . have fallen to his share" so that he ended up with an excess of bodies, so many that he had to hold back drawings from the atlas for fear that it might be "over-

14. Christopher Lawrence, "Alexander Munro *Primus* and the Edingburgh Manner of Anatomy," *Bulletin of the History of Medicine* 62 (1988): 193. There had always been some problems involved in getting enough bodies for dissection. The Murder Act of 1752 ordered the bodies of executed murderers to be either displayed or dissected publicly, but this yielded a limited number of bodies per year. According to Ruth Richardson, John Hunter procured cadavers (by negotiating with body-snatchers) for his brother William's anatomy school during the 1750s. Ruth Richardson, *Death, Dissection, and the Destitute* (London: Routledge & Kegan Paul, 1987), p. 57. This was the period when William Hunter's work on *Anatomy of the Human Gravid Uterus* was under way. And so it is almost certain that Hunter supplied his anatomy school in part with bodies obtained from fresh graves, and perhaps obtained in the same way the bodies of women in pregnancy for his *Anatomy*.

15. Roy Porter, "William Hunter: A Surgeon and a Gentleman," in Bynum and Porter, *William Hunter and the Eighteenth-Century Medical World*, p. 21.

charged." Hunter's success as a capitalist, as a dealer in bodies and producer of an excess of dissections, allowed him to bring his images of mother and fetus into wide currency.[16]

Although the clarity of anatomical detail in the plates from Hunter's atlas is remarkable, the images are not in every respect easy to interpret. They hold back some of the almost infallible truth Hunter ascribes to them. The images of the mother's body invite questions—questions which are ultimately unanswerable—about what happened to the mother. Hunter offers only sketchy information about his primary subject: "A woman died suddenly, when very near the end of her pregnancy; the body was procured before any sensible putrefaction had begun; the season of the year was favorable to dissection; the injection of the blood-vessels proved successful; a very able painter in this way was found; every part was examined in the most public manner, and the truth was thereby well authenticated."[17] Knowing more about the woman is unnecessary to the kind of truth Hunter is after, and so she has been amputated, not only visually and narratively but literally.[18] Her body above the abdomen and below the thighs has been removed. The life-size uterus, depicted with scrupulous detail, fills the oversized page. It is clear that if Hunter had tried to contain the entire body in the image, many of the finer structures of the reproductive organs would have been too small to be readable. But rather than "cropping out" the image of the body above and below his main object of interest, Hunter depicted the amputation of the literal body. The gesture may seem unnecessarily violent to the modern sensibility, but it supports Hunter's claims to absolute truth; the image "repre-

16. Hunter, *The Human Gravid Uterus*, p. i.

17. Ibid.

18. Nevertheless, one can speculate about the origins of the corpse based on what is known about how bodies were obtained for dissection. There were class distinctions made by procurers: for instance, grave robbers concentrated on cemeteries where the poor or vagrants were buried because they were less carefully coffined and buried. What does all this allow us to conclude about this woman? It is impossible to say how Hunter obtained this particular body; but these general circumstances suggest that she did not have strong family connections. It is also likely that she was poor, since few families who could afford burial would willingly give up their dead to a practice they considered degrading to the body.

sents what was actually seen." Nevertheless Hunter's realism is not artless. In part, it is, as Ludmilla Jordinova describes it, an expression of his primarily visual epistemology: "Hunter saw nature's truths as being on the surface, ready to be received by the trained, observant mind."[19]

But what natural truth is brought to the surface in these plates (figs. 1 and 2)? In the first five plates the woman is progressively reduced as the dissection proceeds, leaving only the uterus intact. The impression created by the initial plate—that everything unnecessary to Hunter's project has already been excised—is progressively reinforced until all that is left are the stumps of her thighs and her uterus. Even her external genitals have been cut away. The massive uterus, filling the abdomen and the page, is her nucleus. When everything inessential has been cut away, the core organ, the uterus, is left. At last, in the sixth plate, the wall of the uterus facing the viewer is cut away to reveal the fetus. The dissection then progresses until the uterus is removed entirely, leaving the body an empty shell: the woman has been cored.

In all the engravings containing an image of the fetus, the text tells us that no explanation of the fetus is needed. Although it is possible that Hunter did dissect this fetus, for the purposes of representation, the fetus serves as "the individual in his most complete opacity." The text for this plate tells us that "every part is represented just as it was found; not so much as one joint of a finger having been moved to shew any part more distinctly, or to give a more picturesque effect."[20] Jordinova notes that the body of the fetus "is treated tenderly, while the [mother] appears dissected and mutilated."[21] Once the uterine wall is breached, it seems that the essential nucleus of the woman is no longer her womb but the fetus itself. Once the fetus is revealed, the mother's dissected body serves as the contextualizing frame for its intact body. It is her body that yields the most pertinent information about the child. The body of

19. Jordinova, "Gender, Generation, and Science," p. 399.

20. Hunter, *The Human Grand Uterus*, unpaginated.

21. Jordinova, "Gender, Generation, and Science," p. 390. In his preface Hunter explains that he did not anatomize the fetus because his project had already become too big and too expensive and because others had already made adequate anatomies of the fetus.

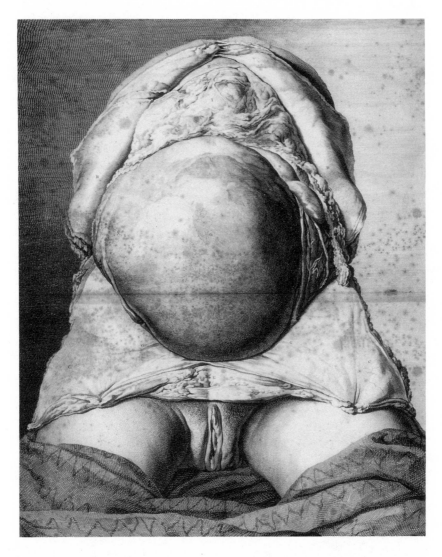

FIGURE 1. Nine-month uterus, William Hunter's *Human Gravid Uterus*, 1779. From the collections of the Owen H. Wangensteen Historical Library of Biology and Medicine, University of Minnesota.

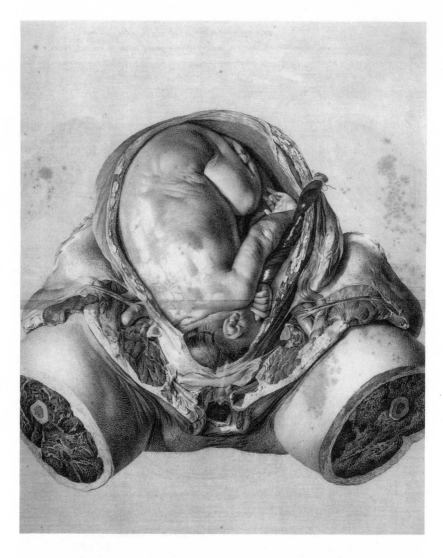

FIGURE 2. Fetus *in utero*, William Hunter's *Human Gravid Uterus*, 1779. From the collections of the Owen H. Wangensteen Historical Library of Biology and Medicine, University of Minnesota.

the child completely fills the uterus, suggesting that it must have been almost ready to be born; the missing parts of the mother's body and the opened uterus confirm that it died with its mother before birth. The fate of the mutilated mother and inviolate, lifeless child are inextricably tied together. The image represents the fetus as simultaneously an irreducible human entity and a body connected with that of the mother in profound, and potentially tragic, intimacy.[22]

But this interpretation of the mother-fetus relationship has been challenged in the contemporary era, when both the physical circumstances for viewing the fetus and the expectations of what that image will reveal have changed.[23] The first attempts at fetoscopy (direct visualization of the human fetus) were made in the 1950s. In the 1970s interest in the procedure was high. Fetoscopy seemed bound to become the founding technology of the new specialty of fetology, but during the 1980s enthusiasm waned. This happened in part because the procedure holds considerable risk for the fetus and in part because of refinements in ultrasound. At present there is very little that can be visualized fetoscopically that cannot be detected with ultrasound. Furthermore, ultrasound can produce im-

---

22. Jordinova calls it "an almost oppressive intimacy" (ibid., p. 406), but later she says that "Hunter's foetuses possess and confidently inhabit their mothers' bodies" (p. 409). She contrasts this with pre–eighteenth-century images in which the fetus "seemed lost in the waters of the womb" (p. 409). To me, the earlier representations suggest a fully sentient and freely active fetus, proportioned like a mature adult. The inconsistencies within Jordinova's discussion of the maternal-fetal relationship in Hunter, as well as the differences between her interpretations and mine, reinforce her final point, that even Hunter's naturalistic images do not simply reveal the truth but are instead constructions that are open to interpretation.

23. As early as the 1960s, the International Symposium on Diagnosis and Treatment of Disorders Affecting the Intrauterine Patient published their proceedings in *Diagnosis and Treatment of Fetal Disorders* (New York: Springer-Verlag, 1968). Beginning in 1984, an annual international symposium on the fetus as a patient began publishing its proceedings, *The Fetus as a Patient* (New York: Elsevier Science Publishing, 1984–). Other books that came out in the 1980s focusing on the treatment of the fetus as a patient separate from the mother include I. Rocker, ed., *Fetoscopy* (New York: Elsevier, 1981); Franco Borruto, ed., *Fetal Ultrasonography: The Secret Prenatal Life* (New York: John Wiley & Sons, 1982); Bruce K. Young, ed., *The Patient within the Patient* (New York: Liss, 1985); E. Peter Volpe, *Patient in the Womb* (Macon, Ga: Mercer, 1984); Michael R. Harrison, *The Unborn Patient: Prenatal Diagnosis and Treatment* (Orlando, Fla.: Grune & Stratton, 1984).

ages of internal organs, cross-sections of the brain and heart, for instance.[24] In Hunter's day the interior of the body was fully accessible to view only after death. Until this century it was impossible to look inside the womb at a living fetus. It is the technology of ultrasound, and to some extent fetoscopy, that has given the gaze the power to sweep backward from death to the first stirrings of individual life.

Foucault says in *Birth of the Clinic* that at the dawn of modern medicine, death—"the great analyst"—"bursts open the wonders of genesis in the rigour of decomposition." He writes, "The slow, natural death of the old man resumes in inverse direction the development of life in the child, in the embryo."[25] Death, in the medicine of Hunter's era, recapitulates the events of gestation in reverse order. The individual was fully knowable only during and after death, when he had reached the final stages of development and was in the process of decomposition. The modern medicine of the twentieth century has not left behind the understanding of the eighteenth; gross anatomy is still a required course of medical study. But developments in mammalian embryology in the nineteenth century and the study of genetics in the twentieth describe a backward movement through the lifetime of the individual. Instead of focusing on the moment of death as the revelatory moment, now the clinical gaze focuses on the first moments of life. Hunter's anatomy takes the viewer through a narrative of decomposition in the sense that in the pictorial story of this woman's dissection, the eye follows her body's progressive disintegration as each layer is removed. Nilsson's chronology takes us in the reverse direction, as he represents a life that is gradually coming into itself, achieving with the turn of each page a more finished form.

The shattered corpse of the mother in Hunter's anatomy would be an incongruous frame for the narrative of a fetus's unfolding life. One might expect that as the revelatory gaze shifts from the corpse to the living embryo, traditional perceptions of women's bodies as

24. Personal conversation with Susan Sipes, M.D., specialist in fetal medicine at the University of Iowa Hospitals and Clinics.

25. Foucault, *Birth of the Clinic*, pp. 144, 143. He notes also that, to Marie-Francois-Xavier Bichat, "knowledge of life finds its origin in the destruction of life. . . . It is at death that disease and life speak their truth" (p. 145).

imbued with decay might recede. But the mother's image retains its associations with death. Wolfgang Lederer, psychiatrist and matriphobe, succinctly expresses in *The Fear of Women* the enduring view of "Mother" as death: "Woman, awesome in fertility, is fearsome in decay. . . . But decay is always inherent in matter, and in so far as Mother is Mater, is Matter and *Materies,* as opposed to the eternal spirit, she is perishable."[26] Perhaps it is less the thought of "Mother's" association with death than her ambiguous identity as the vessel of both life and death ("awesome in fertility . . . fearsome in decay") that causes the dread Lederer expresses.[27] In its search for the root of life, the clinical gaze shifts from the corpse to the living embryo. But rather than resolving the traditional maternal paradox, the refocusing of the clinical eye brings about the erasure of the mother's body. Her body disappears at the moment when the figure of the living fetus arrives in the foreground.

The introduction to the second edition of *A Child Is Born* asserts that because of Lennart Nilsson's high-tech photographs of fetuses, "the new life taking shape inside the mother-to-be thus becomes vivid and more easily recognizable as a new and independent individual."[28] Advanced imaging techniques make it possible to think of the fetus as a whole, fully differentiated human subject from its first moments.

26. Lederer, *The Fear of Women,* p. 249.

27. Fascinated by the memory of an image in one of his high school textbooks of a medieval statue of "a naked woman most bonnie in front, but in the rear covered with sores, ulcers, worms and all manner of pestilence" (ibid., p. 37), Lederer has looked for (and found) similar verbal and visual images of the beauty and putrescence of "woman" from the Middle Ages through the nineteenth century. But he turns to Simone de Beauvoir for evidence of the sentiment in modern times: "This is woman's first lie, her first treason: namely, that of life itself—life which though clothed in the most attractive forms, is always infested by the ferments of age and death" (ibid., p. 41). He quotes De Beauvoir's *Second Sex* (New York: Knopf, 1953), p. 160.

28. Lennart Nilsson, *A Child Is Born,* 2d ed. (New York: Bantam, 1990), p. 8.

CHAPTER 10

Fetal Vision

In Mattapoisett, Marge Piercy's utopia in *Woman on the Edge of Time*, the babies of the future gestate in "brooders." A visitor from the twentieth century, Connie Ramos, is taken on a tour of the facility, where one of her amiable hosts is eager to show her the fetuses.

> He pressed a panel and a door slid aside, revealing seven human babies joggling slowly upside down, each in a sac of its own inside a larger fluid receptacle.
> Connie gaped, her stomach also turning slowly upside down. All in a sluggish row, babies bobbed. Mother the machine. Like fish in the aquarium at Coney Island. Their eyes were closed. One very dark female was kicking. Another, a pink male, she could see clearly from the oversize penis, was crying. Languidly they drifted in a blind school.[1]

Connie Ramos, a mother who was "knocked out" for the birth of her own child back in the twentieth century, cannot completely put

---

1. Marge Piercy, *Woman on the Edge of Time* (New York: Fawcett Crest, 1976), p. 102.

aside her own conception of pregnancy and motherhood as a private experience of intimate attachment and pain. Although the fetuses are almost ready to be born, Piercy emphasizes that they have not opened their eyes. And Connie, unable to overcome the shock of seeing the unborn, refuses to watch anymore. She cannot look at the unborn without seeing again the horrifying image of the three-month fetus a doctor once showed her after her abortion. For Connie, vision should not intrude on a process that has always taken place in the dark. Her intensely negative reaction to viewing the fetuses contrasts sharply with the comfortable, enlightened attitude of her hosts. The processes by which the living embryo metamorphoses and grows, once utterly private, are private no longer; the physical and emotional barriers that prevented people from viewing, and *controlling,* the process of generation have been broken through. The brooder, emblem of a new and better vision of reproduction, is the foundation of utopia.

In her twentieth-century incarnation Connie is a middle-aged, poverty-stricken Chicana who is committed to Rockover State Mental Hospital. Faced with circumstances that seem impossible, Connie refuses the victim role assigned to her under patriarchal capitalism and fights actively to create a better future.[2] Although Connie is never able to rejoice in the idea that her descendants will be born from what she calls "this crazy machine," she makes herself responsible for helping to construct this future because she cannot ignore the advantages of extracorporeal gestation. In Mattapoisett, women like Connie are respected members of a society which has vanquished intolerance. To achieve this end, women have had to sacrifice in-body gestation and all connection to their genetic children. The argument behind Mattapoisett is that we can ensure the birth and survival of an enlightened society by rendering public the processes of generation that once were hidden deep inside women's

2. Piercy asserts that encountering apparently alien characters in fiction is one way of increasing our empathy for them and making them less alien. Of Connie, Piercy says: "Very few people who read my novel *Woman on the Edge of Time* would have anything to do with the protagonist—a middle-aged, overweight Chicana defined as crazy, shabbily dressed, lucky to get off welfare and into a mopwoman's job." Marge Piercy, "Active in Time and History," in *Paths of Resistance,* ed. William Zinsser (Boston: Houghton Mifflin, 1989), p. 114.

bodies. This program of genetic engineering, and the resulting dissolution of the nuclear family, is directly responsible for the dismantling of racial prejudice, male dominance, and class hierarchies. Each person is a unique individual whose social, cultural, and family relationships prevent her or him from developing racist, classist, religious, cultural, or sexist prejudices. In *Woman on the Edge of Time*, the intense, private intimacy of mother and child during gestation has been broken. There is no genetic or gestational connection between a child and the people who mother him or her. An anatomy such as William Hunter's cannot represent this form of reproduction. The powerful physical intimacy between the mother and child in his atlas seems to have been deadly to both. The mother's mutilated body and the death of the fetus—catastrophes essential to Hunter's treatment of reproductive anatomy—would seem barbaric and excessive to the people of Mattapoisett, where maternal-fetal intimacy and its hazards do not exist.

Although the technology that would permit the comprehensive extracorporeal gestation Piercy describes remains in the future, current technologies of fetal visualization—especially those employed in *A Child Is Born*—create images that give the impression of fetal autonomy. The fetus that could be accessed only after death in Hunter's day is now available to view while it lives. The impressive advances in technologies of intrabody visualization that intervene between the works of Hunter and Nilsson produced a profound representational shift. The living body of the fetus, freed from the obscurity of its life in the womb, should outshine the archaic corpse and reveal its truths unambiguously to the curious gaze. But the image of the unfinished body of the fetus has not changed as much as the frame that tells the viewer how to read that body.

An image of a fetus at eighteen weeks shows the complete and seemingly perfect fetus with hands, face, and genitals, all encompassed in a rosy glow.[3] This photograph, the text informs us, was taken during a fetoscopic examination in which a very wide angle lens and fiberoptics were used. The image is framed by a hard circular line in the foreground; the space beyond is black, as though we were looking at the fetus through a porthole or telescope. The

3. Nilsson, *A Child Is Born*, p. 139.

mother's body, the essential contextualizing frame in Hunter's anatomy, is a black void in Nilsson's. Just looking at the image, we cannot be sure that this is a living fetus, still in the womb. The hands are slack; the membrane-covered eyes reveal nothing. We have to take it on faith—faith in the technological advances that made the image possible—that the fetus is only asleep or anesthetized. In any case, its future is doubtful or it never could have become the subject for this portrait. Because the procedure entails great risk for the fetus, experimental work on fetoscopy takes place on women scheduled for abortion (a troubling practice in itself, considering that fetoscopy is a surgical procedure that is also risky to the mother and is unrelated to the abortion she is seeking). Another possibility is that this is a fetus being examined for some abnormality that, in the opinion of its mother's physician, could be diagnosed only through direct visualization. In either case, there is a crisis going on with this fetus that is not inscribed in the photograph.

The ambiguity of this image can be underscored by comparison to another illustration of a fetus at eight weeks. It is barely old enough to be termed a fetus. Like its older counterpart, this fetus is surrounded by black space. The fluid-filled amniotic membrane veils the figure of the fetus, but eyes, limbs, and even blood vessels are quite apparent. To the untrained eye, this fetus seems to be just as viable as its older counterpart, but this is a "specimen" rather than a living fetus. Again it is the frame that conveys the essential information about the fetus. The part of the placenta which should be attached to the (absent) uterus fans out around the amniotic sac. The significance is lost unless the viewer knows precisely what she is looking at. The text is no more forthcoming than the image. The caption for a similar photograph tells the reader that "the cells are seething with life, the heart is beating, blood is being pumped through the umbilical cord and the whole embryo is in constant motion," a complete misstatement of the status of the embryo pictured there.[4] A Child Is Born makes such skillful use of photographic and rhetorical technique that it is almost impossible to sort out the living from the dead.

4. Ibid., pp. 91, 85.

Nilsson's reticence about the origins of some of his photographic subjects and the intentional equivocation of Lars Hamberger's explanatory text all belie Nilsson's manifest principle of the primacy of the visual. Asked by a *Life* reporter when life begins, Lennart Nilsson goes to his portfolio of fetal photographs, noting a series of "historic" events in the development of each embryo. He says, "Look at the pictures. I am not the man who shall decide when human life started. I am a reporter, I am a photographer."[5] Nilsson's deferral to the photographic image recalls William Hunter's conviction that there is more to be learned from viewing either the object or a naturalistic representation of the object than from verbal or textual description. Hunter believed that the value of the printed anatomy was its capacity for making the study of the body "both more easy and pleasant" for humanity in general, a goal which Nilsson has achieved with far greater technical sophistication than Hunter—who also made use of the most advanced visual technologies of his era—could have thought possible.[6] Although both make claims about the truth-telling powers of the faithful image, their works are reticent in certain respects, especially in regard to the origins of their subjects.

In Hunter, however, there is no mistaking the fact that the fetus is a corpse. With Nilsson the facts are difficult to verify. It is not my intention to say that Hunter's images represent the truth of the mother-fetus relationship and that Nilsson's do not. Nilsson's access to advanced technology makes the illusion of fetal independence more credible, and the contemporary political climate makes it vital that the images and the text of his book maintain that illusion. Nilsson's waffling on the issue of when life begins, and his deferral to the ambiguous images in his book, suggests that he recognizes the complexities of the debate over fetal rights and abortion and has no desire to take sides.

But if Nilsson himself remains as silent about fetal rights as he does about the story behind his photographic subjects, his photographs speak volumes. Reproductions of Nilsson's photographs

5. David Van Biema, "Master of an 'Unbelievable, Invisible World,'" *Life* 13, no. 10 (August 1990): 46.
6. Hunter, *The Human Gravid Uterus*, p. i.

have turned up on the placards hoisted at right-to-life demonstrations. I have seen them used on right-to-life displays in the student
union at the University of Iowa, sometimes along with an unpleasant photograph of a postabortion fragmented fetal skull. There is a
certain irony in the use of Nilsson's photos to demonstrate the
integrity of fetal life in right-to-life posters. The dead fetuses pictured in *A Child Is Born* have the same serene aspect as the living;
their images might as readily demonstrate that abortion is a beautiful and peaceful solution to a difficult pregnancy.

Amid this ambiguity, the only consistent "truth" that these photographs seem to tell is that the fetus, whether corpse or living
organism, is essentially an independent individual. But these photographs cannot, in fact, reveal anything about fetal life but what
the viewer expects to see. They tell us nothing conclusive about
how the fetus experiences life in the womb. They are images around
which wildly diverging narratives of fetal development have been
constructed.

Some physicians describe the fetus as a parasite who takes over
the mother's body; others describe it as a prisoner of the mother's
psychological and physical pathology.[7] Prisoner, parasite, philosopher, astronaut, hermit, patient—all the identities ascribed to the
silent fetus have this in common: they are based not on a model of
cooperation or union between mother and fetus but on a model
of maternal-fetal opposition. They all ascribe to the fetus a degree of
intention, a modicum of mature consciousness, and an awareness
of self and other. Whether subordinate or superior, invader or captive, the fetus is always alienated from its immediate (maternal)

---

7. For instance, comments by Frank Hytten, M.D., describe the fetus as "an ego-
ist, and by no means an endearing and helpless little dependent as his mother may
fondly think. As soon as he has plugged himself into the uterine wall he sets out to
make certain that his needs are served, regardless of any inconvenience he may
cause. He does this by almost completely altering the mother's physiology, usually
by fiddling with her control mechanisms." Quoted in Ann Oakley, *The Captured
Womb: A History of the Medical Care of Pregnant Women* (Oxford: Basil Blackwell,
1984), p. 175. Here the mother is a machine. She has "control mechanisms" that *she*
cannot control, but the embryo can. "He" (the embryo) is self-centered and utterly
ruthless, even before the brain develops. And yet the complete selfishness of the
embryo is a quality we should admire: this tiny mite is a real survivor, unlike his
mother, who fails to understand that she is being parasitized.

environment. The fetus in *A Child Is Born* is an astronaut, the prototype for the star child in *2001: A Space Odyssey*. In these images the mystery of human origins appears to be resolved in the blinding revelation that origins are completely internal to the individual, written into his unique genetic code. Nothing of what the fetus is derives from its physiological union with the mother's body. Isolated from all external sustenance, the free-floating body appears to generate its own form—even its own light—from some source beneath its translucent skin. It appears to grow page by page from an undifferentiated blob of cells to a beautifully formed human being, generating itself from the nothing in which it floats.

According to the text of *A Child Is Born*, Nilsson's two-celled embryo is *the* "irreducible human quality," the smallest entity that we can confidently call human. (If Nilsson is unwilling to offer an opinion about when life begins, Hamberger is not so guarded. He describes fertilization as the moment when "a new life begins.") At the fusion of the nuclei of sperm and egg, "instantaneously, numerous hereditary characteristics of the new individual are determined."[8] It is no longer possible to argue as the preformationists did in Hunter's time that the fetus *literally* has a finished human form from its conception. But it is at least possible to argue that it possesses a coded version of that form; it is *virtually*, if not *literally*, a fully realized human individual. This is the contradiction: that the *unfinished* fetus also represents the most *essential form* of man.

8. Nilsson, *A Child Is Born*, p. 56.

CHAPTER 11

Irigaray's *Speculum:*
Views of the Womb

Luce Irigaray writes in *Speculum of the Other Woman:* "Already the prisoner was no longer in a womb but in a cave—an attempt to provide a figure, a system of metaphor for the uterine cavity. He was held in a place that was, that meant to express, that had the *sense* of being, *like* a womb. We must *suppose* that the womb is reproduced, reproducible, and reproductive by means of projections."[1] The figure of the fetus-as-prisoner is locked up inside a system of metaphor from which there is no escape. The uterine metaphor, an infinitely impressionable matrix that envelops, nourishes, and imprisons him, also makes him intelligible.

Irigaray's study of Plato in *Speculum of the Other Woman* takes the reader on a rigorous tour of—among other things—the philosophy that endorses the mother's deletion from the scene of reproduction. Irigaray's commentary on the problematic relationship between the material womb and the Platonic cave suggests how erasure has come to be the natural, essential function of the (metaphoric) mother. Irigaray first invites us to "read [the cave] as a meta-

---

1. Irigaray, *Speculum,* p. 279; subsequent references in this chapter are cited in the text.

phor of the inner space, of the den, the womb or Hystera," but then immediately warns us that "the text inscribes the metaphor as, strictly speaking, impossible" (p. 243). Impossible because, in the Platonic philosophy which gives rise to the allegory of the cave, the womb is formless. Because it has no inherent form, it can project no image and cannot be rendered as metaphor. The cave in Plato's allegory has no material referent in the womb. Although we are permitted to "*suppose* that the womb is reproduced, reproducible, and reproductive," it has always already been superseded by a uterine metaphor. By means of the philosopher's sleight of hand, the womb is a screen that takes the shape of images projected onto (or into) it. "The *womb*, unformed 'amorphous' origin of all morphology, is transmuted by/for analogy into a circus and a projection screen, a theater of/for fantasies (p. 265)."[2]

When the "prisoner" has been led out of the "cave," while his eyes are still dazzled by the light, his education at the hands of the philosopher/obstetrician "begins." But the uterine metaphor that describes the prisoner/fetus's existence prior to the philosopher's influence is a feature of his education under the philosopher's direction. The real origin, the mother, is forgotten. Her space and time vanish into the representation. And the man who unchains the prisoner from his figurative bonds and leads him into the light is the same philosopher/obstetrician who, in the first place, makes the womb a metaphor for the cave.

Irigaray asks, "What lies beneath such an approach to *child-birth?*" (p. 279). But her answer to her own question is that what lies beneath is an impossible, vain dream of ideal origins, a gestation that takes place in the light. The brooder program in Piercy's *Woman on the Edge of Time* shows that the old dream might be practicable, given a favorable technological and social environment. In Mattapoisett the womb is a glass that reflects back the community's principle of racial diversity: babies of all races float freely together, listening to the piped-in heart sounds of an absent mother. These

2. Irigaray's term "screen" is similar to my description of the representational womb as a *frame* that contextualizes the figure of the fetus. The screen, like the frame, is a space that contains images. The screen, however, can also be understood as a membrane overlying, softening, or concealing the figure. Whereas the frame suggests a static, frozen image, the screen suggests a moving picture.

fetuses have already begun their education under the direction of
the philosopher/obstetricians. They have always already been
brought into the light. There is no troubling maternal origin for
them to forget, for their origins lie entirely within the scheme of
representation. The womb in *Woman on the Edge* is a projection
screen for the enactment of revolutionary sociopolitical directives.
In Mattapoisett the womb is extracted from a "timeless" maternal
body whose essential nature bars her from entering into the historical moment of Mattapoisett. The prehistoric maternal body had to
be replaced by another figure that would reflect and reproduce a
large-scale social revolution. Although the political-social program
of Piercy's utopia is well served by this revision of the uterine metaphor, the greater profit goes to the philosopher/obstetrician who
first delivered it. What supplants the maternal body in *Woman on
the Edge of Time* is only another version of the Platonic figure, an
artificial organ that perpetuates the womb's historical status as a
reflective matrix.

Irigaray's rhetorical method of speaking with and through Plato
leaves the impression that he represents not only the ancient history but the summation of all philosophies of subjective generation.
From that point of view, it is hard to imagine how to place theories
of the mother-fetus relationship in historical or cultural contexts.
With the development of techniques for *in vitro* fertilization and
support systems for very premature babies, technology is taking us
ever closer to fully realized artificial reproduction. But that trend
does not indicate that a reproductive revolution is under way; instead, it is a practical validation of the old figurative structures.

Piercy makes it possible to see that the maternal body and its
relationship to the fetus are historical in the sense that our understanding of their relationship is subject to some degree of change,
through technological and political revolution. But she generates
her re-visioning out of the same system of metaphor that Irigaray
describes, and without undermining it in any way. In Piercy's revision, the prisoner has never been chained up in the cave because
the embryo is never in the womb. Connie's counterpart in Mattapoisett, Luciente (whose name means "bright"), is the enlightened being who was not generated within the "cave" of illusions.
Although her body, like Connie's, contains the literal organ meta-

phorized in the Platonic cave, she will never be identified with it, nor experience her own erasure in metaphor, because she will never experience the biological processes of pregnancy and birth. Piercy takes the allegory as far as it will go by completely divorcing the biological-genetic mother and fetus. She ends up back where Plato began, where philosophical enlightenment depends on the (biological) mother's erasure. Her erasure does not refute the traditional identification of women with wombs. Rather, Piercy's presentation of the artificial womb confirms the validity of the Platonic metaphor. The nullified womb corresponds to the unremembered cave that contained the fetus's struggle to achieve form and consciousness. It is amnesia that causes Plato to comment in *Timaeus:* "We must not call the mother and receptacle of visible and sensible things either earth or air or fire or water, not yet any of their compounds or components; but we shall not be wrong if we describe it as invisible and formless, all-embracing, possessed in a most puzzling way of intelligibility, yet very hard to grasp."[3]

Plato defined the literal womb as a "living creature" with a tendency to wander throughout a woman's body; its metaphorical counterpart, the "receptacle" of "all becoming and change," has no form of its own.[4] The "artificial" womb in Piercy's *Woman on the Edge of Time* is the space in which all physical and social forms take shape. The "artificial" womb, having no consciousness, implies no troubling psychological or philosophical questions regarding maternal agency. The artificial womb negates the unasked question at the center of the classical definition of the womb (how can the womb, which has form, even a life and desires of its own, be metaphorized negatively as an invisible and formless "form"?).[5] There is nothing "puzzling" about the artificial womb. All its components and processes are designed by rational minds to (re)produce the proper constituents of the ideal community. Even as mere possibility, an unrealized idea, the "artificial" womb promises to obliterate the fear and desire the idea of "mother" arouses in the amnesiac subject puzzling over his obscure origins. It reveals the precise ge-

---

3. Plato, *Timaeus,* trans. H. D. P. Lee (Baltimore: Penguin Books, 1965), p. 18.
4. Ibid., p. 16.
5. Plato defines the "receptacle of becoming" as "a form that is difficult and obscure" (ibid., p. 16).

netic and environmental coordinates of an individual's origins, rendering conscious and rational processes that—when they occur deep in the unattainable spaces of the mother's body—produce anxiety, frustration, and confusion in the (also inaccessible) unconscious of the adult.

Anyone in Piercy's utopia can be a mother because motherhood there is defined as a rational social function, in strict accordance with the character of the machinery that produces the mothers. Piercy rightly portrays motherhood as constructed in close coordination with sociopolitical processes, but excludes the biological mother from her definition. Because they were born from the "artificial" womb, Piercy's "artificial" mothers exceed the "real" in every way that counts. They are as loving as Connie, but far wiser, and better able to provide physical, intellectual, and emotional sustenance to their children.

"Who or what," writes Irigaray, "*profits* by the credits invested in the effectiveness of such a system of metaphor?" (p. 270). In 1974 Maurice Panigel, then professor of reproductive biology at the University of Paris, described the uterus as permeable to light, sound, and chemicals. "The uterus and fetus are not protected. They are not in a federal reserve cave completely protected from outside changes."[6] Since the uterus is *not* a protected "federal reserve cave," the fetus is not only vulnerable to environmental dangers but also to the study and treatment of the disorders that result from its exposure.

Panigel draws on an already familiar system of uterine metaphors to make his point; the Platonic cave and the "federal reserve cave" are permutations of the same analogy. But he adds an economic component to the system. The fetus here has a value measurable in monetary terms; at birth it is removed from the "federal reserve cave" and put into circulation in a reproductive economy. In Connie's view, her daughter Angelina was made into a commodity when she was "sold off to some clean-living couple in Larchmont."

6. Maurice Panigel, "Biological Perspectives," in *Intrauterine Fetal Visualization: A Multidisciplinary Approach,* ed. Michael M. Kaback and Carlo Valenti (New York: American Elsevier Publishing, 1974), p. 122.

In Mattapoisett women keep their wombs empty so they will no longer serve as the guarantors of reproductive capitalism. Luciente defines childbirth as "the original production."[7] Only when the means of *re*production are communally owned can true communism can arise. Children, like everything else produced in utopia, have no single owner; they belong to the community at large.

Like the broader system of uterine metaphors, the economic analogies between production and reproduction are unstable and subject to change. The fetus and the newborn find their way into the system as both currency and commodity. The mother's body and the womb are bank, factory, and/or warehouse. Viewed from Le Sueur's or Piercy's perspective, the mother under capitalism is a reproductive laborer alienated from the products of her labor. From the perspective of Aldous Huxley's *Brave New World*, where (in a parody of communism) "every one belongs to every one else," mothers under capitalism are owners who obsessively hoard their babies. The instability of this system of metaphor suggests its limitations. The evolving relationship between mother and child and the social systems supporting reproduction and child rearing are too large to be reducible to an economic metaphor. Mary O'Brien, commenting on adverse effects of the health industry on the "unifying female sociability" that once dominated childbirth, suggests the limitations of an economic analysis of reproduction:

> One can exaggerate this effect, but there is a sense in which reproduction has become commodity production, just as the social relations of reproduction have become property relations. . . . The desocialization of childbirth is a part of a general trend towards the isolation of individuals and the efficient "rationalizing" of human events, which are part of the prevailing notion of society as a giant marketplace. The question is: Is this *all* that it is? The answer is clearly no.[8]

7. Piercy, *Woman on the Edge of Time*, p. 105.
8. Mary O'Brien, *Politics of Reproduction* (London: Routledge & Kegan Paul, 1981), pp. 10–11. O'Brien contends that, in those nonwestern cultures in which childbirth has not yet been appropriated into the system of commodity production, women base their own social system on reproduction. Childbirth, for instance, becomes a "celebration of femininity." Women's social systems, however, are still subordinate to the patriarchy. O'Brien calls for a "feminist philosophy of birth" which grounds "sociability and the ethics of integration where they belong: in the essentially social process of reproduction" (p. 40).

According to O'Brien, class analysis cannot wholly account for the current system of reproduction in the West, for it fails to consider the effects of male dominance. She maintains that male dominance is a primary causative factor not only in the desocialization of child-birth but also in the personal isolation that results from reducing social systems to purely economic terms. Although she is careful not to confuse reproduction with the economic system that serves so frequently as its metaphor, O'Brien's argument depends on a tight relationship between analytic metaphors and practice. Historical changes in the social relations of reproduction, including the isolation of laboring women by means of obstetric technology and hospital discipline, are "part of the prevailing *notion* of society as a giant marketplace."

In Meridel Le Sueur's novel about women and the communist movement during the depression, the Girl initially delights in the capitalist metaphor; she thinks of the unborn child in her womb as safely "on deposit."[9] But experience soon teaches her that the socioeconomic system she identifies with will betray her by treating her child like a commodity she is too poor and powerless to own. By the time the Girl is ready to give birth, she sees her act no longer as a way to defraud the system from within, but as a way to exit the capitalist system and create a better one. At birth her daughter is already a member of a women's community in which all hardship and all resources are shared. Like Piercy, Le Sueur sees in communism a more benign model for a reproductive economy.

It may be only at the juncture of patriarchy, capitalism, and Platonic philosophy that the uterus becomes a "federal reserve cave." The metaphor may adequately reflect attitudes toward mothers, their bodies, and reproductive processes prevalent in western obstetric practice, but it does not necessarily represent women's perspectives on their own bodies and reproductive organs or their experiences of childbirth and child rearing. The close relationship between practice and its metaphorical representation applies only when we think of obstetric practice and women's reproductive practice as synonymous. Women's own accounts of childbearing and child rearing under patriarchal capitalism suggest that they are

9. Le Sueur, *The Girl*, p. 85.

as likely to resist as to accept the proposition that a close affinity exists between *their* practice and the prevalent metaphors.[10]

In the novels of Le Sueur and Piercy, the reproductive economy is still thoroughly interconnected with the "productive" economy. Each opposes (re)productive capitalism to utopian communism to show how the latter would make mothers full participants in a radically transformed (re)productive economy. But the net effect is to validate the metaphoric system. Mothers are no longer bank vaults, factories, or warehouses; and as (re)productive laborers they are no longer alienated from their product.

Woman on the Edge, however, leaves some room for skepticism. Connie initially rejects the artificial reproduction that prevails in Mattapoisett, bitterly comparing utopian parents to "that couple, white and rich," who took Angelina: "All made up already, a canned child, just add money."[11] For Connie, bearing a child is an intimate and literal experience, a matter of body and blood, and she is so acutely aware of the hazards of abstracting the experience to an economic plane that she sees in utopia's system of reproduction a perpetuation and expansion of the old system. But then, under Luciente's influence Connie begins to think of her own longing for a baby in a similar light. Luciente admonishes her for obsessing about "birth, birth birth" and reminds her that it is no longer "women's business" (p. 351). In a revelatory moment, Connie envisions Angelina safe and happy in Mattapoissett, and realizes she must give up her desire to have a child of her own: "Yes, you can have my child, you can keep my child. . . . She will be strong there, well fed, well housed, well taught, she will grow up much better and stronger and smarter than I. I assent, I give you my battered body as recompense and my rotten heart" (p. 141).

10. Until lately women have had little opportunity either to refuse theories of reproduction or to produce their own, but they remain the principal agents in childbirth and child rearing. O'Brien calls for a theory of birth generated by women, predicting that "feminist philosophy will be a philosophy of birth and regeneration, not in a simple-minded or metaphorical way, but in an arduous re-examination of traditional philosophy and a vigorous critique of the pervasive oppressiveness of the potency principle as it lurches monolithically to Nirvana" (*Politics of Reproduction*, p. 200).

11. Piercy, *Woman on the Edge of Time*, p. 106.

When Connie assents to Mattapoissett, she is also buying into the metaphoric system that identifies reproduction with commodity production. But long after Connie has agreed to pay with her own life for the future of her descendants, her charge that no one could "know what being a mother means who has never carried a child nine months heavy under her heart" (p. 106) continues to subvert the utopian conviction that subsuming reproduction into production will provide an effective solution to social and economic inequities. Connie's absence—her final erasure from her own present and future—is a sign that suggests the dangers of abstracting the bearing and nurturing of children from their basis in literal bodily experience. The (re)productive metaphor invites mothers to interpret childbearing according to an economic system that devalues them and distorts their experience.

CHAPTER 12

Obstetrics and
the Intelligible Fetus

However fascinated physicians might have been with the fetus before the advent of ultrasound, as long as the living fetus remained inaccessible to the physician's eye, the clinical gaze found the mother its only accessible object. Nonetheless, as Maurice Panigel's derisive evocation of the (now obsolete) view of the womb as a "federal reserve cave" suggests, ultrasound (first tried on obstetric patients in the late 1950s)[1] and other diagnostic techniques have given the obstetrician greater contact with the fetus. As a result, the focus of the profession is shifting. In an optical illusion, whenever the eye focuses on one form, the other fades out of focus and becomes the ground for the newly intelligible figure. Something similar has happened in obstetrics, effecting a change so profound that it has already transformed the ethic and practice of obstetrics.

Viewed in terms of the evolving uterine metaphor outlined in the last two sections, the history of the intelligible fetus begins with the mother's retrospective erasure. As Irigaray writes, "The subject is claimed to have always existed in that perfection of self-identity

1. Oakley, *The Captured Womb*, p. 159.

from before birth."[2] The mother, for her part, is identified with the womb, and the womb is designated as amorphous and unrepresentable in itself. The "puzzling . . . intelligibility" of the formless "receptacle" in Plato is less puzzling if we think of the womb as background, the negative of the form of the fetal images projected onto/ into it. The mother-as-womb is intelligible only in the sense that "she" conforms to the positive image of the fetal form. In this metaphoric transformation, the "intelligible" womb is only a reflection or an inverted form of the phallus.[3] The metaphorized womb makes possible the fantasy of an intimate connection between the positive, masculine figures of fetus and phallus, an illusion that closes the gap that exists in real time and space between the father's ejaculation and the birth of the child.[4]

Under the terms of the metaphor Irigaray describes, the cave/ womb is continually reinscribed in the allegory that erases it. It absence-as-figure is guaranteed by its presence-as-ground, since neither the eye nor the mind can tolerate positing it as both at once. The refocusing of the obstetric gaze from the mother's body to the fetus effects a similarly vain gesture of erasure. The physician reveals the "intelligible" fetus by first making the womb "sensible," or available to sensory apprehension. No matter how intently the eye focuses on the figure of the fetus, it is comprehensible only in relation to its background; even when it is represented as pitch-black space, some trace or recollection of the womb remains to interact with the image of the fetus.

Since the advent of ultrasound, representations of the womb in

2. Irigaray, *Speculum*, pp. 354–55.
3. A graphic representation of the inversion appears in early medical illustrations anatomizing the womb and vagina according to a phallic model. The fetus and the phallus are comprehensible only by virtue of their ground, the womb-made-metaphor.
4. Irigaray suggests the mechanism for this connection—and the negation of the maternal it enacts—in a section of *Speculum* titled "The Forgotten Path": "For metaphor—that transport, displacement of the fact that passage, neck, transition have been obliterated—is reinscribed in a matrix of resemblance, family likeness. . . . Where man, *ho anthropos*—sex unspecified, neuter if you will . . . cannot escape a process of likeness, even though he re-presents or re-produces himself *as* like" (*Speculum*, p. 247).

medical literature have shifted from "black box" images, in which the womb was viewed as an opaque, almost impermeable barrier between the fetus and the outside world, to images of the womb as a penetrable "window" onto the fetus.[5] The "black box" is a figure used to designate another figure that is unrepresentable, and so is a form of erasure. But as an obstetric concept it functions to reinforce the notion of the womb as a whole, irreducible organ, integral to the mother-fetus system. In its new designation as a "window" on the fetus, the womb is reduced to a frame, meaningful only in relation to the figure it delimits.

Contemplating the benefits ultrasound has bestowed on fetal therapists, Michael Harrison, a prominent pediatric surgeon who has both impressed and antagonized his colleagues by attempting experimental surgery on the fetus, focuses on the wonder of making the hidden visible: "The fetus could not be taken seriously as long as he remained a medical recluse in an opaque womb.... The prying eye of the ultrasonogram ... rendered the once opaque womb transparent, stripping the veil of mystery from the dark inner sanctum, and letting the light of scientific observation fall on the shy and secretive fetus."[6]

Harrison's romantic model of the monkish fetus cloaked in a "veil of mystery" is often reproduced (though rarely as eloquently) in the scientific writings of other fetologists and obstetricians.[7]

5. In another context David Porush offers a particularly evocative definition of the "black box" as the term is used in engineering: "The black box is a symbol used conventionally by engineers and draftsmen to indicate a portion of a mechanism which cannot be represented accurately in a given blueprint of it, either because the scale of the diagram is too large or small, or because not enough information about the mechanism can be obtained. The black box, therefore, is a map of something that is unknown, impossible to describe or render symbolically." David Porush, *The Soft Machine* (New York: Methuen, 1985), p. 207.

6. Michael Harrison, "Unborn: Historical Perspective of the Fetus as a Patient," *Pharos* (Winter 1982): 19–24.

7. For example, a 1989 *Science* article describes the fetus before the advent of ultrasound as "a captive of its own environment, an enigma to be protected but left untreated." John T. Hansen, and John R. Sladek, Jr., "Fetal Research," *Science*, November 10, 1989, p. 775. The published proceedings of an international 1982 congress on ultrasound was subtitled "The Secret Prenatal Life." In the preface, Giuseppe Vecchietti claims that "embryo-fetal life, long concealed in the mother's womb, is progressively revealing more and more of its previously secret aspects."

His "opaque womb" and "dark inner sanctum" are versions of the "black box" genre of uterine metaphor; but like Panigel, who invoked the image of the "federal reserve cave" only to dismiss it as archaic, Harrison refers to the "veil of mystery" in order to strip it away. Harrison conflates the physician's eye with the ultrasound machinery; the resulting cyborg exposes the reclusive fetus to the light for the first time (Harrison describes himself as a "sonographic voyeur").[8]

Harrison's "dark inner sanctum" and his depiction of the fetus as its "resident" who does not even know he has never seen the light until the ultrasound's "prying eye" brings it to him, form a modern, cybernetic version of the Platonic allegory. Another view supplies a component of the allegory when it describes the fetus before the advent of ultrasound as "a captive of its own environment."[9] We recall from Plato that the prisoner's painful introduction to the light signals his release from the half-life of shadows he endured in the cave. The physician's invasion of the womb initiates the fetus into a higher level of perception ("scientific observation").

At this point the physician has taken on the identities and functions of the other players in the drama of enlightenment. His voyeuristic penetration of the murky darkness of the womb brings the fetus to life—not only because visual access to the fetus permits him to diagnose disease and prescribe treatment, but also because his seminal gaze rescues the fetus from the oblivion of its union with the mother. The expansion of the physician's identities, mediated by the machine, recreates the physician as father and philosopher, the bearer of life and the light of knowledge: a visionary cyborg. His expansion is a subjective pregnancy, in which he pene-

---

Borruto, *Fetal Ultrasonography*, p. 13. Fernand Daffos (who, significantly, titles his survey of methods of fetal visualization "Access to the Other Patient") describes the (postultrasound) maternal body as "transparent." He also credits ultrasound with opening the "window onto the uterus and the fetus." Fernand Daffos, *Seminars in Perinatology* 13.4 (August 1989): 252.

8. During a fetoscopic examination, a conscious fetus turns its head away and puts up its hands in an effort to avoid the bright light, a reaction that might be interpreted as shyness. Lennart Nilsson's film *The Miracle of Life* (1983) includes real-time sequences of a fetus *in utero* that demonstrates this reaction.

9. Hansen and Sladek, "Fetal Research," p. 775.

trates the maternal space and discovers yet another appropriable identity: that of the fetus. Simultaneously the prisoner/fetus languishing in the dark and the philosopher/obstetrician bearing the light, the sonographer personifies Irigaray's illusory subject, who is "claimed to have always existed in that perfection of self-identity from before birth."[10] He is his own deliverer.

At a 1974 conference on the future of fetoscopy, at which many researchers reported dismal (and often, for the fetus, fatal) results with their experimental efforts to establish direct visual contact with fetuses in animals and women, William A. Liley began his presentation on methods of fetal visualization by musing lightheartedly on the motives of obstetricians:

> I forget just which psychiatrist or psychologist it was who, in categorizing the various medical specialities in terms of the psychological traits of their practitioners, decided that obstetricians were compensating for an ungratified childhood curiosity to know where babies come from. If that is true then many present today could be said to have handsomely over-compensated, for curiosity has progressed through inquisitiveness to investigation or research, and gratification now can be quantified in numbers of publications and grateful parents.[11]

Like Harrison, who refers to "sonographic voyeurs," Liley treads the rhetorical border between sexual and scientific motives.[12] Scientific rather than sexual curiosity motivates the physician's research, but the result is still a "gratification" that generates thriving progeny: "numbers of publications and grateful parents." Liley elaborates the idea of scientific desire by evoking economic and military metaphors. Obstetricians seek compensation for the lack of knowledge and/or gratification dating from childhood; the most successful have "over-compensated" by devoting their professional lives to the pursuit of reproductive knowledge. He comments: "My own revisiting of the world of the fetus was carried by the force of

10. Irigaray, *Speculum*, pp. 354–55.
11. William A. Liley, "Experiences with Uterine and Fetal Instrumentation," in Kaback and Valenti, *Intrauterine Fetal Visualization*, p. 70.
12. Harrison, *The Unborn Patient*, p. 7.

arms." The hostility implicit in Liley's metaphor disturbs me, but his intended audience understands that the instrument of this rape is neither a penis nor a scalpel but pure science, and the object of his assault is not a woman but a "world."[13] He goes on to characterize her even more abstractly as an "environment": "The opportunity to invade fetal privacy allows an exploration of the fetal physical and sensory environment, and it is apparent that the traditional picture of a fetus living in a dark and silent world and blindly maturing structures in anticipation of a life and function to begin at birth is far from the reality." In Liley's view, his attempts to return to the womb "by force of arms" has succeeded in revealing that the "dark and silent world" that daunted his predecessors never existed. Liley's exploration has made it "apparent" that the fetus has always lived in a world of light and sound. The old "traditional picture" is invoked only to be deposed, as Liley inaugurates a revised version of the old allegory.[14]

In this retelling, the cave and its enigmas, the child's frustration over being denied full knowledge of his mother, return to figure again as the negative space of the physician's self-conception. If his research interests have been motivated by a childhood urge to know all, that desire has at last been fully satisfied in the "discovery" that he was never a blind and helpless victim of some (nonexistent) uterine plot to imprison him. In a larger sense it is this negative space, the unreal womb, that grounds the profession. The allegory of the cave, rewritten as a residual fantasy left over from the childhood of obstetrics, describes the enlightenment of the profession as it leaves behind the archaic illusions of the "dark and silent world." What replaces the outdated illusion is not the literal organ, the womb, but another "world," where the light (of scientific observation) has always already penetrated.

13. Liley, "Experiences with Instrumentation," pp. 76–77.
14. Ibid. At the same conference, Carlo Valenti's concluding remarks reveal his frustration when he says, "I still would like to leave with the idea that if a man can go to the moon, then a physician should be able to go into the uterus." Valenti brackets womb and moon as versions of the same frontier, as inner and outer space, as history and destiny. If man is able to venture out to an unknown and inhospitable outer space, he should be able to explore the space of his own origins. Kaback and Valenti, *Intrauterine Fetal Visualization*, p. 269.

The womb that vanishes into the "environment" in Liley's account reappears as a mirror in another researcher's commentary. Michael Kaback subtitles the introduction to *Intrauterine Fetal Visualization* "Through the Looking Glass Lightly." The allusion to Alice's other world reconciles old "black box" images (now designated as fantasy) with the contemporary image of the womb as window. The womb figures here as a reflective surface behind which a fantastic world awaits the adventuring fetoscopist. A mirror that both reflects and receives whatever image is set before it, the womb gives back the physician's image.

I find some compelling connections between the fantasies of the fetal specialists and my own ultrasound dream, with which I began this section. As in the visions of Liley and Harrison, in my dream my identities and capacities expanded; I was not only mother but philosopher/obstetrician, revealing the fetus with the light of my gaze. Looking into its eyes I experienced the deep thrill of discovery. In the dim space between dreaming and waking, I was sure for a few moments that I had met the child I carried. But I had met none other than myself, an aspect of my own (un)conscious desire reflected on the womb/screen I contained.

The transformative experiences of pregnancy, childbirth, and caring for a newborn forced me to confront the dissociation between the dream image that satisfied some half-comprehended desire and the child who gradually became a separate and private self. It is the memory of my old dream that makes me worry now about the integrated fantasies of exploration, triumph, enlightenment, and sexual gratification that permeate the medical literature on fetoscopy and ultrasound. The technologies that produce fetal images also invite the production of fantasy. How many of their own desires and fears have these physicians invested in the figure of the fetus?

The Fear of Mothers

Frederick Leboyer, one of the most influential contemporary "fetal advocates," has led the popular movement to identify the fetus as a fully developed individual. Although his method has met with resistance from other obstetricians, who may be reluctant to change their practices, Leboyer's characterization of the fetus has much in common with those of fetologists. In *Birth without Violence* he credits the fetus with refined senses and complex emotions and thought processes, a characterization that invites the reader to identify with the unborn.[15] Leboyer asks why physicians continue to treat newborns with careless cruelty in an era when, he claims confidently, women have been freed "from the agony of childbirth" (p. 102). He believes that it is the physician's conditioning that prevents him from recalling his own birth as a way of understanding the newborn's anguish:

Anyone present at a birth has got to be profoundly unsettled. . . .

No doubt this is because we have all experienced birth. And the experience echoes deep inside us, as potent as it is suppressed.

Nothing is forgotten—birth least of all. Only its immediate imprint has been blurred.

Thus the doctor and his associates find themselves profoundly but unconsciously involved in every birth they participate in. (p. 103)

Lacking access to their own memories, physicians rely on a traditional mythology of the fetus to explain and dismiss the newborn's wails and contorted features. In the orthodox medical mythology of the fetus as Leboyer describes it, the unborn and newly born feel no significant emotions, do not see or hear, and are incapable of consciousness (pp. 3–4). In place of this fiction, Leboyer offers what he sees as the real experience of the fetus and newborn. He claims that birth, improperly handled, is a frightful experience for the child, who is made to suffer intense physical and emotional pain. Significantly, Leboyer maintains that the brightly lit delivery room blinds the newborn. Birth may leave indelible physical and emotional

15. Leboyer, *Birth without Violence*; subsequent references in this chapter are cited in the text. In fact, Leboyer goes further, crediting the fetus with more acute senses than the adult. Leboyer tells us that "the baby knows everything. *Feels* everything. The baby sees into the bottom of our hearts, knows the color of our thoughts" (p. 112).

scars, and its effects proliferate beyond the personal to leave their mark on religion, art, and social institutions.[16] The pain of birth has left its traces

> In all our human folly.
> In our madness, our tortures, our prisons.
> In legends, epics, myths.
> In the Scriptures.
>
> (p. 31)

In making the point that birth is the root experience underlying our mythology, poetry, and religion (as well as our social ills), Leboyer presupposes that there is a "real" experience of birth which, if it could be remembered, would alleviate the residual pain. If we are blinded by the violence of birth, then the cure is to learn to see the birth scene clearly. If we could recover that real pain, we and our institutions would be healed. Again and again Leboyer directs the reader who doubts the reality of birth pain to the photographs that overwhelm his text, and the final word of *Birth without Violence* bids us simply to "look." Leboyer's confidence in the power of the gaze to convey truth to the mind is comparable to Hunter's and Nilsson's.

Arthur Janov, psychologist and inventor of the primal scream, mentions in his book about "birth trauma" that Leboyer viewed films of adults undergoing "birth Primals" and exclaimed, "I am vindicated! There finally is the proof!"[17] The proven "reality" with which Leboyer replaces the myth is a rewritten version of the parable of the cave. Figuring himself as the philosopher/obstetrician, Leboyer delivers the reader/prisoner (enrolled as a former fetus im-

---

16. Whereas Leboyer finds traces of birth "pain" in institutional cruelty as well as art and religion, Elaine Hoffman Baruch suggests a more positive valuation of the influence of the birth metaphor. Citing Melanie Klein's belief that art and religion represent attempts to recover the body of the mother symbolically, she wonders what will happen when reproduction has moved out of the womb. "What consequences would reproduction *ex utero* have on the relation of the individual to nature, art, other people, the world at large?" Elaine Hoffman Baruch, "A Womb of His Own," in *Embryos, Ethics, and Women's Rights,* ed. Elaine Hoffman Baruch, Amadeo F. D'Amato, and Joni Seager (New York: Haworth Press, 1988), p. 137.

17. Janov, *Imprints*, p. 19.

prisoned by repressed memories of the womb) from the old fantasies into the real world. In Leboyer's allegory of the womb, the maturing fetus "finds itself . . . a prisoner" (p. 24), immobilized by the pressure of the uterine walls. Leboyer approves Hippocrates' belief that the full-term fetus "was forced to abandon the dark cavern which had been its home until then, to search for a way out" (p. 70). Once born, the newborn child suffers agonies in the cold, bright light of the delivery room and longs for the old "prison bars." Nevertheless, Leboyer dramatizes the birth itself as a fierce battle for freedom. The fetus's struggle pits it against the uterine "monster." Having endured months in this prison, the fetus is crushed and cruelly twisted during labor. It responds first with fear, then with anger toward its mother:

Enraged, the infant hurls itself against the barrier. At all costs, it must break through. Free itself.

Yet all this force, this monstrous unremitting pressure that is crushing the baby, pushing it toward the world—and this blind wall, which is holding it back, confining it—

These things are all one: the mother!

. . . It is *she* who is the enemy. She who stands between the child and life.

Only one of them can prevail; it is mortal combat. (p. 26)

The unborn child Leboyer evokes has already recognized itself as an independent entity whose interests are opposed to its mother's. And the fetus being born perceives its mother not just as separate from itself but as an "enemy" who imprisons and tries to destroy her child. The myth demands that someone must intervene, someone who identifies with the fetus's pain and rage. That someone is Leboyer, in his role as philosopher/obstetrician. Leboyer eases the way for the prisoner; he dims the lights so as not to dazzle its eyes and introduces the newborn with infinite gentleness into its new life. Leboyer ministers to the child, massaging and bathing it, inducing it to forget its recent torture. This newborn will be free of the nostalgic longing for, and hatred of, the womb that makes eternal prisoners of most men.

Wolfgang Lederer, a psychiatrist, gathered together a substantial collection of the mythology of woman hatred in his 1968 book *The*

Fear of Women. In his introduction Lederer notes that "in the un-ashamed privacy of our consulting rooms we do from time to time see strong men fret, and hear them talk of women with dread and horror and awe, as if women, far from being timid creatures to be patronized, were powerful as the sea and inescapable as fate."[18] In a chapter titled "A Planetary Cancer?" Lederer, following Karen Horney, relates the fear of women to "the mystery of motherhood." Arguing that modern women feign taking contraceptive measures, Lederer attributes their deceit to a "uterine hunger":

> The threat and pattern of archaic woman, monomoniacally [sic] bent on nothing but the best breeding stock, faithful only to her biological mission, unbound by any man-made, father-made law; eternal Mother using man only as her tool, eternal priestess before the shrine of her own sex—this pattern is potentially and more or less actually still present in every woman: her altar is still her womb, and her god and supreme purpose her child.[19]

In Lederer's fantasy of feminine destructiveness, "woman" alone is responsible for both a worldwide "cancer" and its equally devastating cure. It is tempting to dismiss Lederer's work as an expression of the peculiar gynophobia of one troubled man. But his painstaking research brings together the writings of a host of like-minded men (and more than a few women), journalists, theologians, psychologists, anthropologists, historians, literary figures, and philosophers, to make credible his contention that men fear and loathe women (not merely archetypal "woman" but their wives and mothers). Lederer creates the impression that, in men's eyes, women's powerful sexual seductiveness barely conceals a mindless, voracious fury of reproduction and destruction that is largely responsible for the world's disorder. If "woman's" child is her "god and supreme purpose," he is also her victim.

It is not surprising that a motif of separation from the mother erupts in Lederer's work as the solution to maternal disorder. In a chapter poignantly titled "The Loneliness of Outer Space," Lederer

---

18. Lederer, *The Fear of Women,* p. vii.
19. Ibid., pp. 245–46.

notes that "the alternative to romantic return into the soft, dark, pungent security of the maternal enclosure (the womb, the lap, the arms, the total care in return for the total surrender) would have to be total separation." Lederer's evocation of the pathetically lonely spaceman culminates in a detailed description of a science fiction story he cried over as a boy. The story featured an astronaut who is permanently disconnected from his ship when his umbilical line is severed. But Lederer effectually transforms the funereal narrative of the lost and dying astronaut, floating off into space after he accidentally disconnects himself from his mother ship, into a celebratory story of the death of the mother by her son's hand. Having indulged in the poignancy of man's isolation from his maternal origins, Lederer crisply begins the next chapter: "Still, the separation from mother must be accomplished, if a boy is to become a man. . . . [He must] slay his mother, in so far as she represents to him his inner longing for a return to the security of her bosom."[20]

In this striking inversion Lederer turns the son's recognition of his own mortality into mother murder. Without referring to Jacques Lacan, Lederer gives a concise, if brutal, summation of the familial and social mythology that supports Lacan's analysis of the child's mirror stage. According to Lacan, language, and all social development, depends on the infant's experience of the separation of self and other. A child unconsciously recognizes that a sign has meaning only because it can be distinguished from other signs. He imposes this law on himself: he has meaning, or subjectivity, only if he can be distinguished from his mother.[21] Nevertheless, he longs to return to her womb. To kill his longing, to end the conflict, he must murder her—symbolically. When the mother's absence can be represented by a word that distinguishes her from the child, he has attained some power over their relationship. This accomplishment has been referred to as the "symbolic death of the mother."[22] In Lederer's terms, he slays her "in so far as she represents" the lack her absence has introduced. Thus the mother's absence, a devastating loss which the infant is incapable of imagining or instigating,

20. Ibid., pp. 268, 273.
21. Lacan's generic child, as I have noted, is gendered masculine.
22. See my discussion of the symbolic death of the mother in Chapter 1.

is transformed into his first experience of symbolic agency. The mother did not walk away of her own accord; she was struck down with a word from her son. With her demise, the son is free to enter the symbolic order, or, in Lederer's words, to become a man.

But once begun, the scene of the mother's death, the price of her son's initiation into manhood, must be replayed ceaselessly. The memory of her continues to pose a threat to order and rationality long after the original murder scene. The son's yearning for his mother's womb recurs, so the mythic reconstruction of masculine agency is never finally accomplished. Initially I found it hard to take seriously Lederer's contention that there exists among men a widespread fear and horror of mothers. But now I am convinced that the comprehensive mythology Lederer presents is a valid representation of a system of beliefs so ubiquitous that it is invisible. There are aspects of Lederer's work I find unconvincing, specifically his tendency toward hyperbole and his assumption that the art and poetry of diverse cultures and eras can be appropriated to explain the source of his patients' distress. But the procreative visions of Leboyer, Nilsson, Liley, Harrison, and Huxley are consistent with the mythic structures Lederer describes.

Lederer also cites a few women philosophers and psychoanalysts; "matriphobia" is not entirely gender specific.[23] Marge Piercy, Shulamith Firestone, and Simone de Beavoir also conform to some degree. Marge Piercy's vision of a nonsexist utopia without biological mothers demonstrates that the myth can be adapted to a feminist perspective. Piercy alone represents maternal desire as a form of subjective agency, but the myth of the mother's irrational and all-consuming need (the child's desire projected?), and the need to separate from her, are essential to her vision. The single thread that runs throughout is the child's painful and irresolvable tension between the undying desire for the mother's body and the inevitable anguish of separating from her.

This tension creates an unstable border between the child and the

23. Lederer turns to Helene Deutsch, Karen Horney, and Melanie Klein to support his contention that men live in terror of women. He also cites the work of numerous psychologists—most of them women—whose studies of mental illness in children and adults find that evil, seductive, cold, and/or hostile mothers cause their children's illnesses. Lederer, *Fear of Women*, pp. 2–7.

mother's body. Piercy's sacrificial mother, Plato's allegorical birth scene, Lacan's enactment of the mother's murder, and the physicians' fantasies of conquest of the uterus and rescue of the fetus are all attempts to redraw that border. Defined as a penetrable mirror (recall Kaback's title "Through the Looking Glass Lightly"), the uterine wall is a nonresistant tissue which can neither imprison the fetus nor prevent the free passage of light and vision into its interior. But there is a problem with using metaphor to transform the womb. Liley and Piercy figure the womb as a stable and nonresisting vessel, but Lederer and Leboyer employ the same process to depict the womb as a voracious maw. If the metaphoric mother embodies the origins of psychic, linguistic, and social systems, her mirror image is the ever threatening possibility of their destruction.

Irigaray emphasizes that the cave continues to reassert itself in the *"captive consciousness of the child"*; the maternal darkness will never completely give way to the paternal sun.[24] But whether the mother appears in fantasy as inert space or mindless monster, it is always on the philosopher's terms. These are not a mother's fantasies of her own (re)creation; they originate in the mind of the subject-as-infant and evolve as fantasies that nullify maternal agency. The mother can intend nothing; she can neither expel the child nor imprison him as long as she is incapable of purposeful action.

But an almost insurmountable difficulty appears. How is it that a fetus arises from the inert or blindly ravening body of the mother? The ultimate, and ultimately impossible, answer is that the fetus originates in and of itself. Irigaray refers to the philosopher's assertion of an ideal "Being" beyond physical life as a "second birth, secondary origin." Ideal Being is the "perfection of divine (self) knowledge that had never shared in, never mixed with those material, matrical beginnings that are the blind spots on the souls of mortals." But even mortal man, the lesser copy of a pure original, may hope to achieve "divine self-knowledge" by escaping from his "captive consciousness." If he succeeds in completely forgetting the mother (and he never will, according to Irigaray), "finally the fiction reigns of a simple, indivisible, ideal origin. The fission occurring at

24. Irigaray, *Speculum*, p. 274.

the beginning, at the time of the primitive conjunction(s) is elimi-nated in the *unity of concept.*"[25]

The unity in this fiction is not an eternal union with the mother. Instead, "unity of concept" is achieved by eliminating "the primi-tive conjunction" of mother and child. Leboyer, for instance, would have us avert the rupture of birth by vanishing into the fetus:

> We must disappear.
> So that only the baby remains.
> We must look at this baby. Or better yet, be absorbed into its very being. Without complication. Without prejudice. In all innocence. All newness.
> *Become* . . . this new person. (p. 42)[26]

Once again Leboyer counsels us to look at "or better yet" to assume the form of the fetus. The gaze closes the gap, merging the viewer with the newborn. The mother is nowhere: "only the baby re-mains." Ideal Being, the purest form of the self, is achieved by going back to a time before "fission" was possible, before the mother ex-isted as the principle of separation and mortality. In this state of perfection, birth ceases to indicate the severance of a primitive union with the mother and means only a fuller realization of the ideal. In Lacan's narrative the father fulfills his destiny by interpos-ing the phallic word between mother and child. But in this fiction the father and the fetus are the same being: the fetus sires himself, retrospectively, so that this time, in another revision of Plato's alle-gory, the newborn man by himself enters an "upper world" beyond the prison house that is "the world of sight."[27]

Once this fiction has erased the possibility of fission, the fetus and its physician are no longer discrete entities. They are two phases of the same. Through the drama of escape from his own "captive consciousness," the fetus/father/physician can, for the

25. Ibid., pp. 340, 275.
26. Although Leboyer is not especially popular with his American colleagues, his portrayal of the fetus as a fully differentiated, self-aware individual and of the mother as an enemy to be controlled and placated may not be the motive for the rebuff. Rather, Leboyer's methods differ radically from ordinary hospital routine, and his approach places too many demands on the physician to be widely accepted.
27. Plato, *Republic* 7.

first time, turn himself inside out and deliver himself—the new-born/reborn man—painlessly into the light. The fetus, unable to speak its own mind, is animated to renegotiate the physician's confrontation with maternal origins and mortality.

Deliverance

Although most contemporary versions of the physician-centered birth narrative continue to posit a potentially lethal mother as the constant element, the narrative of deliverance is changeable, responding to and acting on reproductive politics and technology. The fetus *in utero* is more accessible for diagnosis and treatment than ever before; the processes of birth are increasingly controlled by drugs and surgery. But the range of possible birth narratives is expanding faster than the technologies that would render them practicable. Until now, the philosopher's—and the physician's—narrative of "indivisible origins" has always ended where it began, with the mother. But, as the brooder system of reproduction in *Woman on the Edge of Time* demonstrates, the artificial womb presents the most radical and peremptory challenge to the idea of mother as origin and end. For the fetus *ex utero* there is no mother to forget, no dreams of a moment before fission to plague and tantalize.[28] Irigaray aphorizes, "*He who has never dwelled within the mother will always already have seen the light of day.*" Whereas in Irigaray's analysis the hope of achieving the nearest facsimile of this divine deliverance-before-the womb belongs only to those who join with God Himself by "forgetting you have forgotten" the "mother's

---

28. Some proponents of the artificial womb seem to suggest that mortality itself would be held at bay. David Lygre, answering potential objections to the use of artificial womb, writes: "No longer would an embryo or fetus be the helpless victim of the mother's German measles, uterine abnormalities, automobile accidents, drug misuse, malnutrition, kidney disorder, Rh incompatibility, heart disease, and the like. Floating serenely in their incubators of glass and steel, those fetuses would escape the risks and trauma of birth. And it would be easier for doctors to examine them and treat their disorders." Lygre fantasizes about an educational program for the fetus cradled in its glass and steel womb, though what the fetus would be learning is left unexplored. David Lygre, *Life Manipulation* (New York: Walker and Co., 1979), pp. 27–28.

cave," gestation in an artificial womb would give every man a head start.[29] By pushing back the moment of forgetting to long before the nine months' gestation, back all the way to the moment when the egg bursts from its follicle and is collected for fertilization *in vitro,* the struggle for transcendence would be won before it began.

The Platonic mother in Irigaray's reading is forever mute, an unreachable enigma. As a metaphor for the cave, the mother has already been framed as a form of the artificial womb: "As for the mother, let there be no mistake about it, *she has no eyes,* or so they say, she has no gaze, no soul. No consciousness, or memory. No language. And if one were to turn back toward her, in order to re-enter, one would not have to be concerned about her point of view."[30] Irigaray's interpolation ("or so they say") disputes the validity of a definition-by-lack. But the terms of her conversation with the philosophers admit no other definition. The mother remains as mute and amorphous in Irigaray's "Hystera" as she was in Plato's.[31] In this conceptual environment, shared by philosophers and scientists, there is finally little to choose between the artificial womb and the biological mother. Both are valid expressions of the uterine metaphor. But the artificial womb, lined with endometrial tissue, equipped with an organic placenta, and vibrating with recorded heart sounds, suits the needs of the contemporary version of the narrative of fetal deliverance better than a cybernetic woman connected to fetal monitors and intravenous tubes, her labor regulated by drugs. What makes the artificial womb better is that it never contests its function. It is a sanitized mother, cleansed of the mortal threat—maternal agency—posed by the biological alternative. And it is endlessly accessible to view, concealing nothing, admitting and reflecting only specifically chosen images.

The biotechnological mother is a surrogate for an original who is

29. Irigaray, *Speculum,* p. 295.

30. Ibid., p. 340.

31. When, in *This Sex Which Is Not One,* Irigaray does offer a positive definition of woman (if not mother), she defines woman's speech, as well as her mode of experiencing her body and the world, according to the form of her sex organs. Monique Plaza, among others, charges Irigaray with essentialism: "Luce Irigaray pursues her construction, cheerfully prescribing women's social and intellectual existence from her 'morphology.'" Monique Plaza, " 'Phallomorphic Power' and the Psychology of 'Woman,' " *Ideology and Consciousness* 4 (Autumn 1978): 31–32.

forever out of reach. The original exists only in the negative, her lack of qualities her single defining attribute. She is the mother whose body has been erased from the fetal photographs in *A Child Is Born*. The mystery of origins written into Nilsson's photographic chronology is resolved in the blinding revelation that there is no origin.

Browsing through the pages of *A Child Is Born*, I was presented with a pregnancy in which no mother figured. In my dreams I reinserted myself into that scene, appropriating all the roles to myself. The most radically power-hungry dream or fantasy I could have as a mother was the fantasy of agency: I dreamed that I consciously created a child in the womb of my mind, endowed the child with vision and life, ministered to it as mother and physician, and delivered it safely into the world. But that child was a version of myself that was never born "in reality." And so my old dreams resemble those of the philosopher/obstetricians, differing only in that I restore to the mother the subjectivity they deny her. The real difference between me and them—and it is an irresolvable difference—is that I experienced a pregnancy in real time: I felt the constant tumult as the baby hiccoughed, flexed her body, and tested with elbows, knees, and feet the limits of my inner space. She was a bulky, impertinent, spirited presence in my body, simultaneously an integral part of me and an independent entity. In the months before her birth, our relationship was mediated through touch, not vision. The nine-months-long embrace of pregnancy cannot be rewritten as an allegory. The mother cannot be replaced by an inanimate womb without negating a sensual relationship that is essential perhaps *because* it evolves before the child's memory takes hold.

Feminists thinkers who, like Marge Piercy or Shulamith Firestone, envision the end of biological motherhood, or those who, like Gena Corea, continue to define mothers as helpless and unconscious victims of medical terrorism draw from the same myth of motherhood as medical researchers whose focus on the fetus erases the mother. Piercy and Firestone recognize that giving up biological motherhood is a price women might have to pay in order to purchase a valuable commodity: social and economic equality. But only in the contemporary reproductive milieu could women believe that it is reasonable to pay such an exorbitant and unnecessary price. As long as we are working in the realm of fantasy—in the hope that our dreams might provide a basis for building future realities—we may as well dream up a really radical future.

The drifting, disembodied fetus in *A Child Is Born* is a figure for an old myth of self-generation and transcendence. I dream of re-animating it in the service of another myth. In this myth I and my daughter in her turn are part of a historical process that began with an original mother who is recoverable, but only in the evolving continuity of the maternal-fetal relationship. It is a myth in which women are both the space of reproduction and the historically integrated beings produced there. The mother in this myth is an agent who produces herself and then proliferates, generating individuals and the community. Such a mother initiated human time, and her daughters have had a hand in formulating and reformulating every aspect of its processes ever since. She is represented in the unrepentant mother who kills mind-control researchers in *Woman on the Edge of Time,* preventing a future patriarchy even more restrictive and inhumane than the one into which she was born. Connie's heroic self-erasure is inevitable in the mythic structures of the twentieth century. But the myth in which she survives to revolutionize the reproductive economy has yet to be written.

IV Reproducing Postpatriarchal History

Finally, I wish to thank those who passed their imperfect genes on to me, including an Irish vegetable peddler, an Italian cobbler, a laborer in a box factory, and women who, within the confines of a cruel institution of motherhood, somehow managed to raise, nurture and love their children.
—Gena Corea, *The Mother Machine*

Mother Myths

In 1907 a poet and practical nurse named Edith Crawford Adams boarded a nearly empty ferry to cross San Francisco Bay. She held her two little girls, Ruth and Esther, by the hand. At some point during the crossing, she tried to jump overboard with her daughters. But her eldest, the four-year-old Ruth, hung back and begged her mother to stop.

And that, so says the family myth, is how my mother's chance to be born—and mine—was snatched back from the waters of San Francisco Bay.

Edith had reason to despair. She had failed to persuade her estranged husband to reconcile with her, and he refused to support their daughters. Her father had died, leaving her with a mother and unmarried sister in equally dire circumstances. When I heard this story as a child, I concluded that I was lucky—to be alive in the first place, and to have a father. I tried to imagine the alternatives: first, a world in which my grandmother had drowned, a world where I wouldn't exist at all, and then a world in which I grew up as my grandmother had, without a father. My birth, I realized, had depended literally on the vulnerable bodies of my (great-grand)-mothers, and our survival depended on a father's uncertain grace.

Joanna Russ writes, in explanation of the alternative universes inhabited by alternative versions of a woman in her novel *The Female Man*, that it is possible "there is no such thing as one clear line or strand of probability, and that we live on a sort of twisted braid, blurring from one to the other without even knowing it."[1] In this section I examine alternative worlds developed explicitly in women's speculative fiction and implicitly in feminist theory, looking for the imaginative space in which women work through the evolution of the "spindle kin," the flesh-and-blood passage from mother to daughter. Russ's twisting braid is a fitting image for my venture. The worlds that feminist imaginations devise in the late twentieth century are too diverse to be taken collectively to form a "clear line . . . of probability," but there is a constant that connects them: the processes of bearing and nurturing daughters, a braid through which women thread their way from generation to generation.

Feminist SF (speculative and science fiction) writers of the 1970s foresaw that toppling patriarchy would involve definitive and extreme changes in the forms of human reproduction, but their visions were often optimistic in the sense that they believed that patriarchy would initiate its own downfall and provide the tools for building a new and better humanity. Sometime in the early 1980s, however, the mood turned. As Peter Fitting observes, "A retreat from the utopianism of the 1970's" occurred with the appearance of novels such as Margaret Atwood's *Handmaid's Tale* (1985) and Ursula LeGuin's *Always Coming Home* (1985).[2] I would add Joanna Russ's *We Who Are About To . . .* (1987) as the most adamantly antiutopian novel about women's reproductive lives.

Although contemporary feminist SF writers often follow the lead of their predecessors in situating their utopian worlds after a military and environmental holocaust—reflecting the perception that our society is dying of patriarchal capitalism—they have lost the earlier optimism that foresaw an extraordinary cultural and societal rebirth in the aftermath of the death of the heartsick "social body." In part because feminists could see that hard-won gains in civil

1. Russ, *The Female Man*, p. 7.
2. Peter Fitting, "The Turn from Utopia in Recent Feminist Fiction," in *Feminism, Utopia, and Narrative*, ed. Libby Falk Jones and Sarah Webster Goodwin (Knoxville: University of Tennessee Press, 1990), p. 141.

rights were being seriously challenged, it became more difficult to believe in the usefulness of utopian visions.

Similarly, the reproductive technology some feminists in the 1970s believed would help to bring about the revolution no longer seems to hold much promise. In the wake of virulent condemnations of technology-based reproductive methods such as infertility therapy, sex selection, and surrogate motherhood by feminist critics of reproductive "pharmacracy," including Gena Corea, Patricia Spallone, and Rita Arditti, it has become increasingly difficult to see in technology an unproblematic remedy for the reproductive oppression of women.[3]

Visions in American feminism of a "gynocracy" or separatist women's society date back at least to Charlotte Perkins Gilman, but they occur much more frequently and forcefully in the late 1960s and 1970s (in fact, Gilman's 1915 *Herland* was published in book form in 1979). The intensification of separatist visions in the 1970s arose from the affirmation in several branches of feminism that men and women are indeed essentially different, biologically as well as socially, and that therefore women deserve their own forms of culture, exclusive of male influence. In other branches of feminism this idea was countered by those who argued that mother-nurture is mostly a product of socioeconomic forces rather than an expression of women's innate biological facility for caring. The disappearance in the 1980s of feminist-separatist utopias from the literary scene suggests that the "essentialists" failed to win their case for an exclusively women's culture, but the visions contained in the seventies-era utopias I examine in this section still represent some of the most advanced thinking produced in second-wave feminism about the complex interconnections among technological, social, economic, and biological aspects of women's mothering.

Although feminist thinking on these matters has changed, I do

3. Corea gives credit to Dr. Thomas Szasz for coining the term "pharmacracy"; he defines it as "political rule by physicians," but Corea identifies as "pharmacrats" those physicians and scientists involved with producing and applying reproductive technologies. Gena Corea, *The Mother Machine: Reproductive Technologies from Artificial Insemination to Artificial Wombs* (New York: Perennial Library, 1985), p. 2.

not identify a simple historical progression in discrete phases of feminist approaches to theorizing mothering. Rather than a linear progression, I see both theorists and SF writers of the 1980s and 1990s responding to, drawing energy from, and incorporating certain aspects of the models of mothering generated in second-wave feminism.

Feminist SF writers deal explicitly in possible futures, but a utopian urge is also evident to varying degrees in much feminist theory as well. As feminist theorists offer glimmers of a utopian vision, feminist SF writers posit their own theories of mothering in their fiction. In this section I identify many points of connection between the theorists and fiction writers. I look most closely at three theorists: Juliet Mitchell, whose *Psychoanalysis and Feminism* (1974) represented an early attempt to incorporate psychoanalysis into feminist theories of social and familial reproduction; Nancy Chodorow, whose analysis of the effects of the isolation of mothers in the industrialized West in *The Reproduction of Mothering* (1978) is crucially important to understanding how feminist theories of mothering developed in the decade that followed; and Ann Ferguson, who, in *Blood at the Root* (1989), considers feminist psychoanalysis as only one of several powerful theoretical perspectives on social dominance and women's mothering. (Along with psychoanalysis, Ferguson considers radical feminist, lesbian, Marxist, and socialist-feminist theories). Ferguson is important to my discussion because the breadth of her analysis suggests a trend in contemporary feminisms toward taking account of differences in race, culture, sexual preference, and family and community structures. Furthermore, she speculates more explicitly than her predecessors on how we might use these various theoretical perspectives to initiate social change.

In *The Reproduction of Mothering*[4] Nancy Chodorow describes the psychic development of women from the perspective of a feminist psychoanalyst in order to demonstrate how western-style mothering is passed on as daughters reproduce in their own mothering

4. Chodorow, *Reproduction of Mothering;* subsequent references in this chapter are cited in the text.

the infantile relationship they experienced with their mothers. One of the chief characteristics of mothering in our society is the exclusivity and isolation of the mother-child relationship. These exclusive bonds are strongly enforced in western society, for fathers are often absent more than mothers, and women, even when they work outside the home, are usually designated as the primary caretakers. Although we adhere to a principle of a sexual division of labor similar to those that prevail in most other societies, ours is unique in that we expect mothers to perform their duties in the absence of significant family or community support. "My view," maintains Chodorow, "is that exclusive single parenting is bad for mother and child alike" (p. 217). Women's exclusive mothering is bad because under these conditions "the development of a sense of autonomous self becomes difficult for children and leads to a mother's loss of a sense of self as well" (pp. 211–212). For boys, it leads to "conflicts about masculinity and fear of women," which men seek to counteract by asserting their superiority and belittling women (p. 213).

Chodorow's main focus is girls' development. A girl whose mother lacks adult support and "remains ambivalently attached to her own mother" will eventually reproduce in her relationship with her children the conflicts her mother experienced in their relationship. In this case "those aspects of feminine personality which reproduce mothering become distorted" (p. 213). But the "distortion" Chodorow identifies is not, according to her theory, an especially deviant pattern in western society. The pattern she describes is not an anomalous mother-child relationship but a dynamic reproduced to some degree in families throughout our society.

In part, the pattern is susceptible to distortion because women, when they mother, identify with both the maternal and the infantile roles.

> The whole preoedipal relationship has been internalized and perpetuated. . . . Women take both parts in it. Women have capacities for primary identification with their child through regression to primary love and empathy. Through their mother identification, they have ego capacities and the sense of responsibility which go into caring for children. In addition, women have an investment in mothering in order to make reparation to their own mother (or to get back at her). (p. 204)

Whereas traditional psychoanalytic explanations of women's maternal role rely on assumptions of an essential femininity or on arguments of biological destiny, Chodorow finds that this form of mothering reproduces itself in support of a social and economic system that (in turn) depends on it. Attacking the biological argument at its base, Chodorow asserts that many of Freud's claims regarding women's psychology were unsupported and are unsupportable by clinical evidence. His claims "grow from unexamined patriarchal cultural assumptions, from Freud's own blindness, contempt of women, and misogyny, from claims about biology which Freud was in no position to demonstrate from his own research." In her next paragraph Chodorow tempers her critique by stating that psychoanalysis "remains the most coherent, convincing theory of personality development available for understanding fundamental aspects of the psychology of women" (p. 142). Furthermore, she believes that psychoanalysis can be revised to exclude "that which comes from assumptions of the automatically innate superiority and primacy of maleness" (p. 158).

Throughout *The Reproduction of Mothering,* Chodorow works to correct inaccuracies and fill in the gaps in the traditional psychoanalytic account of women's development in order to arrive at an account that more accurately fits the social, economic, and psychological reality of women's lives. Although I identify some important problems in her approach, Chodorow's revisionary efforts result in the most thorough and sympathetic account of western mothering we have today. Her theory of women's mothering analyzes the connections among capitalism, patriarchy, and masculine autonomy as they are perpetuated and intensified under modern capitalism: "An increasingly father-absent, mother-involved family produces in men a personality that both corresponds to masculinity and male dominance as these are currently constituted in the sex-gender system, and fits appropriately with participation in capitalist relations of production. . . . Male denial of dependence and of attachment to women helps to guarantee both masculinity and performance in the world of work" (p. 190). Chodorow sees fathers becoming less involved with the family and women becoming more involved as capitalism marches on. Even as she points out the changing social, familial, and economic circumstances under which women mother, she asserts that "women's mothering is one of the few universal and enduring elements of the sexual division of labor" (p. 3). Chodorow makes other claims to the universality of some essential aspects of women's lives and psychic structure. In *Feminism and Psychoanalytic Theory* she says that "certain features of the mother-daughter relationship are internalized universally as basic elements of the feminine ego structure. . . . In any given society, feminine personality comes to define itself in relation and connection to other people more than masculine personality does."[5]

Chodorow makes two potentially contradictory claims for her theory. First, she claims that it accounts for the psychological consequences of the real, changing social and economic circumstances of women's lives. Second, it delineates "universal" characteristics of women's personalities. The "basic elements" Chodorow finds in women's personalities are culturally derived, but they are to be found universally, in all societies. The only way our mothering system (and all it entails) could be transformed is if men began to mother equally with women. To anyone who (like me) is searching for the social, political, or psychological means by which women could create a more livable experience of mothering, Chodorow's theoretical perspective seems to close out possibilities for change. That the "basic" feminine personality can be altered only if fathers learn to mother—if, in other words, patriarchy dissolves *itself*—leaves little room for hope.

But there may yet be a way out. Margaret Homans, who bases her theory of women's writing in part on Chodorow's ideas, has some trouble reconciling Chodorow's approach with her own view that psychoanalysis produces mythic narratives rather than an objective account of psychic development. In *Bearing the Word*, Homans points out that "Chodorow's argument derives in large part from her feminist manipulations of the Freudian myth. . . . It is possible that Chodorow's account of human development is just as much a myth (if a more palatable one) as Freud's or Lacan's." Homans does not see the mythic quality of Chodorow's work as a disadvantage: "To say that a theory is mythic is hardly to diminish its authority for interpreting culture." She reasserts the relative value of Chodo-

5. Chodorow, *Feminism and Psychoanalytic Theory*, p. 45.

row's theory for explaining women's lived experience, concluding that "Chodorow's account of female life has more explanatory power than Freud's or Lacan's."[6]

Whereas Homans appreciates psychoanalysis as a process of myth making which has a degree of explanatory value for women's experience, Chodorow rejects the myth-making aspect of psychoanalysis, and believes that her own branch of psychoanalysis explains women's real-world experience of mothering: "I have accepted psychoanalysis as a theory of psychological development, one that tells us how social forms and practices affect the individual, but not as a theory of the genesis of civilization and the nature of culture" (p. 53).

In *The Reproduction of Mothering* Chodorow refrains from offering explanations for the origins of women's mothering or the organization of sex roles. She also makes little effort to account for historical changes in women's mothering. By implication, the essential pattern of mothering she identifies resists historical forces, reproducing itself in succeeding generations. This leaves her open to the charge of ahistoricism. In her "Afterword," Chodorow responds to such objections. In regard to the criticism that her account is ahistorical, she claims that although the sex-gender system is subject to change, in "fundamental ways" it remains the same. In addition to assuming a high degree of historical continuity, she also fails to consider cross-cultural differences. Although she points out that we know very little about how differences in class and family structure affect the mothering system, she also claims in her "Afterword" that "it is probable that the issues I discuss are relevant in all societies" (pp. 215, 216).[7]

---

6. Homans, *Bearing the Word*, p. 15.

7. Chodorow uses a comparable strategy elsewhere in *The Reproduction of Mothering* to deflect the charge of ahistoricism. For instance, she acknowledges the historical specificity of psychoanalysis and notes that "we have no evidence that the turn-of-the-century Viennese patriarchal family is universal" (p. 53). At the same time, however, she also makes claims to universality in regard to developmental processes: "Psychoanalytic approaches to mental process, psychic structure and development may be universally applicable (I think they are). Certain capacities may be innate to humans and may unfold according to a predetermined biological pattern, and operations like splitting, fantasy, repression, and so forth may be universal human reactions. Social experience may universally enable the development of an

This also suggests one reason for the charge of pessimism that has been leveled at Chodorow's explanation of women's mothering. Because her theory insists on the universality of a particular pattern of mothering, Chodorow makes no attempt to account for the women whose lives attest to the effects of cultural diversity on mothering within western society; nor does she attend to differences across national boundaries. If she did consider differences in women's mothering across races, cultures, and economic classes, she might be better able to suggest ways of transforming patterns in the white, middle class, late-industrial capitalist society she analyzes.

Chodorow does propose that the grave disadvantages of exclusive mothering can be ameliorated if men take on a greater share of child care. But such changes would "depend on the conscious organization and activity of all women and men who recognize that their interests lie in transforming the social organization of gender and eliminating sexual inequality" (p. 219). Chodorow does not go into the specifics of how such a utopian revolution might be enacted even within the small sphere of American society. There are very powerful economic and social forces working against it, as she recognizes. What would it take to initiate a revolution—a cultural mutation—powerful enough to interrupt the vicious circle in which "the sexual division of labor both produces gender differences and is produced by them"? (p. 38).

---

identity which comes to constitute the self, affect the nature of psychic structure formation, and organize sexuality" (p. 53). Similarly, in regard to the exclusivity of the mother-child relation, Chodorow critiques the psychoanalytic tradition that ignores historical changes in parenting style (p. 74). She cites researchers whose studies show that even significant variations in family structure and the amount of mother-child contact (for instance, in those contemporary families where children spend a great deal of time in day care centers) do not produce the adverse effects psychoanalysis predicts. Yet she notices little relation between changing economic factors and parenting style: "Women have learned that fundamental changes in the social relations of production do not assure concomitant changes in the domestic relations of reproduction" (p. 6). Ann Ferguson criticizes both Chodorow and Adrienne Rich for proposing that motherhood "universally has been appropriated by patriarchy"; she suggests that "Black and working class" families may function very differently from the "middle-class white bourgeois family" and that we cannot look to motherhood for a comprehensive, cross-cultural explanation of male dominance. Ann Ferguson, *Blood at the Root: Motherhood, Sexuality, and Male Dominance* (London: Pandora Press, 1989), pp. 169–70.

13

The Woman in the Machine:
Feminist Writers of
Speculative Fiction

In 1971 Elizabeth Gould Davis wrote:

The ages of masculism are now drawing to a close. Their dying days are lit up by a final flare of universal violence and despair such as the world has seldom before seen. Men of goodwill turn in every direction, seeking cures for their perishing society, but to no avail. . . . Only the complete and total demolition of the social body will cure the fatal sickness. Only the overthrow of the three-thousand-year-old beast of masculist materialism will save the race.[1]

Davis's prediction that a revolutionary return to gynocracy was upon us seems, in retrospect, to have been remarkably naive. Although few even in 1971 would have agreed with Davis that women were about to rise up and retake power as patriarchy crumbled about them, her passionate nostalgia for a "milder, gentler" pre-patriarchal, precapitalist society exemplifies the intense expec-

1. Elizabeth Gould Davis, *The First Sex* (Baltimore: Penguin Books, 1971), p. 339.

tancy that marked the "Age of Aquarius."[2] Something *big* was about to happen.

The mood of optimism that helped to bring Davis's book into being also spawned a renewal of the utopian spirit among certain feminists. Writers such as Marge Piercy, Joanna Russ, Kate Wilhelm, Suzy McKee Charnas, and Sally Gearhart produced feminist utopias in which a golden age follows the collapse—through revolution, plague, or nuclear war—of the old monolithic patriarchal order. Their utopian worlds all arise out of a history in which a ubiquitous patriarchy either produced its own end or lost a large portion of its empire to other social forms. Some novels, such as Russ's *Female Man*, Piercy's *Woman on the Edge of Time*, and Charnas's *Motherlines*, demonstrated faith in the emancipatory potential of reproductive technologies. These technologies, in common with military and industrial technologies, are developed within patriarchy—they are, in a sense, its progeny—but they also may provide the means for disabling their creator. Feminist speculative and science fiction writers, recognizing that revolutionizing the means of (re)production might be as critical a strategy as changing how children are reared, include reproductive technologies in their revolutionary arsenal as essential tools for ending patriarchal rule, and with it the biological and social enslavement of women as mothers.

Chodorow's assertion that we could create a more balanced system of parenting by having men do more mothering leaves us without answers to the vital question of how to bring about this revolution, but feminist SF writers attempt to show how the technologies produced within modern patriarchy could be used to enact the revolution. The form of the postrevolutionary society differs from writer to writer, ranging from the assimilation of men and women as social mothers, as in Piercy, to a radical gynocracy from which men are excluded, as in Russ. Feminist SF writers of the 1970s imply that making men into mothers would require massive changes, not only in the relations between the sexes and in economic, social, and fam-

2. J. J. Bachofen, *Myth, Religion, and Mother Right*, trans. Ralph Manheim (Princeton: Princeton University Press, 1967), quoted ibid., p. 339.

ily structures, but in the human body and mind as well. From this perspective, producing the "humanized" men Piercy believes would be capable of nurturing children is the equivalent of giving birth to an almost entirely new human species. The feminist utopian communities are the result of drastic physiological and social changes that interrupt the cycle in which "the sexual division of labor both produces gender differences and is produced by them."[3]

In common with Chodorow and other feminist theorists, these feminist writers of speculative fiction engage with the questions of the origins, universality, and perpetuation of patriarchy. Their novels serve as a forum for competing theories of mothering, reflecting the unresolved contradictions in the feminist theory of the 1970s. Attempts to establish a specifically feminine subjectivity based on motherhood, and the biological essentialism that implies, are evident in Marge Piercy's *Woman on the Edge of Time,* Kate Wilhelm's *Where Late the Sweet Birds Sang,* and Suzy McKee Charnas's *Motherlines.*

In spite of the similarities in their concerns and their roughly contemporaneous publication (all appeared between 1976 and 1978), these writers have very different perspectives on the value of women's mothering, the revolutionary potential of men's mothering, and the uses of reproductive technologies as transformative tools. I begin with Wilhelm, whose vision of the transfer of mothering duties to men connects with Chodorow's theory in several ways. Wilhelm offers an explanation of the social and technological mechanisms that might bring about the transformation of mothering; furthermore, she demonstrates how that transformation would affect the development of masculine and feminine personalities. She ultimately valorizes a traditional arrangement of reproductive roles in which women provide both biological and social mothering. Following my discussion of Wilhelm, I consider how Piercy's *Woman on the Edge of Time,* in stark contrast, sees the transformative potential of men's mothering as wholly positive. Piercy envisions a society in which technology enables several men and women to share parenting, an arrangement that reinforces community ties while ensuring the development of well-defined individuals. Charnas's

3. Chodorow, *Reproduction of Mothering,* p. 38.

Motherlines moderates between Piercy's wholehearted acceptance and Wilhelm's complete rejection of reproductive technologies, envisioning a world in which women use patriarchal technologies to help themselves reproduce through parthenogenesis and return to the natural world as a separatist utopian community. The last writer of this period I consider is Joanna Russ, whose landmark novel *The Female Man* (1975) goes further than Charnas, envisioning a specifically feminist form of reproductive technology that permits a woman's utopia to thrive, protected from the various forms of patriarchy that persist in nearby space-time dimensions.

Like Marge Piercy, whose dystopian alternative to Mattapoisett was a global corporate nightmare in which only unfortunates are still composed of "animal tissue," Kate Wilhelm saw both the transformative possibilities of reproductive technologies and the potential for their misuse. Whereas Piercy offers her utopian and dystopian worlds as alternatives, however, in Wilhelm's *Where Late the Sweet Birds Sang* (1976) a radically transformed society, produced by cloning, brings about its own demise. The moribund clone civilization is replaced by a utopian agrarian community in which traditional patriarchal reproductive patterns prevail. In Roison McDonough and Rachel Harrison's 1978 essay "Patriarchy and Relations of Production," the authors offer a definition of patriarchy that is particularly appropriate to the feminist utopias of the 1970s: they define patriarchy as "male control of female fertility and sexuality."[4] While Piercy's revolution takes us beyond patriarchy (at least according to McDonough and Harrison's definition), in Wilhelm's journey through pre- and postrevolutionary time, patriarchy consistently prevails. No matter what changes occur, men always control women's reproductive labor, and hence the forms of social and sexual relationships.

The clones whose saga takes up the central narrative are descendants of the Sumner clan, a family of overachievers who decide to wait out a global environmental and political disaster at their fam-

---

4. Roison McDonough and Rachel Harrison, "Patriarchy and Relations of Production," in *Feminism and Materialism: Women and Modes of Production*, ed. Annette Kuhn and Ann Marie Wolpe (Boston: Routledge and Kegan Paul, 1978), p. 38.

ily retreat in the Shenandoah Valley. The Sumner men have anticipated the universal infertility that brings about the end of the world
they have known. Their plan is to create several generations of
multiple clones of each individual in the family. When the world
outside their fortress can support life again, the Sumner clones will
emerge and master the new world.

Wilhelm's account of the origins and structure of the clone community addresses the issue of how a greater commitment to child
rearing among men might restructure society, but she arrives at
different conclusions about the effects of men's mothering than
Chodorow does. Wilhelm hypothesizes a pattern of male mothering
that destroys the individual before she or he ever has the chance to
develop. No longer able to depend on their women for biological
mothering, the Sumner men take responsibility for conceiving, gestating, and nurturing the next generation. They intend to perpetuate cloning only through several generations, until the environment recovers to the point where the women's clones can become
biological mothers, but the tiny society they initiate tries to reproduce itself in succeeding generations. The clones consider themselves a new species, and their creators find them not quite human.
Multiple clones are kept together continually, producing an excep-
tionally strong bond among clone siblings, more compelling than
anything experienced between lovers or family members in a society of "singletons." When the first generation of clones observes
that men have succeeded in nearly destroying the world, the new
"species" reasons that humanity pays "a high price for individuality."[5]

Chodorow's observation that "the basic feminine sense of self is
connected to the world, the basic masculine sense of self is separate" is revised in the clone society to apply to both sexes, as men
lose their traditionally "greater sense of rigid ego boundaries and
differentiation" and become more like women, who "experience
themselves as continuous with others."[6] According to Chodorow,
women's sense of themselves as continuous with others is due to

5. Kate Wilhelm, *Where Late the Sweet Birds Sang* (New York: Harper & Row,
1976), p. 50; subsequent references in this chapter are cited in the text.
6. Chodorow, *Reproduction of Mothering*, p. 169.

their unique psychic development. In women, the "preoedipal relationship has been internalized and perpetuated."[7] In Wilhelm's
novel, clones of both sexes remain forever in their "preoedipal"
relationship with their siblings. Each group of clones is an entity.
Having no experience of the traditional nuclear family, emotionally
"healthy" clones possess no sense of the self as individual. Clone
siblings dress identically, live together in a single large room, work,
eat, and have sex with one another. They communicate telepathi-
cally, and each clone feels what the others feel. Ben, a clone who,
following a temporary physical separation from his siblings, finds
that he has individuated to some degree, compares the clones' psychology with that of their individual forebears: "Always before us,
in infancy there was a period when ego development naturally occurred, and if all went well during that period, the individual was
formed, separate from his parents. With us such development is not
necessary, or even possible, because our brothers and sisters obviate
the need for separate existence, and instead a unit consciousness is
formed" (p. 108).

Like an individual in our society struggling to "keep himself together," each group of clones struggles to maintain its single identity. In order to perpetuate this family structure, they reject natural
reproduction and instead try to establish a program of sustained
cloning and extracorporeal gestation. But in spite of the social transformation the dawning of clone society represents, and in spite of
the blurring of personal boundaries both sexes experience equally,
gender differences are still evident. Women work as artists and
teachers, but whenever they demonstrate fertility, they are pressed
into service as breeders and allowed no other work or interests.
All scientists are male, and it is they who direct the reproductive
program.

The men find that genetic laws dictate they must adopt some
form of sexual reproduction to ensure species survival, but they
cannot overcome their extreme distaste for in-body gestation and
individuality. Their solution is to select certain fertile young wom-
en to become breeders. Although male and female clones do engage
in group sex, breeders are artificially inseminated. A woman se-

7. Ibid., p. 204.

lected to be a breeder undergoes a ceremonial death and is banished from the community to live in a separate compound. Breeders must be physically restrained, drugged, and behaviorally conditioned to prevent them from trying to rejoin their sisters. Cut off from continuous multiple reflections of their emotions, thoughts, sensory perceptions, and sexual experiences, breeders do not become individuals. They fail to develop an ego, and live in a perpetual psychic limbo. Once their reproductive usefulness ends, either they work in the nursery or the men "put them to sleep" (p. 122).

As the clone community develops, Wilhelm complicates the issue of reproductive technology by showing that it might be used simultaneously for social revolution and patriarchal oppression. In the clone community it cannot be (as Chodorow argues) women's exclusive mothering that gives men a sense of superiority over women.[8] The technology that creates cloned groups of men with fluid ego boundaries has also multiplied by five the basic masculine drive to power. Male scientists now make all important decisions and control every facet of social and biological development; women's maternal role has been reduced to a minimal biological involvement. But even that much maternal involvement is unnecessary, given the advanced state of the clones' reproductive technology. Since they regularly gestate cloned embryos from conception onward in artificial wombs, the breeder compound would be unnecessary if the scientists switched to *in vitro* fertilization à la *Brave New World*.[9] There is no practical reason for them to perpetuate a cruelly subjugated class of mothers.

Some of the evils that annihilated their ancestors' world, such as the "me first" mentality of capitalism and the instability men's emotional isolation creates, are eradicated in the new species. But the clones' inability to individuate creates many of the problems Chodorow associates with the mother-daughter relationship.

8. "Women's mothering in the isolated nuclear family of contemporary capitalist society creates specific personality characteristics in men that reproduce both an ideology and psychodynamic of male superiority." Chodorow, *Reproduction of Mothering*, p. 180.

9. Louise Brown, the first baby successfully born following *in vitro* fertilization (IVF), was not born until two years after the appearance of *Where Late the Sweet Birds Sang*. But as an idea, IVF had already been widely available since the publication in 1932 of Aldous Huxley's *Brave New World*, which also brought into currency the idea of multiple cloning.

Clones think of themselves as meaningful only in relation to their siblings. Because they cannot imagine existing as a separate entity, they are vulnerable to coercion from their siblings. Any assertion of individual thought or desire threatens the cohesiveness of the entity, so there is immense pressure on each clone to conform to the others' attitudes and beliefs. The clones' inability to individuate also partly explains their insensitivity to the breeders' suffering. Only a group of sibling clones can be thought of as a complete human entity. A single clone is, in effect, no longer human, and a breeder is no more than a collection of amputated reproductive organs.

The oppression of breeders by an otherwise benign people whose entire existence is devoted to the maintenance of a peaceful, stable community constitutes the most biting anti–reproductive technology message of *Where Late the Sweet Birds Sang*. But the only other alternative method presented in the novel, sexual reproduction, has already contributed to the near-death of the species by producing an atomized society which could not define or work toward common goals. Wilhelm's narrative closes out all paths to a feminist utopia.

But then Wilhelm turns her attention to a heroic clone, Molly, who defies her breeding and socialization to become a natural mother. When Molly gives birth, she hides her child, fearing the consequences if they are discovered. Molly is a perfect mother. She gives her son intense mother love, but also the freedom to grow as an individual. She teaches him to read, introduces him to the natural world, and exposes him to the artifacts and ideologies of their dead hosts' culture.

Because there are no mothers in the culture she comes from, her display of mothering skills is puzzling. Molly has had no models to learn from. Her example suggests that mothering skills are innate, and that a good mother is so powerfully inclined to teach her children the values of our present culture that even a radically different origin and upbringing cannot dissuade her. Molly is captured and placed in the breeder compound. Her young son resents her "abandoning" him, thus achieving one of the developmental milestones of the incipient masculine personality. Eventually, after making contact with her son and validating his progress, she escapes and disappears from the narrative altogether.

Her son, Mark, grows up fearless, strong, and quick-witted. Eventually he kidnaps the breeders and establishes his own community in which sexual reproduction is the rule. As the new Adam, he fathers a new breed on his grateful women and plans to rebuild a society based on that of his individuated forefathers. The clone colony, meanwhile, dies out as its laboratory equipment fails.

Although Wilhelm's novel does not represent an "authentic" psychology of mothering, like psychoanalytic theory it does have some mythic "authority for interpreting culture."[10] Wilhelm travels much farther afield with her speculative fiction than Chodorow does with the utopian implications of her theory, but Wilhelm arrives back where she started. Her speculation ends with an apparently impossible choice among three varieties of patriarchy, each of which results in the subjugation of women for reproductive purposes. She offers as consolation the ideal of transcendent, natural mother love in which women can find fulfillment. Nevertheless, the novel implies that women will not be able to develop a manifesto for liberation from the futile dichotomies between technological versus "natural" reproduction and communal versus individualistic social forms. Molly's ability to mother must be natural, since her conditioning has given her no models for mothering. Like the breeders her son eventually "liberates," Molly helps to create patriarchal utopia by giving herself fully to her motherly role. An essential component of utopian motherliness is the women's turning away from the lesbian sexuality of their former sisters. For the women in Wilhelm's novel, a healthy, natural motherliness and heterosexuality go together. They are the utopian alternatives to incestuous homosexuality, the loss of personal identity, and ultimate race suicide.

Furthermore, Wilhelm's unexamined assumptions about the nature of mothers lead her to create in Molly a character of remarkable inconsistencies. Molly educates her son to revere and reproduce the "individuated" patriarchy of her ancestors, which she knows has already proved itself to be utterly self-destructive. Although she is a sympathetic woman of great courage and resourcefulness, she does nothing to help end the breeders' misery, even after she has had a taste of their foul existence herself. Her only contribution to hu-

10. Homans, *Bearing the Word*, p. 15.

manity's survival is the production of a son who can demolish the clones.

I anatomize Wilhelm's novel so thoroughy because it engages many of the questions that preoccupied feminists in the 1970s. Since patriarchy seems to be universal, is it also immortal? Is it universal because of certain, possibly natural, differences between men and women (such as women's ability to mother)? Could radically different family structures in which women's "natural" (or at least "universal") tendency to mother is subverted through the use of reproductive technologies bring patriarchy crashing down? The anachronistic mother in Wilhelm's postrevolutionary novel demonstrates the impossibility of blocking out one's own "social conditioning" under patriarchy in order to think clearly about what might replace it. In a 1977 letter reprinted in *Frontiers*, Wilhelm describes being faced daily with the expectation that she will put her responsibilities to her husband and children above her writing.[11] It is not surprising, then, that those expectations impress themselves on her writing. Among the feminist SF novels of the era, *Where Late the Sweet Birds Sang* is remarkable for its heterosexism and focus on male characters (Molly is the only female character developed in depth), but perhaps Wilhelm's observation that the "material the writer uses . . . is determined to a large extent by unconscious factors"[12] suggests one reason for her approach to postrevolutionary mothering in *Where Late the Sweet Birds Sang*.

In her 1974 essay "On Freud and the Distinction between the Sexes," Juliet Mitchell argues that Freudian psychoanalysis provides a key to understanding how patriarchy and the oppression of women are perpetuated. Mitchell says that the Oedipus complex, which "reflects the original exogamous incest taboo . . . is thus about what Freud regarded as the order of all human culture." Freud derived the myth that explains Claude Lévi-Strauss's kinship theo-

---

11. Kate Wilhelm, "Dear Frontiers," *Frontiers* 2.3 (1977): 75; reprinted from *The Witch and the Chameleon*, April 1, 1975. Wilhelm cites as the "one positive point" about the life of a woman writer the fact that "a writer who is a housewife and mother also generally is not the financial support of the family" and therefore she need not write for money but rather according to her desire (p. 76).

12. Ibid., p. 76.

ries "from his analysis of the individual's unconscious." According to Mitchell, "The myth that Freud rewrote as the Oedipus complex epitomises man's entry into culture itself."[13] Patriarchy, then, constitutes our entire cultural context: "We have at least the beginnings of an analysis of the way in which a patriarchal society bequeaths its structures to each of us (with important variations according to the material conditions of class and race), gives us, that is, the cultural air we breathe, the ideas of the world in which we are born and which, unless patriarchy is demolished, we will pass on to our children and our children's children."[14]

Two points are important here. The first is Mitchell's contention that psychoanalysis analyzes not just the individual unconscious but the institution of patriarchy itself. The second is that patriarchy applies universally, though its form varies according to material conditions. Therefore, psychoanalysis—adapted to the various economic and racial conditions of patriarchal society—is universally applicable and perpetuates itself in each succeeding generation. Although Mitchell is no more convinced than Wilhelm that reproductive technology is the proper tool to end women's oppression—and complains about feminists who believe in its revolutionary potential—she does not contend that we are stuck with patriarchy forever. "It is not a question of changing (or ending) who has or how one has babies. It is a question of overthrowing patriarchy."[15]

13. Juliet Mitchell, *Psychoanalysis and Feminism* (London: Virago Press, 1974), pp. 371, 377. Nancy Chodorow disagrees with the claim that psychoanalysis is a theory of cultural origins (*Reproduction of Mothering*, p. 53). And she later criticizes Mitchell for her claim that "Freud solves the universal Lévi-Straussian exchange problem" reflected in the Oedipus complex, stating that she does not think it is universal in any event (*Feminism and Psychoanalytic Theory*, p. 234).

14. Juliet Mitchell, *Women: The Longest Revolution* (London: Virago Press, 1984), pp. 231–32. McDonough and Harrison argue that Juliet Mitchell's attempt in *Psychoanalysis and Feminism* to reconcile Marxism with psychoanalysis fails. In the Freudian psychoanalysis she works with, "the structure and functioning of the unconscious are immutable in form," although "they may be filled with varying 'contents' dependent upon the mode of production and corresponding social relations." Her analysis cannot integrate Marxism and psychoanalysis, they argue, because "both these things are conceptualized at different levels of abstraction and there is therefore no homology between the concepts and that to which they allude." If the processes of the unconscious are universal, psychoanalysis is immune to historical analysis. McDonough and Harrison, "Patriarchy," p. 24.

15. Mitchell, *Psychoanalysis and Feminism*, p. 416. Mitchell's comments on feminists' attempts to find solutions to women's oppression reflect her irritation

And it is a question to which there are not, so far, any answers. Wilhelm, along with Mitchell, seems to equate civilization with patriarchy. She confounds the idea that patriarchy, capitalism, and masculine autonomy can survive only as a unit when she shows how patriarchy might persist after the death of capitalism and individuality.[16] But in her description of the psychic development of Molly's son, Mark, she follows a recognizable psychoanalytic line. The boy's initially strong, pre-Oedipal attachment to his mother is broken by the intervention of his father's clone siblings, who take the boy to be educated and send the mother to the breeders' compound. For a while Mark despises his mother for being too weak to prevent their separation (her weakness, absence, and maternal subjugation indicate that she is no longer the all-powerful phallic mother of his early childhood). In spite of the evidence of women's inferiority, Mark does not turn for sexual fulfillment to other men. In a revision of Freud's primal scene (according to Mitchell, the myth that, rewritten as the Oedipus complex, describes man's entry into culture), he abducts the breeders who have served the reproductive needs of his father's identical siblings. His coup brings about the immediate death of one of his uncles and contributes to the death of the society over which they rule. This act represents not the overthrow but the reinitiation of patriarchy. Just as Wilhelm's circular narrative negates the possibility of a feminist revolution, the psychoanalytic account, produced within and informed by patriarchy, can only continue to reinscribe itself and the psychological and social system it describes. The psychoanalysis of patriarchy will not work as a blueprint for its demolition or for the society that might replace it.

In part, it is the specific perspective of the feminist psychoanalytic account—its focus on the white, bourgeois, industrial, hetero-

---

that they have entirely missed the point, because, she contends, biology is irrelevant. "It has been suggested that we struggle for an 'ecological revolution'—a *humanized* brave new world of extra-uterine babies. . . . In [this] proposition, technology conquers the biological handicap of women—their greater physical weakness and painful ability to give birth. . . . It is no surprise that in these circumstances the feminist revolution has nowhere to come about. . . . It is the specific feature of patriarchy—the law of the hypothesized pre-historic murdered father—that defines the relative places of men and women in human history" (p. 409).

16. See Chodorow, *Reproduction of Mothering*, p. 190, for a discussion of the conventional psychoanalytic model I refer to.

sexual family—that limits its potential for revolutionary insight and inspiration.[17] Ann Ferguson, in *Blood at the Root* (1989), points out that Mitchell and other Freudian feminists cannot "provide us with a vision of a nonpatriarchal society." Mitchell calls for a revolution, but as long as patriarchy is reproduced in the unconscious, Ferguson says, there is no way to bring it about. Ferguson offers her own view of what a socialist-feminist vision of the future involves. She limits her discussion to the United States, where "community and autonomy" have always been conflicted goals. Given our history, she says, we need an egalitarian, participatory democracy and "political structures which set individual civil rights as non-negotiable rules of the game."[18]

In Marge Piercy's novel *Woman on the Edge of Time*, the intense, private intimacy of mother and child during gestation and early childhood has been broken to create a society founded on the values Ferguson outlines. Connie Ramos, the novel's time-traveling protagonist, is repulsed by the "alien" method of reproduction she finds in the society of the future, but ultimately admits that it creates a better situation for children (by undoing the exclusive mothering bind Chodorow describes as "distorted"). Piercy's representation of the benefits of the artificial womb parallels arguments advanced by Shulamith Firestone in *The Dialectic of Sex* (1969) that artificial reproduction would help replace "the psychologically destructive

17. Ann Ferguson criticizes Chodorow for assuming that the polarized gender identities evident in our culture are the rule in other cultures. Ferguson's own view is that "oppositional personalities" uniquely describe advanced capitalism. Focusing on what she sees as Chodorow's error in generalizing our gender structure to other societies, Ferguson says that the concepts of a feminine self "with permeable ego boundaries" and a masculine self with an "oppositional sense of self" "presuppose our public/private split, with the particular types of competitive practices (market relations) *vs* incorporative practices (the entwined individual interests and identities of those involved in family/household systems) characteristic of our society, and more specifically the male breadwinner/female housewife nuclear family." Ferguson, *Blood at the Root*, p. 40.

18. Ibid., pp. 39, 228, 229. In Ferguson's model, the values inherent in this form of "council socialism" include a breakdown of gender divisions in labor; a revaluing of wage labor and household jobs traditionally assigned to women; the provision of food, health care, and education for all; acceptance and support of diverse family structures; vastly expanded civil rights and material support for children; the breakdown of compulsory heterosexuality; and universal access to techniques of artificial reproduction.

genetic 'parenthood' of one or two arbitrary adults with a diffusion of the responsibility for physical welfare over a larger number of people."[19]

In Piercy's Mattapoisett, there are no biological mothers. Every woman, no matter what her racial or cultural identity, has sacrificed in-body gestation for the good of the whole community. But within the world of the novel, the woman who is immediately confronted with the need for sacrifice is a poor Chicana. Already in late twentieth-century America, Connie has been devalued as a mother. She represents a version of the "genetic profile" white racist eugenicists have historically been eager to eradicate. In a moment of weakness Connie almost agrees with her oppressors that she should not reproduce. After bearing a single daughter, Angelina, Connie was sterilized, and now she wonders if "maybe those bastards who had spayed her for practice, for fun, had been right. That she had borne herself all over again, and it was a crime to be born poor as it was a crime to be born brown."[20] This is a vulnerable moment, when she is grieving for her lover and suffering the effects of intense poverty, and it demonstrates that Connie has internalized society's hostility toward her. For a moment she accepts the "logic" of her own (and her daughter's) erasure, and she strikes out at her daughter. Although Connie feels personal responsibility for her action, the

19. Shulamith Firestone, *The Dialectic of Sex: The Case for Feminist Revolution* (New York: Morrow Quill Paperbacks, 1971), p. 271.

20. Piercy, *Woman on the Edge of Time*, p. 62. Involuntary or coerced "voluntary" sterilizations have historically been used for "eugenic" purposes with disproportionate frequency on the poor and on women of color. Adele Clarke catalogues cases of coercive sterilization, including the Madrigal case dealing with sterilization of Hispanic women in Los Angeles, in "Subtle Forms of Sterilization Abuse," in *Test Tube Women: What Future for Motherhood?*, ed. Rita Arditti et al. (Boston: Pandora Press, 1984), pp. 191–92. Daniel Kevles discusses involuntary sterilization of mental patients, blacks, and American Indians, and describes the court cases that have resulted from failure to obtain informed consent, in *In the Name of Eugenics: Genetics and the Uses of Human Heredity* (Berkeley: University of California Press, 1985), pp. 275–76. Gena Corea, in *The Hidden Malpractice* (New York: Harper & Row, 1985), p. 181, notes that poor women are more likely to be coerced into sterilization following abortion or childbirth, both as a solution to what one doctor referred to as "the welfare mess" and because hospitals need teaching material. For further discussion of the sterilization of welfare mothers, see Germaine Greer, *Sex and Destiny: The Politics of Human Fertility* (New York: Harper & Row, 1984), pp. 311–33; and Scully, *Men Who Control Women's Health*, p. 145.

scene leaves little doubt that both Connie and Angelina are victims of the omnipresent social hostility toward the poor and women of color. The scene strongly suggests that Connie's momentary violence and her inability to provide adequate care for Angelina is a social failure, not the result of an essential maternal pathology. Her life in twentieth-century America demonstrates convincingly that children suffer because society, denigrating mothers, makes it nearly impossible for women to thrive, or even survive, as parents. But the utopian solution she ultimately works for hinges on the final exclusion of biological mothers.[21]

In the 1950s the natural childbirth movement responded to the transfer of birth from the home to the hospital and the increasing use of anesthesia and surgical interventions by arguing for childbirth without drugs, treatments, or surgical procedures that would interfere with women's "natural" labor processes.[22] The methods of natural childbirth could be as prescriptive and coercive as the standard hospital birth, but the movement was important because it helped to open up the question of who would control the mother's body, and what tools would facilitate that control. In *With Child* Phyllis Chesler, who had planned a "natural" birth in the late 1970s, remembers her experience of the hospital's coercive, highly technologized methods, wondering afterward if she had resisted admitting anything was wrong with her treatment "because I don't want to admit—to myself—how powerless I am?"[23]

21. The cover of the paperback Fawcett Crest edition of *Woman on the Edge of Time* declares, "Only her sacrifice could save the future," a claim that aptly reflects the theme of maternal sacrifice and mother-child separation that threads throughout the novel.

22. Among the early books on natural methods of childbirth are Grantly Dick-Read's *Childbirth without Fear* (1944), Barbara Gelb's *ABC of Natural Childbirth* (1954), and Marjorie Karmel's *Thank You, Dr. Lamaze* (1959). "Natural childbirth," as Suzanne Arms pointed out in the mid-seventies, was interpreted in practice to mean many different things: employing breathing techniques learned in childbirth training, receiving regional rather than general anesthetics, having a husband or companion present during labor, avoiding a cesarean section, or giving birth at home with a midwife. Suzanne Arms, *Immaculate Deception: A New Look at Women and Childbirth in America* (Boston: Houghton Mifflin, 1975), pp. 138–39.

23. Phyllis Chesler, *With Child: A Diary of Motherhood* (New York: Thomas E. Crowell, 1979), p. 253.

Feminist concern for "choice" in regard to high-tech versus natural childbirth has been concentrated primarily in the middle-class white women's movement. Patricia Spallone points out that "for women in 'Third World' countries, and for Black, disabled and poor women in industrialized countries, 'choice' was not the issue, but rather how to resist sterilization abuse, eugenic abortion, and the lack of options in contraceptive practice."[24]

Although Chesler describes herself as "powerless" to make her own decisions about her obstetric care, her child's birth also reflects the experience of many white, middle-class women, who are more likely to be *allowed* by their physicians to have a choice in their treatment. A 1987 survey of court-ordered obstetric interventions shows that, of those women forcibly detained in hospitals or compelled to undergo intrauterine transfusions or cesareans, 81 percent were black, Asian, or Hispanic, and all were on public assistance or receiving care at teaching hospitals.[25]

Chesler's position as a white, middle-class feminist means that she enjoyed a degree of privilege—or "choice"—not available to many others, but she found herself with far less control over her treatment than she had anticipated. The line that separates the middle-class obstetric patient from the impoverished one is not a clear-cut division between those who have choices and those who are disenfranchised. Although there is no question that poor women are far more likely to suffer humiliating treatment and even bodily harm, both are subject to the ideologies of the profession, and both may be invalidated as reproductive agents.

After her son's birth, Chesler discovered that she was as likely to

---

24. Patricia Spallone, *Beyond Conception: The New Politics of Reproduction* (London: MacMillan Education, 1989), p. 83.

25. Veronika Kolder, Janet Gallagher, and Michael Parsons, "Court-Ordered Obstetrical Interventions, *New England Journal of Medicine* 316.19 (1987): 1192–96, cited ibid., pp. 43–44. Diana Scully's book about the training of obstetrics residents, *Men Who Control Women's Health*, describes how obstetricians in training classify women as either private paying patients (who deserve some personal consideration) or as nonpaying patients, who are learning material, and therefore more vulnerable to coercion. The bodies of these women—usually poor, young women of color—are more deeply embedded in the obstetric machinery than those of white, middle-class women. Residents subject these women to more interventions because they need to gain as much practice as possible before they go into private practice.

be invalidated by her "sisters," her feminist friends and colleagues, as she had been by her doctor. A feminist editor refused to publish *With Child*, claiming that "biological reproduction has been the downfall of women." Chesler considered her women friends' refusal of help or understanding a refusal of the maternal body: "Is our female flesh so painful you deny it in the name of woman's survival, woman's freedom?"[26]

The rejection of motherhood among many feminists found its logical basis in the argument that a woman's reproductive body is her enemy. Shulamith Firestone represented the most extreme version of this position, arguing in *The Dialectic of Sex* (1969) that women would not achieve liberation until they were altogether free of their reproductive biology. Reproductive technologies seemed to offer a solution to the mother's dilemma. Just as forceps, cesarean section, and anesthesia had once promised women freedom from the dangers and pain of childbirth, now Brave New World technologies that were either already in an advanced stage of development, such as *in vitro* fertilization, or seemingly on the horizon, such as cloning and artificial wombs, promised to relieve women of the tyranny of their reproductive bodies.[27]

The initial enthusiasm for reproductive technologies was tempered by the lessons of the natural childbirth movement. Recognizing that neither the natural nor the technological approaches to birth were unproblematically liberating, Adrienne Rich identified as her ideal a world in which "women would choose not only whether, when and where to bear children, and the circumstances of labor, but also between biological and artificial reproduction."[28] During the following two decades, however, concerns about the exploitative potential of reproductive technologies mounted steadily. In the mid-1980s both Gena Corea and Rita Arditti and her colleagues, arguing that male physicians will inevitably use the technology to control women's bodies, offered vehement arguments against a large range of technologies, including infertility treat-

26. Chesler, *With Child*, pp. 220, 198.
27. Baruch, "A Womb of His Own," p. 138.
28. Rich, *Of Woman Born*, p. 174.

ments such as *in vitro* fertilization, sex selection, and surrogacy.[29] The debate about whether mothers are victims of medical oppression or slaves of biology who can escape oppression only by technologizing or eliminating internal gestation has given way to a more activist approach.

Patricia Spallone, whose background in medical research and membership in FINRRAGE (Feminist International Network of Resistance to Reproductive and Genetic Engineering) gives her a unique perspective, says that women must "actively protest against the proliferation of reproductive and genetic engineering in both 'First World' and 'Third World' countries" and "look for alternatives to address women's needs."[30] Elaine Hoffman Baruch argues that "rather than be its passive recipients, women must become actively involved in determining the development and values of reproductive technology to end or at least mitigate the male domination of reproduction."[31]

The class differences Spallone identifies in women's experience of "choice" regarding reproductive technology are apparent in Piercy's approach to high-technology reproduction. Whereas Spallone imagines women in the future who have freely chosen to give up in-body gestation, Piercy's Connie Ramos, standing "on the edge of time," struggles unsuccessfully in the twentieth century to resist abuses

29. Corea, *The Mother Machine*, Arditti et al., *Test-Tube Women*. Among many feminists, distrust of reproductive technology is still the rule. Emily Martin finds that the drive to develop an artificial womb reflects "the same kind of denigration of women's bodies that led to a belief in the 1950's . . . that a scientifically formulated bottled milk product was better for babies than breast milk." Emily Martin, *The Woman in the Body: A Cultural Analysis of Reproduction* (Boston: Beacon Press, 1987), p. 146. Patricia Spallone maintains that reproductive technologies may be used to bring about "a destruction of women's physical integrity, an exploitation of women's procreativity, and yet another attempt to undermine women's struggle for control of our own reproduction" (*Beyond Conception*, p. 1).

30. Spallone, *Beyond Conception*, pp. 190–91.

31. Baruch, "A Womb of His Own," p. 139. Adrienne Rich anticipated this approach in the 1970s. Warning that it may "seem naive and self-indulgent to spin forth matriarchal utopias" in which women have somehow seized control of the technology, Rich remarks that we need women active at all levels in the research and practice of medicine who will gather and distribute information. Rich, *Of Woman Born*, p. 282.

similar to those Spallone mentions. In an essay about her experience as a Latina and nascent lesbian, Mirtha Quintanales addresses the reproductive concerns of poor women and women of color, pointing out that "Third World women" have found "little room in the women's movement (let alone anywhere else) for us to talk about our individual lives and thoughts, our shared experiences and concerns."[32] The editors of *This Bridge Called My Back* comment that "Third World women have become the subject matter of many literary and artistic endeavors by white women, and yet we are refused access to the pen, the publishing house, the galleries, and the classroom. . . . In leftist feminist circles we are dealt with as a political issue, rather than as flesh and blood human beings."[33]

Piercy is among those leftist feminist white women who have taken third world women as a political issue and literary subject. Her social and political identity problematizes her portrayal of Connie's encounters with institutional medicine, both reproductive and psychiatric. Piercy's working-class upbringing, however, makes her especially sensitive to issues of economic and racial oppression and helped lead her to her radical stance. It is from this perspective that she proposes advanced reproductive technologies as a tool for liberating humanity from racism, sexism, and classism.

Each child in Mattapoisett has three "coms," or co-mothers, but children may also have important relationships with other adults. In some ways the formation of mothering groups in Mattapoisett resembles what Karen Lindsey, in *Friends as Family* (1981), terms

32. Rita Arditti and Shelley Minden, "An Interview with Mirtha Quintanales, From the Third World Women's Archives," in *Test-Tube Women*, p. 129. Similarly, black feminists object to the "racism and elitism" within the feminist movement that suppresses the concerns of "Black, Third World, and working women." Combahee River Collective, "Black Feminist Statement," in *This Bridge Called My Back: Writings by Radical Women of Color*, ed. Cherríe Moraga and Gloria Ansaldúa (New York: Kitchen Table–Women of Color Press, 1981), p. 211. Marilyn Frye compares the tendency of white feminists (a group to which she belongs) to generalize their experience to a similar tendency among men: "White people also speak in universals. A great deal of what has been written by white feminists is limited by this sort of false universalization. Much of what we have said is accurate only if taken to be about white women and white men within white culture." Marilyn Frye, "On Being White," in *The Politics Of Reality* (New York: Crossing Press, 1983), p. 117.

33. Moraga and Ansaldúa, *This Bridge Called My Back*, p. 61.

"chosen families."[34] Chosen families are domestic groups formed at will rather than as the result of involuntary genetic connections. In Piercy's utopia, "coms" raise children together; the biological mother has neither full responsibility for her children nor exclusive rights in them. Breaking the "nuclear bond" between biological mother and children allows the society to instill in its newborn citizens an appreciation of egalitarian values.

Carol Stack's study in *All Our Kin* (1970) of an impoverished African American community found that the nuclear family structure (and the intense, exclusive mother-child bonds such a family structure promotes) had a negative survival value among people who are effectively barred from realizing the capitalist dream of affluence.[35] She found that harsh socioeconomic circumstances favor extended-kin networks, which permit people to share scarce resources as well as child-rearing responsibilities. In extended-kin networks, no firm boundaries exist between family and community.

In Piercy's socialist-feminist utopian vision, alternative family structures such as those Stack describes provide a model for subverting the nuclear family (still often considered the standard form of the white bourgeois family).[36] But in many ways, her vision appeals to the ideal of the commune in the American counterculture of the 1960s and 1970s. Communes represented a white middle-class attempt to create versions of extended-kin networks. Some communards and the sociologists who studied them maintained

34. Karen Lindsey, *Friends as Family* (Boston: Beacon Press, 1981).

35. Carol Stack, *All Our Kin* (New York: Harper & Row, 1970).

36. Piercy's vision of the utopian community includes many of the attributes of the extended-kin networks Stack describes. People in Mattapoisett share mothering duties, community responsibilities, and material resources. Their sexual relationships and friendships tend to be fluid; the exclusivity of marriage has no place in a society without personal possessions. Among the many problems Stack noted—all the result of severe poverty—was the overcrowding of large extended families into inadequate housing. In Mattapoisett, by contrast, each person has private space, and children too young to be left alone at night sleep in nurseries. No one, not even a mother, gives up his or her privacy in order to care for children. Extended-kin networks in the community Stack observed are necessary for meeting basic physical and emotional needs in a hostile society structured to maintain social inequalities. In Mattapoisett "chosen families" are a strategy for eradicating social inequalities.

that dismantling the nuclear family would level sexual inequalities.[37] Many studies of the movement found, however, that, even in
communes that succeeded in sharing work and resources equitably
among families, the traditional sexual division of labor prevailed,
and men continued to dominate.[38] Furthermore, in some successful
communes virulently patriarchal nuclear families are the norm,
calling into doubt the notion that male dominance and the nuclear
family are inevitably tied to capitalism.[39]

American communes are nonetheless conceived and embedded
in the American economic system. In addition, they often function
as corporations, participating directly in the larger economy. For
her utopia Piercy extracts the commune from its capitalist context
and weds it to the civil rights and feminist movements. She recalls
that in writing *Woman on the Edge of Time*, "my first intent was to
create an image of a good society, one that was *not* sexist, racist, or
imperialist: one that *was* cooperative, respectful of all living things,

37. Rosabeth Moss Kanter reported that women are likely to achieve greater
status and participate more fully in the community when family loyalties are deem-
phasized. Rosabeth Moss Kanter, "Family Organization and Sex Roles in American
Communes," in *Communes: Creating and Managing the Creative Life* (New York:
Harper & Row, 1973), 287–307. In *The Future of Motherhood* (New York: Dial Press,
1974), Jessie Bernard quotes Judson Jerome on the greater freedom and security enjoyed by mothers in communes: "For many women, the commune is the only real
option available if they want to have children, but don't want to be locked into a
couple relationship" (p. 319). Rick Margolies equates the family with the state, and
asserts that radical communities should reject the nuclear family in order to liberate
"men and women from this kind of mechanical, enfeebling and narrow definition of
how they relate." Rick Margolies, "Building Communes," *Alternatives* 3.2 (1972): 2.

38. Bernard notes that mothering experiments in communes vary from "simple
sharing of motherwork among women to complex plural mothering," but rarely do
men take on much responsibility for child care (*Future of Motherhood*, p. 311).
Gilbert Zicklin places the responsibility for maintaining the sexual division of labor
on women, claiming that "countercultural women in the late sixties were prone to
play traditional female roles." Gilbert Zicklin, *Countercultural Communes: A So-
ciological Perspective* (Westport, Conn.: Greenwood Press, 1983), p. 95. Jon Wagner
writes of the incongruity, given "expert testimony" to the effect that communes did
not favor male dominance, of his discovery that many communes "were also ori-
ented toward charismatic leadership and, in some cases, toward male supremacy."
Jon Wagner, ed., *Sex Roles in Contemporary American Communes* (Bloomington:
Indiana University Press, 1982), p. vii.

39. See, for instance, Jon Wagner, "A Midwestern Patriarchy," in *Sex Roles in
Contemporary American Communes*.

gentle, responsible, loving, and playful. . . . To try to imagine people of such a society was my hardest task."[40] Piercy's solution to the problem of producing the proper citizens was to engineer them. In Mattapoisett careful genetic conservation preserves racial differences, but children are not matched with co-mothers who share their racial or ethnic heritage. The mothers' sex and sexual orientation are likewise unimportant. Connie, embodying the disadvantages of exclusive biological motherhood, contrasts starkly with the co-mothers. The "artificial" mothers exceed the "natural." They are as loving as Connie, but they are better able to provide physical, intellectual, and emotional sustenance for their children.

In view of assertions by Mirtha Quintanales, Audre Lorde, and others that the deepest concerns of third world women have received little notice in the (white) women's movement, Piercy's approval of high-tech reproduction as a solution to Connie Ramos's disenfranchisement misses a vital point.[41] Long before Luciente appears to her, Connie already has ample experience of those who, claiming to know what is best for Connie, her child, and society, seize control of her reproductive body. Doctors and social workers coerce her into undergoing sterilization and give her daughter to a white couple who, according to the dominant ideology, can provide Angelina with love, security, and a chance for a better life.

Connie is the maternal ancestor, imaginatively and ideologically, of the society in which her other self, Luciente, and her daughter's counterpart Dawn thrive. But Connie is a shadow in Mattapoisett. Although she can converse with and even touch its people, she exists there only fleetingly, a poignant reminder of the misguided and cruel world her sacrifice has negated. Since Connie's visits to Mattapoisett leave no traces on her physical body, the novel does

40. Marge Piercy, "Mirror Images," in *Women's Culture: The Women's Renaissance of the Seventies*, ed. Gayle Kimball (Metuchen, N.J.: Scarecrow Press, 1981), p. 193.

41. As Lorde writes: "Now we hear that it is the task of black and third world women to educate white women, in the face of tremendous resistance, as to our existence, our differences, our relative roles in our joint survival. This is a diversion of energies and a tragic repetition of racist patriarchal thought." Audre Lorde, "The Master's Tools Will Never Dismantle the Master's House," in Moraga and Ansaldúa, *This Bridge Called My Back*, p. 100.

not exclude the possibility that the utopia exists only in Connie's mind as a fantasy derived from her unearned guilt over giving birth to a child who has already suffered traumatic upheavals. Coming back from her last trip to the future, Connie says, "I dreamed of my daughter, safe, happy, in another place."[42] From this point of view, Mattapoisett is a fantasy in which Angelina is protected from (maternal) violence.

Connie endorses the definition of motherhood as sacrifice even when, recognizing the similarity to her own tragedy in the contemporary world, she initially rebels against the utopian reproductive program: "How could anyone know what being a mother means who has never carried a child nine months heavy under her heart, who has never borne a baby in blood and pain, who has never suckled a child. Who got that child out of a machine the way that couple, white and rich, got my flesh and blood."[43] "What being a mother means" in this context is an acceptance that reproductive biology is a source of pain: the pain of birth, of love, and of separation. Whereas the twentieth-century sections of the novel demonstrate that mothers are "enchained" not by their wombs (or by their children) but by the politics enacted on the metaphor of the womb-as-prison, the utopian sections perpetuate the gynophobic metaphor in the philosophy and reproductive practice Luciente advocates.

Some of Piercy's contemporaries, including Joanna Russ and Suzy McKee Charnas, created separatist utopias in which women use adapted reproductive technologies to reproduce without men.[44] Like Piercy, they advocate group mothering and the deliberate imposition of emotional and physical barriers between biological mothers and their children. Yet women give birth to their own children. Viewed from the perspective of a separatist utopia, Piercy's use of artificial wombs becomes a gesture of patriarchal affirmation, of

42. Piercy, *Woman on the Edge of Time*, p. 371.
43. Ibid., p. 106.
44. Russ's Whileaway in *The Female Man* employs a program of egg merging, which demands high technology without doing away with in-body gestation. In Suzy McKee Charnas's *Motherlines* (New York: Berkeley, 1978), women who have been genetically altered by male experimenters to conceive parthenogenetically from horse semen found their own community and, rejecting technology in the form of artificial insemination, choose to mate with the horses in order to reproduce.

approving men's inability to accept women's bodies and their reproductive capabilities, and placing the burden on women to validate men as "mothers." Women take an active role in planning and
carrying out the utopian reproductive program, and Connie's most
revolutionary actions are intended to bring Mattapoisett into being.
Connie creates the possibility of a new world, but it is a world in
which she, as a biological mother, would have no place.

Luciente, Connie's contact and alter ego in Mattapoisett, has
achieved the happy and fulfilling life denied to Connie. Her extended family includes lovers, co-parents, and children, but her responsibilities to her family are limited, leaving her free to pursue
her profession (plant geneticist) and participate fully in her community. She represents what women could be if they were no longer
responsible for bearing and raising children. Luciente tries to persuade Connie to abandon her ideals of mother-child unity, reasoning that women had to stop giving birth in order to complete the
transformation of society:

> It was part of women's long revolution. When we were breaking up all
> the old hierarchies. Finally there was that one thing we had to give up
> too, the only power we ever had, in return for no more power for
> anyone. The original production: the power to give birth. Cause as
> long as we were biologically enchained, we'd never be equal. And
> males never would be humanized to be loving and tender. So we all
> become mothers. . . . To break the nuclear bonding.[45]

In Mattapoisett women no longer circulate in the reproductive
economy. The resulting collapse of that system creates a new social
context in which the old forms (capitalism and patriarchy) have
no place. Although Piercy and Wilhelm differ on the question of
the unity of capitalism and patriarchy, they both arrive at the con-
clusion that the exchange of women-as-breeders is the linchpin of
patriarchy.

Rather than being biological mothers in nuclear families, Mattapoisett's mothers are chosen kin and "experts" in child rearing.
Together they represent a sort of community-sponsored nurturing,
housing and supervising children from birth onward. Piercy's uto-

45. Piercy, *Woman on the Edge of Time*, p. 105.

pian resolution of present-day hierarchies of race, gender, and class received a mixed reaction.[46] Among those who responded positively, Susan Kress applauded Piercy's assessment of the benefits of artificial reproduction, saying that Piercy answered the horror of Aldous Huxley's *Brave New World* by making "the future work for women."[47] Nancy Breeze and Dorothy Berkman praised Piercy's vision of communal child rearing.[48] Even those who were disturbed by the prospect of extrauterine reproduction often found the resulting utopian society appealing.[49]

However promising Mattapoisett appears overall, in its reproductive program it preserves the patriarchal fear and distrust of the mother. Judith Gardiner argues that in some feminist fiction (of which Piercy's novel is a primary example), whereas the masculine

46. Elaine Hoffman Baruch recounts a brief history of feminist responses to artificial reproduction in "A Womb of His Own."

47. Susan Kress, "In and Out of Time: The Form of Marge Piercy's Novels," in *Future Females: A Critical Anthology*, ed. Marlene Barr (Bowling Green, Ohio: Bowling Green State University Popular Press, 1981), p. 118. Kress notes, however, that in Piercy's earlier novels, "wars" rage "between 'real' parents and children" (p. 117), a portrayal of family relations that accords with Huxley's unfavorable description of nuclear families. Ironically, although Piercy and Huxley have diametrically opposed perceptions of how genetic engineering and artificial reproduction would affect sex roles and class structure, they do agree that eradicating biological mothers and preventing a one-to-one bond between parent and child is an essential prerequisite to creating a citizen fit to function in a planned society.

48. Nancy Breeze called *Woman on the Edge* "a visionary movement" away from isolated, biologically assigned child care, in "Who Is Going to Rock the Petri Dish?" in Arditti et al., *Test-Tube Women*, p. 400. (Other essays in this volume challenge her optimism, critiquing current birth technologies such as *in vitro* fertilization and surrogacy.) More recently, Dorothy Berkman focused on the accomplishments of Mattapoisett, such as the abolition of social hierarchies and the vision of a new, nurturing, maternal man who has a personal stake in child rearing, improvements that result directly from the technologization of birth. Dorothy Berkman, "So We All Became Mothers: Harriet Beecher Stowe, Charlotte Perkins Gilman, and the New World of Women's Culture," in *Feminism, Utopia, and Narrative*, ed. Libby Falk Jones and Sarah Webster Goodwin (Knoxville: University of Tennessee Press, 1990), pp. 100–115.

49. In "So We All Became Mothers: New Roles for Men in Recent Utopian Fiction," Peter Fitting admits his reservations about the use of "brooders" in the novel, saying that extrauterine gestation unnecessarily complicates reproduction and deprives women of "the experience of motherhood" (*Science Fiction Studies* 12 [1985]: 175). In "The Turn from Utopia in Recent Feminist Fiction," however, Fitting describes Mattapoisett as one of the "utopias in which I would most like to live" (p. 154).

villain is responsible for oppressive social institutions, "the female villain is the bad mother, and what women are guilty of, circularly, is irresponsibility, falling asleep on the impossible job of caring for the children of the world, that is, of caring for our collective future."[50] To refine Gardiner's argument, it is specifically the *biological* mother, the mother whose body reproduces the nuclear family, who must be replaced. Luciente's indictment of in-body gestation names both the mother and the child as victims of maternal biology. The mother is enchained by her biology—by her own womb—and the child is chained up within the mother, first literally, as a fetus, then, after birth, by the "nuclear bonding" that follows in-body gestation. In the twentieth century, Connie is permanently separated from her child and incarcerated in a mental institution, where she undergoes psychiatric experiments designed to deprive her of will, consciousness, and memory. As attractive as Mattapoisett appears in comparison to this hell, utopia demands from Connie the same sacrifice as that exacted by a malevolent contemporary patriarchy, for its existence depends on her personal destruction. The supreme irony, in view of Connie's eventual (although reluctant) acceptance of Luciente's logic, is that Mattapoisett reproduces and valorizes the elimination of mothers, which, in the twentieth century, is a particularly barbaric expression of patriarchal oppression. The self-sacrificial biological mother is no new thing in our maternal mythology. The feminist utopia, built on the traditional principle of motherly sacrifice and effacement, takes that principle to its logical extreme with the self-willed erasure of the biological mother.

Connie erases herself so that Mattapoisett's egalitarian values may thrive. When she poisons the physicians who are developing technologies of mind control, she also, in effect, brings her own life to an end (thereafter, all we know of Connie is what her medical records state). Connie as she is cannot survive. She must be "reincarnated" as Luciente, a woman whose psyche is undamaged. Connie is a product of, and therefore represents, the ills of twentieth-century capitalism: alienation, the drive to amass capital (monetary

50. Judith Kegan Gardiner, "Evil, Apocalypse, and Feminist Fiction," *Frontiers* 7.2 (1983): 79.

or generational), and the unhealthy nuclear family. Her maternal body is at once singular and communal, doubling as a figure for the daughter's need to separate and her desire to merge, and for western society's tension between autonomy and community. The maternal sacrifice erases the conflict between Connie, the "desocialized" individual whose place in both worlds and on both sides of the political and psychological dichotomy is one of exile, and the community.

Ann Ferguson breaks down the dichotomous model by identifying not two but three conflicting tendencies in the women's movement, tendencies which she labels "separatist," "assimilationist," and "coalitionist." Each term describes a strategy for feminists in relation to men. Assimilationists "attempt to persuade the dominators that their own interests will be best served if they allow the oppressed into their ranks," and separatists organize "the oppressed to separate and prioritize values endemic to their subculture."[51] The coalitionist takes a middle course, maintaining autonomous feminist networks and, as the need arises, working with men in coalitions to effect social changes. Ferguson sees coalitionism as the solution to the limitations of assimilation and separatism, but notes that the other strategies are necessary to coalitionism.

It is tempting to map the political strategies of assimilationism and separatism onto Chodorow's gendered dichotomy of feminine connectedness and masculine separation, and to see in coalitionism the happy solution to the social asymmetries that prevent men and women, mothers and fathers, from working together for a better world. Thus assimilationism, defined as the absorption of women into the central cultural body, takes after the traditional psychoanalytic maternal personality, which is defined by its inability to detect where one's own body ends and that of the other begins. Separatists, by contrast, secede from the central cultural body, defining themselves by their difference from it. Separatism seems to take after the traditional masculine personality in that it establishes itself as a separate identity by reference to an "other"—a disparate entity and adversary. In Ferguson's terms: "Such a strategy does not eliminate

51. Ferguson, *Blood at the Root*, p. 246. Ferguson also applies this "trichotomy" to the civil rights, lesbian/gay, and workers' movements in the United States.

dualism: it just reverses it. Women are now seen, implicitly or explicitly, to be superior to men."[52]

Nevertheless, separatism is an important move toward a future
free of gender-based oppression. Women in an all-female community could not reproduce the traditional heterosexual feminine role
in which mothers define themselves only in relationship to the
other members of their immediate nuclear family.[53] Although in a
separatist community women would mother exclusively, as Chodorow argues women in the postindustrial West do, they would not
mother in isolation from the community at large. Instead, mothers
and daughters would be continuous with the community as a
whole. In such a community every relationship, including those
between friends, co-workers, adversaries, and lovers, would partake
of the bodily and psychic continuum that is the mother-daughter
bond. A society entirely composed of mothers and daughters would
seem, from the psychoanalytic point of view, endlessly similar;
there would be no way to differentiate persons, there would be no
individuals, since the "pre-Oedipal" unity of mother and child
(which, as the idea is formulated, belongs always to the subject's
forgotten past) would never have been broken by the father's phallic
interference. How might a girl without any experience of men—a
girl who never experiences penis envy, or recognizes her mother as
castrated, or looks to a man to help her escape from her mother—
create that ambiguous love-hate relationship with her mother, the
tension between the desire for fusion and the desire for separation,
that marks "feminine" subjectivity?

In the literary separatist utopias, one strategy for dealing with
this thorny problem is to provide male outsiders as foils for feminine subjects. These utopias specifically exclude men, but the values of the feminist separatist culture are most thoroughly disclosed
at the site of the women's encounters with male outsiders, who
represent extreme versions of the traditional masculine personality

52. Ibid., p. 245.
53. Ferguson uses Chodorow's theory of the construction of gender to define the
"mediation problem" mothers encounter as they intercede in conflicts between their
partner and their children. Women in this position work to keep other family members in harmony as the only way of finding emotional satisfaction for themselves
(ibid., pp. 173–75).

type. Feminist utopias redefine femininity as a *process* in which the struggle to resolve the conflict between the individual and the collective describes a woman's relationship to her body, her children, her lovers, and her community. Nevertheless, the utopian woman whose redefinition explodes gendered categories still requires the "othered" male, with his atavistically rigid ego boundaries intact, for contrast. In Joanna Russ's 1972 short story "When It Changed," a precursor to the utopian Whileawayan sections of *The Female Man* (1977), the protagonist, Janet, confronts spacemen for the first time and derides them as "apes with human faces." The men are irretrievably different and inferior, but Janet recognizes their power and finds herself worrying that when men have put into action their plan to use the bodies and genes of Whileawayan women to replenish human stock, she will see her "children cheated of their full humanity or turned into strangers."[54]

Janet describes to a "monomaniacal" spaceman the Whileawayans' budding industrial age: "This was a delicate point in our history; give us time. There was no need to sacrifice the quality of life for an insane rush into industrialization. Let us go our own pace. Give us time."[55] From the point of view of the spacemen and the patriarchy they represent, the women of Whileaway had been cast out of time; the men's arrival (coinciding with the reader's first contact with Whileaway) marks the moment of their reinsertion into patriarchal history. The same event initiates language. Janet's narrative begins—in other words, she is inaugurated as a speaking subject—on the occasion of her first encounter with men. Janet entreats an unidentified power to halt the march of patriarchal time: "Keep it as it is. Don't change." But Janet, her wife, and their daughters are on the verge of being revalued as commodities and put into circulation in the masculine reproductive economy.

The coincidence of patriarchy with history demonstrated in "When It Changed" finds a theoretical corollary in Juliet Mitchell's account of the beginnings of culture and society. She draws on Lévi-

---

54. Joanna Russ, "When It Changed," in *The Norton Anthology of Literature by Women*, ed. Sandra Gilbert and Susan Gubar (New York: W. W. Norton & Company, 1985), p. 2268.
55. Ibid., p. 2265.

Strauss's theories of language and kinship, contending in 1974 that the recognition of difference, based on the exchange of women by men, is essential to the "movement of culture." The incest taboo "establishes that smallest of differences which is necessary to inaugurate society."[56] It is clear that the overthrow of male dominance, capitalism, and excessive individualism would succeed only at great cost. According to this view, *post*patriarchy is a state—or rather a stasis—in which the "movement of culture" grinds to a halt, signification fails, and the individual loses sight of her bodily and psychic boundaries in an incestuous union with the collective maternal body. It is, therefore, unrepresentable.

If patriarchy is synonymous with culture and society, Russ's attempt to imagine a postpatriarchal society cannot succeed. But the energy generated by patriarchy's self-destruction may initiate postpatriarchal history, as the big bang theoretically initiated the space-time we experience. In fact, in *The Female Man* the alternative worlds of Russ's multidimensional narrative allude to the sociopolitical conditions of this world. The movement of culture in postpatriarchy always refers itself to its point of initiation, the death of the ancestral patriarch. If the symbolic order in our culture depends on the absent or dead mother, signification in a postpatriarchal world also depends on an absent referent: the banished or dead father.[57]

And so, when Russ resurrects Janet and Whileaway, she situates them in another space-time, where men cannot invalidate women's global utopia. The most authorial of the multiple voices of *The Female Man* explains that Whileaway is the Earth, "but not our Earth"; it exists in the future, "but not *our* future." It exists as only one in a network of infinite universes from which it was generated.

56. Mitchell, *Psychoanalysis and Feminism*, p. 376.

57. From the Lacanian perspective, the symbolic death of the mother occurs as the child learns to use language to represent her loss. This death is an essential element of Lacan's account of the child's introduction to language: "The replacement of the mother by a symbol may be considered equivalent to the 'death' of the mother." Muller and Richardson, *Lacan and Language*, p. 94. Similarly, in developing her argument for viewing Lacan's theories as one expression of a culturewide "myth of language," Margaret Homans stresses the hostility inherent in this concept: "The symbolic order is founded, not merely on the regrettable loss of the mother, but rather on her active and overt murder" (*Bearing the Word*, p. 11).

In its turn, Whileaway generates other universes. Its physics, therefore, is as antipatriarchal as its social organization. Western patriarchy—the form that Russ's utopia rebels against—depends on the concepts of linear time (that is, the march of time in a single unbroken line) and the single universe as much as it depends on a single paternal god and the valorization of the individual man. The network of universes that includes Whileaway is based on a reproductive model; each universe continually gives birth to others, and the "individual" also multiplies as each new universe is generated. Time and space multiply infinitely as "every choice begets at least two worlds of possibility." In view of the endless "fecundity of God," the patriarchal insistence on singularity becomes as absurd as the rabid insistence of the Inquisition, when faced with Galileo's heliocentric model of the solar system, that the Earth was the center of the universe.[58]

The congruence of physics with biopsychology in *The Female Man* makes it possible for women—but not for men—to theorize time travel and construct a time machine. Women in two different space-time dimensions come up with time travel. Jael, Janet's genetic double, seeks her other selves along the "twisted braid" of multiple strands of probability that blur "from one to the other without even knowing it" (p. 7).[59] The women's ability to imagine (and then forge) connections across dimensions that men cannot even perceive suggests a more positive valuation of the feminine personality, which in Chodorow's formulation is marked by a maternal "boundary confusion" which daughters make "rather unsatisfactory and artificial" attempts to overcome.[60] The ambivalent psychology that makes it difficult for women to operate as fully sep-

58. Russ, *The Female Man*, pp. 6–7; subsequent references in this chapter are cited in the text.

59. Russ explains her attraction to writing science fiction on the grounds that SF, among other genres, implies "that human problems are collective, as well as individual, and takes these problems to be spiritual, social, perceptive, or cognitive—not the fictionally sex-linked problems of success, competition, castration, education, love, or even personal identity with which we are all so familiar." Joanna Russ, "What Can a Heroine Do, or Why Women Can't Write," in *Images of Women in Fiction: Feminist Perspectives*, ed. Susan K. Cornillon (Bowling Green, Ohio: Bowling Green University Popular Press, 1973), p. 19.

60. Chodorow, *Feminism and Psychoanalytic Theory*, p. 59.

arated subjects under patriarchy might also, at least in another dimension, make them capable of developing an extremely high technology in accord with their social and familial "connectedness."

The women's matter-of-fact approach to time travel shows men at a distinct disadvantage. The men whom the Whileawayans meet in their experiments with space-time travel are comically emasculated in the encounter. For instance, an unwilling visitor to Whileaway lands in a field of turnips and immediately faints when he sees the women's gargantuan farm machinery ("That is a real Earth Man," a tractor driver, standing over his prone body, remarks drily). The women decide to "send it back" (pp. 5–6). Janet, visiting a version of modern-day America, effortlessly disables a hostile marine at a cocktail party who has threatened to "cream" her (p. 47). Though rendered ludicrously ineffectual, men in *The Female Man* still provide a necessary "other" against which women define themselves. It is a familiar strategy. Men in *The Female Man* are as essential to the "movement of culture" in the dimensions occupied by Janet and Jael as breeding women are under patriarchy.

The need to refer to men and their institutions is most fully evident in Jael's world. On her version of Earth, Womanlanders and Manlanders live separately and sustain a perpetual cold war of the sexes; Jael, a cyborg whose body is a weapon, thrives off the sex wars. Their bisected culture is no longer based on the exchange of women but on the exchange of babies. On a mission to Manland to negotiate the sale of male babies, Jael derives an intense physical rush from killing a man who plans to reinstitute a reproductive economy based on the exchange of women by men. Whereas the Janet of "When It Changed" found herself helpless and unprepared for the men's invasion, and the Janet of *The Female Man* knows her planet is fully protected from all trespasses, Jael's body and values are constructed in direct confrontation with the male threat. She is who she is because of men. Seeing herself through the eyes of the man she is about to kill—a faculty Janet lacks—Jael assesses herself: "*I'm* the other self, the mirror, the master-slave, the rebel, the heretic, the mystery that must be found out at all costs" (p. 174).

Marilyn Hacker, in her introduction to *The Female Man*, says that the "J's"—Janet, Jeannine, Joanna, and Jael, the four genetically identical women who inhabit different universes—"are four discrete women, but they are also . . . components of the whole of one even more complex woman" (p. xxi). They are simultaneously a multiple subject and four individuals, bound together and kept apart by the tension between "community and autonomy" which Ann Ferguson identifies as characteristic of American society.[61] Russ's physics makes them one another's mothers, (twin) sisters, and daughters, but it also divides them, placing each in her own universe, where it is difficult, though not impossible, to make connections with the others.

The psychology informing Russ's cosmic reproductive scheme has a more familiar counterpart in Whileawayan developmental psychology. The mother keeps her child with her for the first five years while she enjoys her first "vacation," and the child enjoys her continual presence and the indulgent attention of her other mothers—members of her biological mother's chosen family. After five years a radical change occurs in an effort to construct the child as an individual: "Whileawayan psychology locates the basis of Whileawayan character in the early indulgence, pleasure and flowering which is drastically curtailed by the separation from the mothers. This (it says) gives Whileawayan life its characteristic independence, its dissatisfaction, its suspicion, and its tendency toward a rather irritable solipsism" (p. 52). This sudden traumatic change is another Whileawayan strategy for ensuring the movement of culture.

On Whileaway, falling in love (with its implications of mutual absorption) is considered an embarrassment, to be endured and speedily overcome. Marriages do not involve legal ties, a lifelong commitment, or monogamy, and women tend to travel a great deal, only periodically returning to their homes. In explaining the sexual restlessness that characterizes women, "Whileawayan psychology again refers to the distrust of the mother and the reluctance to form a tie that will engage every level of emotion, all the person, all the time. And the necessity for artificial dissatisfactions" (p. 53).[62] The separation of mother and daughter, and the individualism women

61. Ferguson, *Blood at the Root*, p. 228.
62. The Whileawayans' cultivation of individualism stands in stark contrast to the Manlanders' harsh training for masculinity in Jael's world: "Manlanders buy

prize so highly, develops in the context of a safely maternal and sisterly society. The planet itself is maternal: "You cannot fall out of the kinship web and become sexual prey for strangers, for there is no prey and there are no strangers—the web is world-wide" (p. 81).

The tension between community and autonomy that characterizes Whileaway is summed up in an encounter between Janet, in her capacity as Safety and Peace Officer, and an older woman, Elena Twa, who "run[s] mad" and "flees above the forty-eighth parallel." Elena leaves behind a note for her companions containing a stinging insult: "You do not exist" (p. 55). She is not the first to commit this "crime"; Janet reports that women do, occasionally, go mad: "We are so bloody cooperative that we have this solipsistic underside" (p. 143). At the woman's insistence (but also in accordance with her duty), Janet kills her. Elena is an unpleasant reminder that the carefully engineered (in both the genetic and social senses) Whileaway-an mind still sometimes snaps under the tension between community and autonomy.

Whileawayan psychology resembles psychoanalysis in its initial focus on the mother-child bond and its severance, even to the extent that it arranges for the child to harbor a certain sense of resentment over her mother's "betrayal." This "artificial" conflict keeps the society in motion. Without the early separation of mother and child, according to Dunyasha Bernadettson, the premier Whileawayan philosopher, "we would all become contented slobs" (p. 52). In their radical revision of psychoanalysis, Whileawayans negate the father's role and thus erase the entire labyrinth of castration fears, penis envy, Oedipal dramas, and the "difficult development to femininity."[63]

---

infants from the Womanlanders and bring them up in batches, save for the rich few who can order children made from their very own semen: keep them in the city nurseries until they're five, then out into the country training ground, with the gasping little misfits buried in baby cemeteries along the way. There, in ascetic and healthful settlements in the country, little boys are made into Men—though some don't make it; sex-change surgery begins at sixteen. Russ, *The Female Man*, p. 167.

63. Sigmund Freud, *New Introductory Lectures: Standard Edition of the Complete Psychological Works*, vol. 22 (London: Hogarth Press, 1933), p. 117.

CHAPTER 14

Postpartum/Postmortem

In the 1970s, during a decade of especially energetic efforts to envision postpatriarchal society, my grandmother Ruth passed on to me her own vision of a matriarchal utopia. I was then a teenager ploddingly and painfully lodged in the material world and inclined to dream of escape; Ruth was in her late sixties and convinced that she was at any moment going to be snatched up into a maternal community "on the other side" of death (she is now eighty-nine). Her utopia was, in most ways, nothing like Joanna Russ's. Ruth believed in a paradise after death of mothers and daughters, located beyond the reach of all social and economic constraints. Everyone *there* was bodiless (and so never experienced hunger or pain), but they all lived in two worlds at once: the immaterial plane, where time and space meant nothing, and—through us—in the material, mortal world. These were our mothers. As such they surrounded us and were intimately concerned with the lives of their "embodied" daughters. For Ruth there was no dominating patriarchal god; the "afterlife" was not patterned on the material one. It was not that she specifically excluded men from the afterlife; in fact, she was sure that the best of her three husbands awaited her "on the other side." But she had hardly known her male blood relatives. She was inclined to trace her lineage through women, and her theology followed suit.

I did not then recognize the connection between Ruth's unconventional theology and her history. She had spent her childhood in a household of women without men. Her aunt and mother were practical nurses, and, with their widowed mother, they rented a house in Oakland, California. There they lived and ran a nursing home for elderly women and sick newborns. Ruth spent her days amid the endless practical processes of caring for the very old and the very young. My mother has a photograph of Ruth at the age of four, holding one of her favorite "patients"—a child of about two who had been left with them ever since birth. At the age of six, when she went to school, Ruth was made responsible for washing and sterilizing the dishes for everyone in the house. Ruth's mother and aunt took the babies to bed with them to keep them warm at night. In spite of their industriousness, their lives were a continuous, and sometimes desperate, struggle for survival. Ruth was chronically malnourished, eventually developing, among other debilitating conditions, scoliosis and deformities of her legs and feet. I now believe that she fixed her hopes for a utopian community resignedly on the afterlife because of the suffering of the involuntarily "separatist" women's community in which she grew up. In spite of her physical deformities, she grew up to be a delicately beautiful woman who had an immense talent for making men happy and inducing them to care for her. Ruth's carefully cultivated beauty, and her talent for adapting her desires to the rules of patriarchy, were essential tools of survival.

I am not at all sure that Ruth would understand Russ's Whileaway. The women of Whileaway, with their raucous humor, frankly sexual bodies, rude good health, and quick tempers, would be alien to her class-conscious feminine aesthetic. Nevertheless, Ruth, like Joanna Russ, envisioned a postpatriarchal community far removed from, and yet emphatically a response to, the adversities of capitalism and male dominance. For Ruth, the alienating term *father* represented both the personal pain of abandonment and a political economy in which lone men thrived but an entire household of industrious mothers and daughters could not make an adequate living. Though absent, "father" made himself felt continually in the form of emotional and bodily hunger. "He" was the ultimate cause of her own suffering and her mothers'. As a young woman, she learned to ally herself with "him." It was an alliance that allowed her to survive, but she never felt herself to be fully protected from poverty. She transformed the traumatic memories of her childhood into a vision of a maternal paradise, where male domination, and hence material want, were irrelevant concepts. The exit from patriarchal history that defined her theology negated that early paternal "absence" and its lifelong physical and emotional effects. For Ruth, death marked the exit, and it was always in the future.

Read against the backdrop of socialist-psychoanalytic feminist theory,[1] the literary utopias women SF writers (such as Joanna Russ and Marge Piercy) generated in the 1970s are graphic demonstrations of alternative "movement[s] of culture" in postpatriarchy.[2] Often they portray worlds in which women have reevaluated, and found destructive, the masculine-identified drive to amass political, geographic, and technological capital. There are no fathers in The Female Man; "father" is not a personally felt absence but a destructive political and social economy. Of the masculine-dominated dimensions in The Female Man, one is marked by a ruthless and counterproductive form of technological and economic "progress," and another stagnates in an everlasting Great Depression. Both serve as antitypes. For Whileaway, Russ validates cautious technological and social progress, postulating a community in which cultural and social movement is ultimately based not on the ownership and exchange of bodies but on the slow processes of directed social and biological evolution—the caring of mothers for their daughters. Their cultural movement is fueled by desire for (and conflicts with) one another as lovers and friends, mothers and daughters, the birth of new forms of art, philosophy, and technology, the collective effort to provide food and shelter, the inexhaustible psychological tension of living an individual life that is also

1. See Kuhn and Wolpe, *Feminism and Materialism;* Ferguson, *Blood at the Root;* and Mary O'Brien, *The Politics of Reproduction* (Boston: Routledge & Kegan Paul, 1981).

2. See also Charnas, *Motherlines;* Sally Gearhart, *The Wanderground: Stories of the Hill Women* (Watertown, Mass.: Persephone Press, 1979); and Tiptree, "Houston, Houston Do You Read."

tightly bound to the community, the cyclical movement of the seasons and the generations, of caring—as Ruth learned early on—for old and young.

Attended by her mother, Edith, Ruth gave birth to my mother on the front porch of her family's nursing home in 1925. Ruth was sick during her entire pregnancy, she recalls. She could not hold food or water. She never saw a doctor because she was sure a doctor would "take the baby." Edith—with the combined force of her nursing expertise and mother love—sustained her throughout. The labor lasted almost two days, made more difficult because of Ruth's chronic malnutrition.

This is for me the "primal scene" in which I ground my early understanding of mother-daughter relationships. I reeled under the weight of the knowledge that my mothers—my mother, and grandmother, and great-grandmother, and great-great-grandmother, and the countless "greats" before her—had borne a daughter, as Marge Piercy put it, "in blood and pain," and that daughter bore her own daughter in turn. I understood this not as an abstract principle, like the symbolic "blood and body" my Catholic friends consume in communion, but as the endless, literal, visceral process that had produced my body.

My own daughter was born in a hospital. I had felt well during most of the pregnancy. Nicole was born about six hours after I arrived at the hospital. My mother visited me twice in the labor room. I recall that she tried to persuade me to put on lip gloss, and I refused rudely. I also offended a good friend by barking at her to leave me alone. My husband, my "coach," looked on, bemused. A fetal monitor was strapped around me, and there was an I.V. line in my arm. As my pain deepened, I heard myself growl and moan, and I heard a nurse impatiently tell me to stop. It all seemed irrelevant, the people and the machinery, their noise and mine, as pain drove me down into the knotted center of my body. When they thought I was close, they gave me a regional anesthetic, and I went dead from my chest downward.

Nicole emerged calmly from this fury. She was put in my arms for a few minutes. She sucked a finger and looked back at me—I thought—with philosophical curiosity. Then she was taken away and I was wheeled into the otherwise empty "recovery" room. For the first time I was frightened. My body was no longer my own. Though I could not form the words to describe it, I felt that I had been gutted, and my confused remains belonged to the hospital staff, who for three days thereafter drugged it, examined it, and tried, unsuccessfully, to feed it. For months afterward I could do nothing with my body; it refused food, it refused sleep, and I became increasingly disconnected from it.

Cyborg Survival

The chronic postpartum depression I experienced after Nicole was born was incomprehensible to me. I knew that I had lost something essential to my survival, but it was an unnameable loss. If I had thought to compare my experience of giving birth with that of my grandmother, I would have concluded that mine benefited from all the progress that medical science had made. During my mother's lifetime birth moved from the home into the hospital, and maternal mortality fell from almost 7 per 1,000 births to about 1 per 1,000 births.[3] By the late 1970s, it was near zero (although these figures do not reflect class and race differences). If anything had gone wrong with my labor or the baby's vital signs, all the proper equipment and expertise would have been immediately available.

And yet something *had* gone terribly wrong. My absorption into the ordinary medical machinery marked the moment when I began to lose the sensation of being inside my body, a sensation I recognized only when it was gone. The progressive merging of my body with the machinery meant that, whenever and wherever the body-machine overlap occurred, I lost perception and control. Amniotomy, fetal monitor, I.V., anesthetic, episiotomy, forceps: I retreated from my body more with every intervention, until I could no longer connect my consciousness to the abject body that contained it.

I cannot romanticize my grandmother's experience of giving birth—her poor health and poverty made it a grim and dangerous

3. Judith Leavitt, *Brought to Bed: Childbearing in America, 1750–1950* (New York: Oxford University Press, 1986), p. 184; Oakley, *The Captured Womb*, p. 298.

process—but in the mythology she constructed around it, she figures as a hero who defied death and medical authority. In her birth
myth she solidified her bond with her mother and, thus fortified,
forged a new one with her daughter. My grandmother patterned her
heretical theology after the bodily connections among mothers
and daughters; accordingly, death was the labor that delivered our
spirits back into our mothers' care.

My daughter's birth provides no material for a myth of this kind.
My well-managed body labored efficiently and delivered up not
only a daughter but a new mother, a mother-cyborg, whose origin
myths must reflect her own origins in the wedding of body and machine. In Chapter 1, I discussed how Elizabeth Baines's portrayal of
Zelda, the "Frankenstein beauty" whose labor is controlled by medical machinery, reveals the disturbing implications of the woman-
as-cyborg model that Donna Haraway develops. Haraway's cyborg
myth calls for *"pleasure* in the confusion of boundaries," but I experienced my "regeneration" as the creation of dead spaces at those
points where my body joined the machine.[4] During my recovery
(my formative years as a maternal cyborg) I learned, slowly and
painfully, to compensate for the loss—forced my consciousness
back into my body, learned to sense basic bodily responses such as
hunger and fatigue. Long before forceps, cesarean section, or obstetric anesthesia, women may have experienced something akin to the
somatic disconnection that marked my birth into motherhood. It
may be that a sense of fragmentation and paralysis is a "natural"
condition for new mothers even after technology-free births, but for
me there is no separating the "natural" from the "artificial." Looking back at my own (re)genesis, I feel no nostalgia for the purity of
lost "nature." What I lost was control, not an essential "nature."

Haraway describes her manifesto as "an effort to contribute to
socialist-feminist culture and theory in a post-modernist, non-
naturalist mode and in the utopian tradition of imagining a world
without gender, which is perhaps a world without genesis, but
maybe also a world without end."[5] I search the feminist utopias

4. Donna Haraway, *Simians, Cyborgs, and Women: The Reinvention of Nature*
(New York: Routledge, 1991), p. 150.
5. Ibid., p. 150.

looking for an imaginary space the cyborg-mother can inhabit, but I am certain she will not find her place in a world without gender, genesis, or end. "A world without genesis" is a world without limits, conditions or contexts. It bears no relation to consciousness, and so it is unimaginable. Similarly, a world without gender bears no relation to any imaginable world. Marge Piercy, whose utopian vision is committed to a world without sexual domination, draws the borders of Mattapoisett along the lines of class, race, and sex. The space she clears—a space where these signs of difference no longer describe structures of dominance—arises explicitly as a response to (and is bordered on all sides by) patriarchal capitalism. If Mattapoisett lacked borders—if Piercy did not define it in relation to patriarchal capitalism—the utopia would vanish from the reader's imagination.

For the same reason, I am wary of Haraway's contention that the cyborg, whom she describes as "the illegitimate offspring of militarism and patriarchal capitalism," disrupts gendered dichotomies. First of all, the cyborg she describes has a father, which contradicts her earlier statement that the "cyborg incarnation" promises a world without origins. Haraway argues that the confusion of borders between the human and the machine which results in the cyborg implies, theoretically at least, that further confusions and fusions of categories are possible. And, as Haraway says, "illegitimate offspring are often exceedingly unfaithful to their origins."[6] But (as Haraway recognizes in her discussion of the "informatics of domination") the body of the cyborg is penetrable and appropriable. She can be divided against herself. The organic aspect of her body may reject its marriage to the machine, which is, after all, an organ of the "militarism and patriarchal capitalism" which fathered her. The machine aspect of her body owes its allegiance to that father, who continues to control it after penetration and uses it to control the organic aspect of her body. The machines that united with my organic body to "manage" my "labor" were the tools of physicians. At that time I experienced myself as outside the mother-daughter continuum that had produced me. Far from disrupting gender categories or propelling me into postpatriarchal history, the process that

6. Ibid., p. 151.

made me a cyborg-mother reproduced in me the sexual and political conditions of patriarchal capitalism.

I am dismayed to be wedded to this "father." But the "unnatural" union cannot be undone because I have no nature to return to.

Gyno Auto-Fabricus

In Joseph Fletcher's fantasy in *The Ethics of Genetic Control*, the scientist orchestrates the genesis of a new being, peeping in on its conception in a consummately primal scene:

> Biological research has shown that genes are genes; they can combine across species lines. . . . If human females reject copulation with, for example, a pongid (high primates such as chimpanzees, gorillas, and orangs) hybridization could be done by artificial insemination or by fertilization *in vitro*, followed by implantation of the embryo in a human, pongid, or artificial womb. If this was unacceptable a pongid female could be inseminated or implanted, to do the gestating. If neither method proved possible or desirable it could be done by implanting an embryo in a glass womb for artificial gestation to birth.[7]

Although the fantasy presents practical difficulties (a human-pongid mating would not produce offspring), its logic conforms to the conventions of patriarchal creation. Fletcher begins with the assertion that people and animals are much the same ("genes are genes"), but in the rest of the passage it is only women who figure as the human half of the equation. The "human females" copulating with chimpanzees to produce "hybrids" are interchangeable with "pongid females" and the artificial womb. Any or all might serve as convenient receptacles. The scientist who stages this human-animal-machine sex scene does not appear in it; he disappears into the passive construction ("hybridization could be done"). While he engineers the fusion of animal and human, man, as scientist, remains the guarantor of order. Men as a class are pointedly absent

7. Joseph Fletcher, *The Ethics of Genetic Control: Ending Reproductive Roulette* (Buffalo: Prometheus Books, 1988), p. 4; subsequent references in this chapter are cited in the text.

from the scene; Fletcher does not imagine a human male, the scientist himself perhaps, copulating with a pongid female, although it would certainly be more convenient than persuading a reluctant woman to cooperate. When all other options have been dismissed as unpleasant or unfeasible, the final and decisive solution remains: the artificial womb, a cyborg without desire, will, consciousness, or mobility.

Fletcher suggests that human-ape chimeras would prove useful; they could perform the dangerous and demeaning work that is now "shoved off on moronic and retarded individuals, the victims of uncontrolled reproduction" (pp. 172–73). Having asserted that our society would be improved if no mentally retarded people were born, Fletcher then proposes that scientists create "parahumans" to fill their jobs, a class of beings created specifically to be exploited. In addition to beings of low intelligence, Fletcher imagines that we could create people with "tremendous" brain power by growing them in artificial wombs (p. 75). Among the arguments Fletcher puts forward for using the artificial womb, one he traces back to "the so-called vaginal politics of the women's liberation," is that women should not have to bear full responsibility for reproduction: "In any case women are not baby machines" (p. 5). If women didn't have to have babies, they could be people rather than "machines."

Nancy Chodorow's theory of the reproduction of mothering cannot explain the "test-tube woman," the cyborg-mother who has no experience of original mother-daughter unity on which to found a maternal personality. Haraway's utopian cyborg—the cyborg with no origins, no mother, no gender, and no pretensions to "organic wholeness"—takes no part in a feminist theory of women's development that refers itself to the masculinist psychoanalytic drama of separation from the mother. Haraway identifies "one route to having less stake in masculine autonomy" as the "plot" in which women "have less selfhood, weaker individuation, more fusion to the oral, to Mother." But she prefers another route, one that "passes through women and other present-tense, illegitimate cyborgs, not of Woman born, who refuse the ideological resources of victimization so as to have a real life."[8] The cyborg Haraway mythologizes in

8. Haraway, *Simians, Cyborgs, and Women*, p. 177.

her essay, originally written in 1985, bypasses mothers, Oedipal complexes, and the doomed quest for psychic holism. It is an updated, sophisticated version of the utopian citizen Shulamith Firestone dreamed of in 1969, when she advocated that women refuse reproductive victimization and insist on artificial reproduction, for only then could women have a "real life."

I cannot find a place for the cyborg-mother in Haraway's myth (this figure is, in fact, specifically denied, since cyborgs have no gender and no origins; they are "not of woman born"). But there are other mythic routes that lead away from a masculinist, unitary identity. Cyborg or chimeric mothers have an important place in some feminist speculative fiction. I examine two narratives, Suzy McKee Charnas's *Motherlines* (1978) and Octavia E. Butler's *Xenogenesis* trilogy.[9] A group of illegitimate cyborgs, cut off from the control of their creators, initiates Charnas's separatist feminist utopia. Charnas's myth suggests that reproductive technologies, appropriated from a gutted patriarchy and stripped of ideologies of dominance, might be used to initiate a new race of women with a uniquely gynocratic history. Butler's *Xenogenesis* series represents a firm break with the 1970s tradition of feminist utopias, of which Charnas was a part. Although Butler's Great Mother, Lilith, pressed into reproductive service by smoothly manipulative aliens, is also a founder of a new race, the result is not a separatist utopia but a complex, multigendered society in which boundaries based on species, race, sex, and sentience are breached to open the way for exotic pleasures and seductive forms of domination. In the fiction of both Charnas and Butler, the cyborg-mother survives and even thrives— but stripped of the innocence, the potential for victimization, that Haraway identifies as an obstacle to living a "real life."

The Riding Women of Charnas's *Motherlines* are the descendants of experimental subjects who outwitted "government men," who used the women in genetic research. A worldwide "wasting," similar to the environmental and political disasters that motivated the

9. Octavia E. Butler, *Dawn* (New York: Warner Books, 1987); *Adulthood Rites* (New York: Popular Library, 1988); and *Imago* (New York: Popular Library, 1989). In *Motherlines*, Charnas begins the novel's standard disclaimer ("any resemblance to actual persons, living or dead, is purely coincidental") with regret that "this book is, alas, a fantasy."

cloning project in Kate Wilhelm's *Where Late the Sweet Birds Sang*, drove scientists to investigate alternative modes of reproduction. The foremothers of the Riding Women were altered in the laboratory to reproduce parthenogenetically. One of the Riding Women, a black woman named Nenisi, explains the basics to a new arrival, Alldera: "Our seed, when ripe, will start growing without merging with male seed because it already has its full load of traits from the mother. The lab men used a certain fluid to start this growth. So do we."[10]

The "certain fluid" was horse semen—readily available from another group of "lab animals." But whereas the government men used artificial insemination, the women, once free, reject the reproductive technology and much of the genetic knowledge they had gained from the government's "information machines." Instead, they teach their daughters to breed horses for transportation, food, sport, and mating. They define themselves as Riding Women, and their lives are merged into the lives of their animals.

This, then, is Fletcher's fantasy turned about: the scientist is indeed absent from the scene he dreamt of, but he no longer directs the proceedings or benefits by them. Instead, the animal and the woman have entered into a pleasurable and mutually beneficial alliance that renders the scientist *de trop*. *Motherlines* suggests that men and women interpret the border-shattering hybrid of human-animal-machine in gender-specific ways. Whereas men ally themselves with the machine and treat the animal-woman chimera as an ignoble servant, women ally themselves with the animal and reject the machine as tainted with masculinity, a strategy that limits their transformative potential. Although the Riding Women have created a society superior to that of the men, both societies are vulnerable because of their inability to accept a blurring of the borders between the human/animal and the machine. Their refusal amounts to a total rejection of the other sex. The men fail to achieve a separatist utopia like that of the Riding Women because they continue to subjugate women (as animals) for reproduction, sexual service, and other forms of labor. The Riding Women, by contrast, reproduce themselves and live in harmony with their animals.

10. Charnas, *Motherlines*, p. 61.

Among the Riding Women there is a distrust of all technological innovation. Even when a group of fems, women slaves, escaped from the dissolving patriarchy, try to show them new ways of protecting food supplies from predators, the Riding Women consider this a breach of the natural order of their lives. They think of themselves as merged with the land and animals in an inevitable cycle of death and renewal, and they often refer to the "pattern" that ties them to the land and excludes all other people. Generation after generation they repeat the lives of their mothers, whom they resemble precisely. Anything that might disturb that cycle—that might cause, in effect, a social mutation—creates conflict. They make decisions by working laboriously toward consensus. But consensus does not mean they all agree, only that individuals who disagree are so tightly bound to the community that they have little choice but to submit to the will of the others.

The Riding Women, like Russ's "four J's" and Wilhelm's clone siblings, continually experience the internal tension between "community and autonomy" which Ann Ferguson identified as characteristic of American society.[11] But the "twisted braid" of cultural and physical dimensions that formed the multiple bodies and psyches of Russ's four J's is unraveled in *Motherlines*. As the title implies, there is no confusion of identities for a Riding Woman but rather a pure line of descent that guarantees her place in the pattern.

The free fems have no place in this closed system. When they learn to ride horses and try to join the women's community, the Riding Women barely tolerate them, and many see the fems' arrival as a rift in the pattern. A Riding Woman who is irritated by the fem she has taken as a lover wonders: "If I killed a fem, if she had a spirit, where would it go? It couldn't rise to the spirit country above the clouds and rejoin its Motherline because it has no real Motherline." Another woman, moved to rage by a fem's claiming to own a horse, stops herself from killing the fem by remembering: "I am never alone. . . . My line and my kindred and our ways are always with me. If I killed now, I would not be a woman. I would be responsible to no one, solitary, worthless. I would be like this fem."[12]

11. Ferguson, *Blood at the Root*, p. 228.
12. Charnas, *Motherlines*, pp. 185, 191.

Her loyalty is not to her mother but to her Motherline. The children of the Riding Women, like those of Whileaway, are discouraged from bonding with their biological mothers. To prevent mothers and daughters from experiencing themselves as merged, a special danger considering they share the same genetic pattern, they are separated early. Women mother in groups, forming an ad hoc family until the child is old enough to wander off and join the "childpack." Once in the childpack, girls lose sight of their "sharemothers" completely and bond only with others of their generation. The women take turns leaving out food for the children, but otherwise they do not interfere. The fittest of the girls survive. If a girl survives until menarche, she is ejected from the childpack and her sharemothers reintroduce themselves, give her a name, and initiate the new woman into their society.

As in other separatist utopias, the women's society forms itself in resistance to men and "masculine" values. Their distrust of most technology, a skepticism that affects every facet of their lives, is a direct response to the origins of machinery in a masculinist culture. Much of the women's energy is spent in remaining separate from other cultures. They share little more than mutual suspicion with the free fems, who, unlike the Riding Women, still think hierarchically, love jealously, and value material goods—all flaws resulting from their upbringing in a masculinist culture.

The men of the Holdfast, remnants of the powerful patriarchy that preceded the Wasting, pose another threat to the Riding Women. The women watch for signs of men vigilantly, and kill them on sight whenever hunters or explorers venture out of their city-fortress. To Riding Women men exist only as targets and as history. Male culture spawned the women, and continues to apply pressure at the borders of their community. The men's society, however, seems to be dying out—destroyed by men's fear of nature (woman) and their efforts to isolate and control nature (woman) with material and social technologies. Charnas does not rely on their threat to propel her narrative. Instead, she focuses on a free fem, Alldera, who is taken into the women's camp when she escapes from men. Alldera is pregnant when the women find her, and soon gives birth to a girl who, some of the women hope, will grow up to start a new

Motherline to replace those that have died out. Before she gives birth, the Riding Women feed Alldera on their milk, and they nurse the baby as well in the uncertain hope that she will one day be able to reproduce herself.

The Riding Women are cyborgs who have renounced their technological aspect. The fems continually look for any means, spiritual and technological, that would allow them to reproduce, but there is nothing left of the science that produced the Riding Women. The women's nomadic life and their determination to prevent mother-daughter bonding create very harsh conditions for their older children, among whom the mortality rate is high. Not only for practical reasons, but because they recognize a need for diversity, some Riding Women are interested in starting new Motherlines, but their foremothers long ago abandoned the technology that would have permitted them to create new lines among the free fems. Their insistence on purity and consistency and their rejection of anything that might be associated with masculinist culture threaten their existence. If the patriarchy self-destructs by dissociating from the natural world, the Riding Women's future is in doubt because they dissociate from their own technology. Having rejected their origins in the machinery of patriarchy, they are forever divided against themselves.

Critics of reproductive technologies that could theoretically be used to breed selectively for race, intelligence, or sex fear that engineered human beings would lose their individuality. Embryos with slightly or severely disabling genetic abnormalities would never develop to full term. Physicians and psychologists would screen potential parents, as they do in current *in vitro* fertilization (IVF) programs, for genetic abnormalities, homosexuality, unconventional life-styles, alcoholism, mental illness, and history of abuse. Selection and screening could, potentially, add strength to class systems by sorting out those who could afford to pay to endow their fetus with all the advantages from those who, for lack of means, would have to depend on random gene mixing or forgo children altogether. Some proponents of the new eugenics have favored preventing "undesirable" people from reproducing. In the early 1960s Francis Crick and a group of eminent scientists got together to discuss mandatory childlessness for the masses and the licensing of certain desirable women to bear (genetically engineered) children.[13] The scheme is extravagant, but it is not out of line with more recent fantasies, such as the dream of a "superbaby" expressed in 1981 by the leader of an Australian IVF team, or even the more tentative approach of two researchers who ask, "Should we allow ourselves to remain at the mercy of genetic accident and blind evolution when we have before us the prospect of acquiring supremacy over the very forces that have created us?"[14]

Becoming our own creators (overlooking for the moment the chill of the term "supremacy" in our post-Hitler world and the question of who "we" are) means accepting the fusion of human and machine, since only through an intimate coupling with highly advanced technologies could we hope to gain control over the genetic "forces that have created us." Haraway, speaking to a different audience about a different "us," asserts that the cyborg is not concerned with supremacy.

> To be One is to be autonomous, to be powerful, to be God; but to be One is to be an illusion. . . . Yet to be other is to be multiple, without clear boundary, frayed, insubstantial. One is too few, but two are too many.
>
> High-tech culture challenges these dualisms in intriguing ways. It is not clear who makes and who is made in the relation between the human and machine."[15]

Scientists' efforts to master human evolution with high technologies might result, paradoxically, in the loss of mastery—which was always an illusion anyway. The cyborg has no anxiety about divisions, or the disruption of divisions, between self and other. The Chodorovian analysis of feminine personality, with its emphasis on the struggle between maternal symbiosis and masculine separation, loses meaning for the cyborg. So does the tension between

13. Corea, *The Mother Machine*, pp. 28–29. See also Kevles, *In the Name of Eugenics*, p. 263.

14. Peter Singer and Deanne Wells, *Making Babies: The New Science and Ethics of Conception* (New York: Charles Scribner's Sons, 1985), p. 158.

15. Haraway, *Simians, Cyborgs, and Women*, p. 177.

community and autonomy which Ferguson identifies as a definitive American trait. And with these go hierarchical thinking, and the concept of ownership.

A fully cybernetic society could not be grounded in the principle of separatism. The suspicion and disgust the Riding Women in *Motherlines* have of anything different, anything that might change the set pattern of their lives, prevents them from becoming fully integrated into their world and their bodies. Octavia Butler, in her *Xenogenesis* series of the 1980s, offers a very different view of the merging of species and technology. The Oankali, aliens who travel the universe in a huge womblike living ship, salvage a few humans from their dying Earth following an environmental holocaust similar to those that assaulted Earth in the novels of Piercy, Wilhelm, and Russ. Although Butler shares this convention with the writers of the previous decade, and although she continues to be concerned with the conflicts and pleasures of the individual-community relation, in her vision, separatism, whether based on gender, species, or race, is a very poor survival strategy. Attracted rather than repelled by difference, the Oankali work according to a principle of assimilationism rather than separatism. The Oankali send Jdhaya, an alien diplomat, to make contact with Lilith, the African American woman who will, they hope, help them found a new species. Jdhaya must first help Lilith overcome her disgust of his gray, tentacled body. When he speaks of trading genetic material with humans, Lilith is immediately wary, but he assures her that he is not talking about mating: "We do what you would call genetic engineering. We know you had begun to do it yourselves a little, but it's foreign to you. We do it naturally. We *must* do it. It renews us, enables us to survive as an evolving species instead of specializing ourselves into extinction or stagnation."[16]

The implied criticism of human genes suggests that the Oankali suffer from the same paternalistic desire to set right humanity's evolutionary missteps which guides the western eugenics movement. The Oankali, however, have the science to make it happen. Jdahya is not completely candid with Lilith, since the Oankali plan for "naturally" engineering a new species does involve sexual con-

16. Butler, *Dawn*, p. 41.

tact between the species. He is reticent because he understands and appreciates Lilith's difference from him. Although humans, anxious about preserving their purity, do not "trade" genetic material with animals, and many even avoid sexual mating with other races, the Oankali are biologically driven to such trades. Jdahya explains that they "carry the drive to do this in a minuscule cell within a cell."[17] Similarly, the human disgust for difference, as well as the tendency to dominate, is written into human genes. The humans' combination of intelligence and hierarchical thinking is the genetically determined handicap that drove them to self-destruction. This argument is similar to one advanced by Edward O. Wilson, the eminent sociobiologist, who maintained that many human behaviors, such as aggression, xenophobia, and genocide, might have genetic origins.[18]

Lilith, who is initially horrified by the prospect of "Medusa children" with "nests of night crawlers for eyes and ears," is eventually taken in by the Oankali's manipulations, literally seduced by the sexual pleasure they offer and by her own determination to survive. An ooloi, a gender-neutral alien who mixes others' genes within its body to create embryos, eventually impregnates Lilith with an embryo whose genetic material derives from Lilith, her dead human lover, and the ooloi's two Oankali mates. This will be her daughter, the ooloi assures her, but she will "be better than either of us."[19] Their children will be able to regenerate limbs and make many other physical changes, and they will not have the humans' suicidal tendency to make war. Lilith's futile protest that "they won't be human. . . . You can't understand, but that *is* what matters"[20] makes no difference, for she has no choice in the matter. Furthermore, her resistance is meaningless, since the Oankali have already made the humans sterile. From the Oankali point of view, Lilith's desire for species survival—for another chance at a separatist community—is evidence of her genetic "handicap."

Lilith's stalemate with the Oankali is even more disturbing

17. Ibid.
18. See Kevles, *In the Name of Eugenics*, p. 275.
19. Butler, *Dawn*, p. 263.
20. Ibid., p. 263.

when considered in relation to the history of the reproductive oppression of black women. Angela Davis, in an essay on the blindness of the white women's reproductive rights movement to its own racist history, points out that Margaret Sanger embraced the racist ideology of the eugenics movement, defining " 'the chief issue of birth control' as 'more children from the fit, less from the unfit.' "[21] The Oankali's insistence that humans are genetically flawed and should not reproduce themselves is a species-based eugenic argument similar to arguments promoted in the race-based American eugenics movement of the nineteenth and twentieth centuries.[22] However, as in Marge Piercy's *Woman on the Edge of Time*, in the *Xenogenesis* series the woman whose reproductive rights are abrogated is a woman of color. Lilith bears many children who carry some portion of her genetic material, but she performs this reproductive labor under duress and in the service of the Oankali's evolutionary plans. Lilith is the involuntary surrogate mother for those who consider themselves her betters. The Oankali's use of Lilith recalls black women's reproductive oppression under slavery as well as the contemporary surrogacy industry.

Davis notes that in 1939 the Birth Control Federation of American planned to recruit black ministers to help persuade blacks to use birth control. Margaret Sanger wrote in a letter that the federation did not "want word to go out that we want to exterminate the Negro population and the minister is the man who can straighten out that idea if it ever occurs to any of their more rebellious members." Neither Davis nor her source, Linda Gordon, is clear about whether Sanger meant they secretly wanted to use the birth control program to exterminate blacks, or whether they did not want the black community to get the wrong idea about their intentions.[23] In

21. Angela Davis, "Racism, Birth Control, and Reproductive Rights," in *Women, Race, and Class* (New York: Random House, 1981), pp. 213–14.

22. For instance, Daniel Kevles reports that Charles Davenport, a turn-of-the-century biologist who believed that people of different national origins were "biologically different races," promoted "negative eugenics," or the prevention of reproduction among the "unfit." Kevles, *In the Name of Eugenics*, pp. 46–47.

23. Davis, "Racism," p. 215. Davis's source is Linda Gordon, *Woman's Body, Woman's Right: A Social History of Birth Control in America* (New York: Grossman Publishers, 1976), pp. 332–33.

either case, the racism of the birth control movement and the concerns of the black community are clear from Sanger's comment.

The Oankali decide to use Lilith for a similar purpose. Once she is superficially reconciled to her new life and bonded with an ooloi, the Oankali assign her the task of preparing a group of humans to cooperate with the Oankali evolutionary program. Lilith agrees, but hopes to betray the Oankali by helping the humans escape the bondage that awaits them. Her plan fails, but Lilith renews her determination to help other humans to freedom: "If she were lost, others did not have to be. Humanity did not have to be."[24] Nevertheless, resisters, or humans who refuse the gene trade, consider Lilith a betrayer who "sold first herself, then Humanity."[25]

The Oankali would never recognize their control of humans as a form of slavery; they are incapable of the hierarchical thinking that produces the human urge to subjugate the alien. Rather, they reason that the humans' genetic defects meant they were doomed as a species. Humanity can survive only if it evolves, rapidly and radically, through gene trading. The nuclear holocaust that nearly wiped out humanity supports the Oankali perspective, and the irrational and violent behavior of many of the humans (especially men) suggests that the fatal genetic flaw is continually working to destroy its host.

It is not possible to locate absolute villains and victims in *Dawn*. The Oankali are incapable of race hatred; they are "xenophilic" rather than "xenophobic." There is no malice in their oppression of humans. Passionate assimilationists, they control Lilith and other humans by absorbing them into their community. The Oankali enslave humans with pleasure and use anesthesia rather than chains to restrain the rebellious. When they are finally convinced that only a few humans are assimilable, they permit the others to return to Earth alone—and sterile. Davis identifies genocide as one of the prime motivations for sterilization and birth control programs aimed at people of color in the United States. Lilith's human lover Joseph draws an analogy between their captors' (or rescuers') plans and eugenics programs, speculating on what Hitler might

24. Butler, *Dawn*, p. 264.
25. Butler, *Adulthood Rites*, p. 48.

have accomplished if he had had the technology for genetic engineering.[26] The shadow of genocide looms over Butler's narrative, and the novel's implications for our own racially divided society should not be overlooked. But among the trilogy's most radical propositions is that racism and our concern for species purity (our disgust, for instance, at the idea of mixing our genes with those of apes) are related human flaws deriving from our genetic makeup.

Since she does not share the Oankali ability to read DNA, Lilith must accept that she will never know herself or her species as well as the Oankali know her. She becomes their sardonic apologist, implicated in her own bondage. When her ooloi tells her that he has made her pregnant against her expressed wishes because this is what she really needs, Lilith has no basis for refuting the ooloi's explanation. The child she will have is a construct, empty of the tragic human flaw. She will have no purely human children because, as her ooloi explains, "We wouldn't dare trust you to raise them. You would be kept only for breeding—like nonsentient animals."[27] Lilith, the sentient animal, goes on having construct babies almost endlessly. Caught in the web of her complex family, Lilith becomes more accepting of the fate the Oankalis have engineered for her. After the first novel in the series, Lilith's role is reduced to bearing, nursing, and worrying about her many children. Once she is a mother, her story comes to an end, and she serves as a minor character in her children's narratives in the later novels.

Adulthood Rites focuses on her first son, Akin, a human-Oankali construct who is a dangerous experiment from the Oankali point of view. Akin shares many genetically determined traits with human males, who, according to the genetic wisdom of the Oankali, are especially dangerous because of their propensity to violence. Less disturbing genetically determined characteristics are their distaste for monogamy (they grow bored with one woman) and their tendency to wander (family life means little to them). Lilith is made pregnant with Akin at her request after she feels she has had enough daughters.

With Butler, the gender-based personality structures that Chodo-

26. Butler, *Dawn*, p. 150.
27. Butler, *Adulthood Rites*, p. 10.

row identifies are stripped of their cultural component and hard-wired into every cell in the human body. Women have a talent for connection and a desire to settle down that destines them to mother. Men, by contrast, strive for separation, wandering from woman to woman in order to broadcast their seed. This characteristic cannot be weeded out in human-born male constructs, so while humanity gives way to chimeras and cyborgs, its bipolar sexual structure survives intact.

Complementing Butler's affirmation of genetic sexual difference is her preservation of heterosexuality.[28] Butler introduces a third term, the nonsexed ooloi, into the sexual and reproductive equation, but rather than upsetting the gendered dichotomies that reinforce heterosexuality and the sexual division of labor, the ooloi functions as a greatly enhanced husband/father/physician. The union of Lilith and the ooloi does not take us beyond gender, or out of patriarchal history. Although the ooloi contributes nothing of its own matter to its children, it determines their form and initiates their development, as the father does in Platonic reproductive theory. The ooloi is the paternal scientist (the IVF researcher is its closest modern analogue) who has at last taken his place in the primal scene, manipulating the genetic code according to some model the mother cannot understand. It penetrates Lilith sexually, but its sexual organ goes deeper than a man's penis, piercing her to her true "core," the DNA that determines her nature. Its intense desire for contact with the alien humans is both scientific and sexual. It has achieved what researchers in genetic engineering are looking for: "supremacy over the very forces that have created us."

28. Haraway objects to the lack of alternative sexualities in the *Xenogenesis* series on the grounds that Butler has left "too much of the sacred image of the same" intact and failed to provide "the different genders that could emerge from another embodiment of resistance to compulsory heterosexual reproductive politics." Donna Haraway, *Primate Visions: Gender, Race, and Nature in the World of Modern Science* (New York: Routledge, 1989), p. 380.

Conclusion:
The Original Test-Tube Woman

It seems we may find our common ancestry, our common mother, in a test tube. In 1987 geneticists from the University of California at Berkeley and the University of Hawaii published a paper in *Nature* relating a startling connection they had uncovered between mitochondrial DNA and evolution. (Mitochondria are organelles that generate energy in cells. Mitochondrial DNA does not participate in the mixing of genes in sexual reproduction, and so it is inherited only through the mother.) They reported that samples of mitochondrial DNA drawn from 147 people of varying races and geographic locations "stem from one woman who is postulated to have lived about 200,000 years ago."[1]

Michael Brown, a science reporter, produced a book titled *The Search for Eve,* in which he relates the sometimes vicious debate that has sprung up among paleoanthropologists and geneticists about the mitochondrial mother of us all. Perhaps more interesting than the saga of scientific rivalries, however, are Brown's attempts to visualize Eve's body and environment. Brown opens by narrating

1. Rebecca Cann, Mark Stoneking, and Allan Wilson, "Mitochondrial DNA and Human Evolution," *Nature* 325.6099 (1987): 31–36.

the daring hunting feats of a tribe of early men, and then follows them home to meet the elder, the male tribal leader, who "exchanged vowels with a woman who passed by with a small parade of children." This is Eve, who is "highly respected by the men, not only because of her prodigious childbearing but because of her meticulous care of them."[2] Brown views "that incredible woman" in various scenes, such as nursing an infant, watching for leopards, and surrounding her hut with thorns to keep the wild beasts away from her miraculous progeny.

No one can say what color she was. The races as we know them would not yet have existed. But Allan Wilson, one of the researchers who traced her DNA to her distant descendants, thinks she was "a member of the archaic *sapiens* species, and was not yet an anatomically modern human."[3] Brown describes the "disappointment" of her being an archaic: "She would have been a brute. Her brows would still have had the unsightly thick ridge. Her head would have been rather low and sloped, with not much of a forehead to caress—and no chin. She would have smelled like a goat. And if she got mad, she may have whacked Adam over the head with a hand ax."[4] This is not Eve but Lilith, Adam's uncooperative first wife. She is the early counterpart of Butler's Lilith, who, in spite of her many genetic flaws, possessed traits worthy to be passed on to a dramatically new and "improved" species. She puts to shame our treasured regard for racial and species purity. Racial, geographic, religious differences all disappear in her. Hers is a body fractured in countless divisions. Her original identity is lost, but an essential part of her survives the millennia, endlessly regenerating according to her original coding. This mother/animal, speaking to us in code from her test tube, mothered a new species, without the benefits of reproductive technologies or obstetric care.

Perhaps she spoke only in grunts, and yet she speaks in every cell of our bodies. Since we can only imagine her—the genes she bequeathed have nothing to say about the shape or color of her body—I like to think of her as one of the last of her archaic "species." Having

2. Michael Brown, *The Search for Eve* (New York: Harper & Row, 1990), p. 6.
3. Cited ibid., p. 195.
4. Ibid.

just given birth, she considers in some dismay her mutated daughter's bulbous forehead and chin. This new one, sadly, lacks the brow ridge that, among her mother's people, is a mark of beauty and intelligence. Perhaps the mother of us all debated whether it would be kinder to smother the malformed child. But somehow she overcomes her uneasiness at the child's difference—at least enough to help the child survive—and so sends her genes, her enduring word, tumbling down through the generations.

Eve, the "good mother," is a problematic figure in our search for origins. Tracing our origins to her body leads us back ultimately to a space-time of unimaginable sameness, where the individual merges with the collective body, and where the collective cannot be envisioned as a community with a specific racial, national, religious, or political identity. Eve's maternity is the critical juncture at which the potential for difference arises. Her body represents the miraculous original division that created family and, ultimately, community. Chodorow's "feminine personality" may well have found its mythic origin in her image. Eve overflows her corporeal boundaries to take up permanent residence in her children, who might try to forget or discredit her but will never oust her. She is a woman defined by her relationships, her identity as an individual sacrificed in the name of the (re)production of imperialism, patriarchy, capitalism. Although she serves the institutions her sons founded, she remains their "other" term, always threatening a return to undifferentiated collectivity, forever withholding the secrets contained in her prolific womb. She reminds us that, when it comes to origins, we are all incurable amnesiacs.

Elizabeth Fox-Genovese's controversial book *Feminism without Illusions: A Critique of Individualism* sets out to explore "some ways of imagining the claims of society—the collectivity—as prior to the rights of the individual, some ways of imagining and protecting the rights of the individual as social, not private, rights."[5] By placing priority on the rights of the (female) individual, she argues,

---

5. Elizabeth Fox-Genovese, *Feminism without Illusions: A Critique of Individualism* (Chapel Hill: University of North Carolina Press, 1991), p. 9; subsequent references in this chapter are cited in the text.

feminism has contributed to social atomization. Although "communities of women, grounded in the fellowship of sharing work, childbearing, recreation, religion, are as old as human history," things have changed for us, owing to the misdirection of feminism. "The path that feminism is treading leads inexorably to the final erosion of community, nor will any amount of nostalgic rhetoric be able to wish it back" (p. 53).

Given this pessimistic account of feminists' contribution to the seemingly irrevocable "erosion" of community, it is not surprising that Fox-Genovese (as she reminds the reader) "does not offer a political program" (p. 9). Nevertheless, she believes that "the best of the old values and practices may yet be reinvigorated in new form," and she calls for "a new and essentially corporatist social vision" (p. 54). *Feminism without Illusions* is, for my purposes, important less as an analysis of how feminists misuse the principle of individualism than as a demonstration of the difficulties of negotiating a theoretical or practical balance between the individual and the community.

Although Fox-Genovese may not speak for great numbers of feminists, I think her concern for the influence of "individualism" on feminism reflects a general trend. To some degree, many branches of feminism, including not only those feminisms concerned with issues of race and ethnic or cultural diversity, but also the materialist, lesbian-separatist, and white-liberal-academic-heterosexual (the branch that has, as Fox-Genovese points out, professed to speak for all women) strains, are working through the daunting question of *how* women can renegotiate their relationships within family, community, and society. Among the pleasures the feminist SF writers offer are candid advancements of political programs and the hope, however distant, that we can create a society where the rights and responsibilities of the individual would be in harmony with the needs and values of the community.[6]

Imagining and working toward such balanced communities should be one of feminism's ongoing projects, but the current politi-

6. We must, Fox-Genovese contends, "reject the siren calls of nostalgic and utopian communitarianisms," a statement that might be read as a condemnation of attempts by second-wave feminists such as Marge Piercy and Suzy McKee Charnas to imagine radically different utopian communities (ibid., p. 54).

cal climate (shadowed by the rise of the New Right) suggests it is too early for women to begin placing the claims of the community before the rights of the individual (woman). We should delay this in part because the history of women's immersion in community interests suggests that this strategy might lead to an intensification of women's oppression as productive and reproductive laborers. Feminists are already embedded within and serving the "community." In spite of its limitations, the ideal of individual freedom has provided a conceptual space in which feminists can analyze their relationship to the community and consider the possibility of a postpatriarchal society.

Having been denied the status and many of the rights of individuals for most of our history, many women focus, understandably, on obtaining the privileges (white male) individuals enjoy. Fox-Genovese criticizes the emphasis on the achievements of individual women, especially when women who accrue some privileges on the basis of their race and class claim their good fortune as a victory for the "sisterhood" of all women. This is a crucial point, but Fox-Genovese goes further, claiming that white middle-class women who achieve professional success are responsible for pushing women of color and their male partners further into poverty: "The gains reaped in the name of sisterhood frequently result in the sharpening of class lines by pushing lower-class and minority women, singly or together with their men, further down the socioeconomic scale" (p. 22). Fox-Genovese wants individual women to stop pursuing their own selfish pleasures and ambitions and to take back responsibility for maintaining community standards of morality, sexual and reproductive behavior, and family life. The example of the selfish white professional woman illustrates the problem she perceives in women's claiming individual rights: that women who compete successfully under capitalism will forget their responsibility to the larger community, and that (therefore) the vast majority of women and men of color will remain impoverished and oppressed.

Although Fox-Genovese rarely mentions women's mothering, the feminism she espouses takes a traditional maternal model as its ideal. It is as wives and mothers that women have been responsible for protecting the family from the ravages of industrial capitalism, for salvaging the souls of individual men, and for reproducing and monitoring moral standards in the new generation. Self-interest had no place in that "ideal" model, and it has little more in Fox-Genovese's reconstruction.

In Part I, I argued that the processes involved in creating a new (maternal) self during childbirth suggests that motherhood is one experience through which women (re)negotiate the terms of their subjectivity. Women in pregnancy and labor embody a community—in the most basic sense, by producing a life that brings together the genetic material of two parents, and by sharing their internal systems with a fetus. The processes women relate in narratives of birth, however, deal not only with their experiences as communal entities but also with their struggles to reestablish themselves as speaking individuals. I share Julia Kristeva's conviction that the unitary individual who remains the same over time is an illusion. As subjects-in-process, we are never wholly separated from nor merged with our mothers, children, lovers, or friends. But if a woman is to speak and act in the interests of herself, her family, and her community, she can do so only as an individual. One of the most disturbing implications of Fox-Genovese's demand that feminists give up their antisocial pursuit of individualism is that it reinstates the traditional dichotomy between the (masculine) individual and the (feminine) community.

Fox-Genovese's thesis recalls Nancy Chodorow's description of the feminine personality as "connected," and therefore potentially more sensitive than men to the needs of family and community. But Chodorow finds that women's "connectedness" becomes a major problem for women who do not separate from their mothers and (therefore) fail to develop a reasonable degree of individuality. Although I cannot agree with the universalizing tendencies of Chodorow's model, it does suggest why women might be wary of communitarian values as they are expressed in our society. The (male) individual, defined by his firm ego boundaries and sense of himself as separated, can act in the public sphere as a discrete individual capable of personal agency. By contrast (according to this same gendered model of the individual/community dichotomy), women's love and labor reproduce the community, but their absorption into the community erases them as individuals and denies them agency.

I argued in Part II that the differences between communist and capitalist economies have been ordered according to gendered terms. Communism has been decried—equivalent, in some eras, with satanism—at least in part because it seemed to represent a socioeconomic model based on motherhood. For instance, Richard Nixon vetoed the Comprehensive Child Development Act of 1971, which was designed to provide federal funds for child care. Susan Mann makes the cogent point that by "arguing that this legislation should be rejected because it sided with a 'communal approach' to childrearing over a 'family-centered approach,' Nixon subtly reinforced right-wing propaganda that day care would 'Sovietize' American children."[7] Communism has popularly been interpreted in the West as deemphasizing individual rights in favor of an inevitably oppressive "collective" will. The promise that communism would resolve alienation by restoring to workers the means of production has been read as a threat to market competition, individualism, and therefore—since men depend on women to reflect and validate them as individuals—to gender difference and the sexual division of labor. According to this thinking, families would disappear under communism, and with them the psychological processes by which we become individuals. Under communism we would never really grow up, but would be forever infantile. The state would be our (suffocating) mother, making all our decisions for us. The socioeconomic hierarchies of capitalism would be wiped out, along with the promise of order and progress, supplanted by a state resembling a vast maternal organ in which we would be lost as individuals.

Along with the fear of the consuming mother/state, however, is the (male) individual's need for his mother—his original community—to serve as the background for his pursuit of self-identity. As I argued in Part III, images of the mother in representations of fetal development identify her as environment, nurturing and constant, with no needs or desires of her own. She cannot be an individual herself and still serve to reflect and pass on the image of the individual. The fetus, as visualized by ultrasound, fetoscopy, or postabortion photography, is a figure whose incomplete formation and

7. Susan Mann, "Women's Access to Abortion and Day Care," in *Family, Economy, and State: The Social Reproduction Process under Capitalism*, ed. James Dickinson and Bob Russell (London: Croom Helm, 1986), p. 242.

dependence on the mother's body make it an evocative visual expression of our anxieties and conflicts about our own questionable status as individuals. As this scenario is played out in contemporary fetal medicine, technologies of representation make the mother a backdrop for the newly clarified image of the fetus, who now, as a conceptually if not literally complete individual, is entitled to state protection from the effects of the mother's pursuit of her own selfish sexual agendas. According to this extreme view, a woman abdicates her individual rights when she becomes pregnant. At conception the woman's body is placed in the service of the community.

In the theory and practice of medicine, psychology, and economics, mothers are often represented as nonentities, nonparticipants, environments, or functions. As obvious at this may seem, it still needs to be said: women, whether or not they become biological or social mothers, do not experience their lives and bodies in these terms. By means of feminist theory and practice that emphasizes women's claim to the status of individuals, women have tried to undo the erasure. We as women live within, and help to compose, a culture that valorizes the individual: Although we have been designated as its other term, the collective, we experience the conflicts and tensions of the individual-community relation; our theory and practice as feminists must refer to that relation.

Although Fox-Genovese reprioritizes the individual-community relation, she does not question the formulation itself. She states that feminists who argue for reproductive choice on the basis of the individual's right to privacy and for comparable worth on the basis of collective values contradict themselves (and "insult the intelligence of the American people" [p. 57]). We cannot, then, be for the individual and for the community at the same time. But this argument leads us into a dead end because it reproduces the individual/community dichotomy that Fox-Genovese opposes. Furthermore, the formulation that considers the individual as separate from her community, and positions her in conflict or accord with it, fails to take into account that communities, like "individual" subjects, are in process. The cohesive, holistic community is as much a fiction as the autonomous subject.

A similar problem arises in Fox-Genovese's argument for limiting the "right to choice." She "emphatically den[ies] that women have, or that a man has, an absolute right to the disposition of her or his body," and urges us to agree on a moment when life begins so that we can define the limits of our right to abortion (p. 10). As my discussion in Part III of technologies of fetal visualization demonstrates, our obsession with defining the individual in terms of his bodily boundaries and point of origin is an expression of our devotion to the principle of (male) individualism. The fetishization of the individual Fox-Genovese decries is a vital aspect of her desire to determine when life begins.

The problem is reflected also in Fox-Genovese's attempts to impose an either/or logic on abortion: "Either abortion entails the killing of babies or it does not." "Are we dealing with two lives or one?" Her pursuit of clarity leads her to validate attempts to "define life in the abstract," although she acknowledges that the methods of logical abstraction serve patriarchal interests: "If a rigid and abstract definition of life embodies dichotomous male thinking, it also embodies the highest standard of civilization—the greatest respect for human life in all its diversity—that human beings have been able to devise" (pp. 83–84). But respect for life-in-the-abstract does not easily translate into respect and care for those who are actually living. Mother versus fetus, individual versus community: these oppositions are essential to the process of formulating a "rigid and abstract definition of life." They pit us against one another and divide us from within.

By reproducing in her own argument the perspective she criticizes, Fox-Genovese demonstrates the difficulties of separating one's own thinking from the influences of history and community, a difficulty none of us avoids. By basing demands for unrestricted access to abortion on women's rights as individuals, feminists may have missed the opportunity to argue from a logic that more accurately reflects the diversity of women's experience of their bodies and relationships. After reflecting on my own early experience as a single mother in the late 1970s, when for a few years I barely survived without financial or emotional resources, and after considering the stressful reproductive lives of many of my friends, I am convinced that women's demand for abortion does, in fact, reflect the values and needs of the community—even of those factions that claim a "pro-life" stance. Mothers who seek abortion are abiding by the unspoken values expressed in the community's treatment of mothers and children.

Except for the rare professional woman, most single mothers (of whom many are single not by choice but because the father abandoned their relationship) find it almost impossible to provide for their children even such basic supports as food, shelter, and medical care. Ann Ferguson, pointing to significant changes in the demography of poverty, reports that between 1969 and 1978, "10,000 additional women with children fell below the poverty line. . . . In 1979 the number surged to 150,000, and was matched in 1980.[8] Efforts to pass laws in the United States providing for day care have had little success, and many existing government programs effectively exclude families with low-to-moderate incomes.[9] Many women who mother in isolation do so not because they are staunch individualists flouting the values of their community, but because they receive little practical support or emotional sustenance from their families and communities.[10]

For these reasons I believe that most women who seek abortion do so not as an expression of selfish individualism but as the result of listening carefully to the voice of their community. A high rate of abortion is a necessity in a "community" that avows its concern for life while denying the basic needs of mothers and children. In a community with safe and easily accessible birth control—in a community that, at the least, offered mothers practical support for their reproductive labor, or better yet considered parenting a community responsibility—fewer women would find it necessary to end their pregnancies.

Abstract dichotomies between mother/fetus and individual/ community are continually reproduced at multiple sites of cultural construction, including not only feminism but the theory and practice of medicine, law, and psychology. As long as we continue to think in these terms, our conflicts about our most intimate bodily and emotional relationships—conflicts that are manifested every

8. Ferguson, *Blood at the Root*, p. 173.

9. Mann, "Women's Access," p. 243.

10. By the late 1980s woman-headed households accounted for 15 percent of all households; their numbers continue to grow. Ferguson, *Blood at the Root*, p. 173.

day in families, in the physician-patient relationship, in court-rooms, and on the front lines of the abortion war—will have only limited and temporary possibilities for resolution. It may be, how-ever, that we have to keep arguing for reproductive choice on the basis of the individual's right to privacy, since that seems to be the only argument our legislative and judicial systems understand.

I have argued throughout this book that the mother-fetus rela-tionship cannot be properly thought of in terms of a contract, al-liance, or conflict between individuals, but, given the current polit-ical climate, I am prepared to reproduce in my own argument the theoretical contradictions I have criticized. I am convinced that the mother, as the speaking and acting "member" in the mother-fetus relationship, must for all practical purposes be considered a fully autonomous individual. As it is constituted in our era, the debate that pits the fetus-as-individual against the mother is irresolvable, but it is still critically important to continue negotiating the great-est possible degree of social and reproductive autonomy for women. The strong feminisms of the 1960s and 1970s created the emotional and intellectual space in which some women could renew their efforts to form communities and work toward woman-centered so-cial, spiritual, sexual, and reproductive practices. Feminists SF writers such as Charnas, Piercy, and Butler are reworking the ideal of community to suit a feminism that seeks to rupture the artificial boundaries between our bodies and our minds, machines, the land, and other forms of life. They are sensitive to conflicts between the individual and the community, but they also understand that myths of origins and the initiation of the individual must be bal-anced against a consciousness of the tensions and pleasures of shared bodies and communal lives. If we can look back on Eve as the woman who encoded in each of us a genetic history of our arrival into the bodies and social relations we now inhabit, we can also look to the myth of Eve for the transformative energy to consider how we might meet again across the barriers of gender, race, and space-time.

Bibliography

Arditti, Rita; Renate Duelli Klein; and Shelley Minden, eds. *Test-Tube Women: What Future for Motherhood?* Boston: Pandora Press, 1984.

Arms, Suzanne. *Immaculate Deception: A New Look at Women and Childbirth in America.* Boston: Houghton Mifflin, 1975.

Atwood, Margaret. *The Handmaid's Tale.* New York: Random House, 1986.

Axelson, D. "Women as Victims of Medical Experimentation." *Sage: A Scholarly Journal on Black Women* 2.2 (Fall 1985).

Baines, Elizabeth. *The Birth Machine.* London: Women's Press, 1983.

Barr, Marlene. *Alien to Femininity: Speculative Fiction and Feminist Theory.* New York: Greenwood Press, 1987.

Baruch, Elaine Hoffman. "A Womb of His Own." In *Embryos, Ethics, and Women's Rights,* ed. Elaine Hoffman Baruch, Amadeof D'Amato, and Joni Seager. New York: Haworth Press, 1988.

Baudrillard, Jean. *The Mirror of Production,* trans. Mark Poster. St. Louis: Telos Press, 1975.

Beazley, John. "Active Management of Labor." *American Journal of Obstetrics and Gynecology,* May 15, 1975.

Bernard, Jessie. *The Future of Motherhood.* New York: Dial Press, 1974.

Bleich, David. *Utopia: The Psychology of a Cultural Fantasy.* Ann Arbor: UMI Research Press, 1984.

Borruto, Franco; Manfred Hansmann; and Juri W. Wladimiroff, eds. *Fetal Ultrasonography: The Secret Prenatal Life.* New York: John Wiley & Sons, 1982.

Brown, Michael. *The Search for Eve.* New York: Harper & Row, 1990.

Butler, Judith. *Gender Trouble: Feminism and the Subversion of Identity.* New York: Routledge, 1990.

Butler, Octavia E. *Adulthood Rites.* New York: Popular Library, 1988.

———. *Dawn.* New York: Warner Books, 1987.

———. *Imago.* New York: Popular Library, 1989.

Charnas, Suzy McKee. *Motherlines.* New York: Berkeley Publishing, 1978.

Chesler, Phyllis. *With Child: A Diary of Motherhood.* New York: Thomas E. Crowell, 1979.

Chester, Laura, ed. *Cradle and All: Women Writers on Pregnancy and Birth.* Boston: Faber and Faber, 1989.

Chodorow, Nancy. *Feminism and Psychoanalytic Theory.* New Haven: Yale University Press, 1989.

———. *The Reproduction of Mothering: Psychoanalysis and the Sociology of Gender.* Berkeley: University of California Press, 1978.

Cixous, Hélène. "Laugh of the Medusa." In *Feminisms: An Anthology of Literary Theory and Criticism,* ed. Robyn Warhol and Diane Price Herndl. New Brunswick: Rutgers University Press, 1991.

Comers, Lee Sanders. "Functions of the Family under Capitalism." Pamphlet reprinted by the New York Radical Feminists.

Corea, Gena. *The Mother Machine: Reproductive Technologies from Artificial Insemination to Artificial Wombs.* New York: Perennial Library, 1985.

Coward, Rosalind, and John Ellis. *Language and Materialism: Developments in Semiology and the Theory of the Subject.* Boston: Routledge & Kegan Paul, 1977.

Davis, Angela. *Women, Race, and Class.* New York: Random House, 1981.

Davis, Elizabeth Gould. *The First Sex.* Baltimore: Penguin Books, 1971.

Davis-Floyd, Robbie. "Obstetric Training as a Rite of Passage." *Medical Anthropology Quarterly: The Anthropology of Obstetrics* 1.3 (1987).

———. "The Technological Model of Birth." *Journal of American Folklore* 100 (October–December 1987): 479–95.

Delblanc, Sven. *Homunculus: A Magic Tale,* trans. Verne Moberg. Englewood Cliffs, N.J.: Prentice-Hall, 1969.

Derricotte, Toi. *Natural Birth.* Trumansburg, N.Y.: Crossing Press, 1983.

Diagnosis and Treatment of Fetal Disorders. New York: Springer-Verlag, 1968.

Dye, Nancy Schrom. "Review Essay: History of Childbirth in America." *Signs* 6 (Autumn 1980): 97–108.

Eagleton, Terry. *Literary Theory: An Introduction.* Minneapolis: University of Minnesota Press, 1983.

Eccles, Audrey. *Obstetrics/Gynecology in Tudor and Stuart England.* London: Croom Helm, 1982.

Edwards, Robert. *Life before Birth.* London: Hutchinson, 1989.

Ehrenreich, Barbara, and Deirdre English. *150 Years of the Experts' Advice to Women.* Garden City, N.Y.: Anchor Books, 1979.

English, Deirdre. "A Bit of an Ego Trip: Becoming a Doctor." *Mother Jones* 5 (July 1980): 40.

Ferguson, Ann. *Blood at the Root: Motherhood, Sexuality, and Male Dominance.* London: Pandora Press, 1989.

The Fetus as a Patient. New York: Elsevier Science Publishing, 1984.

Figlio, K. "Sinister Medicine? A Critique of Left Approaches to Medicine." *Radical Science Journal* 9 (1979): 14–68.

Firestone, Shulamith. *The Dialectic of Sex: The Case for Feminist Revolution.* New York: Morrow Quill Paperbacks, 1971.

Fitting, Peter. " 'So We All Become Mothers': New Roles for Men in Recent Utopian Fiction." *Science Fiction Studies* 12 (1985): 156–83.

——. "The Turn from Utopia in Recent Feminist Fiction." *Feminism, Utopia, and Narrative,* ed. Libby Falk Jones and Sarah Webster Goodwin. Knoxville: University of Tennessee Press, 1990.

Fletcher, Joseph. *The Ethics of Genetic Control: Ending Reproductive Roulette.* Buffalo: Prometheus Books, 1988.

Foucault, Michel. *The Birth of the Clinic: An Archeology of Medical Perception,* trans. A. M. Sheridan Smith. New York: Vintage Books, 1973.

——. *Discipline and Punish,* trans. Alan Sheridan. New York: Vintage Books, 1979.

Fox-Genovese, Elizabeth. *Feminism without Illusions: A Critique of Individualism.* Chapel Hill: University of North Carolina Press, 1991.

Freud, Sigmund. *New Introductory Lectures: Standard Edition of the Complete Psychological Works.* Vol. 22. London: Hogarth Press, 1933.

Furuhjelm, Mirjam, et al. *A Child Is Born.* New York: Delacorte Press, 1966.

Gallop, Jane. *Thinking Through the Body.* New York: Columbia University Press, 1988.

Gearhart, Sally. *The Wanderground: Stories of the Hill Women.* Watertown, Mass.: Persephone Press, 1979.

Gerson, M., et al. "Mothering: The View from Psychological Research." *Signs* 9.3 (1984): 434–53.

Gieve, Katherine. *Balancing Acts.* London: Virago, 1989.

Gilman, Charlotte Perkins. *Herland.* New York: Pantheon Books, 1979.

Goodlin, Robert. *Care of the Fetus.* New York: Masson Publishing, 1979.

Goulianos, Joan. *By a Woman Writt.* Indianapolis: Bobbs-Merrill, 1973.

Haraway, Donna. "A Manifesto for Cyborgs: Science, Technology, and Socialist Feminism in the 1980s." *Socialist Review* (January 1985): 65–105.

——. *Primate Visions: Gender, Race, and Nature in the World of Modern Science.* New York: Routledge, 1989.

——. *Simians, Cyborgs, and Women: The Reinvention of Nature.* New York: Routledge, 1991.

Harris, Seale. *Woman's Surgeon: The Life Story of J. Marion Sims.* New York: Macmillan, 1950.

Harrison, Michael R. *The Unborn Patient: Prenatal Diagnosis and Treatment.* Orlando, Fla.: Grune & Stratton, 1984.

Hemingway, Ernest. *In Our Time.* New York: Scribners, 1925.

Hendricks, Melissa. "The Limits of Life." *Johns Hopkins Magazine* (October 1989).

Homans, Margaret. *Bearing the Word.* Chicago: University of Chicago Press, 1986.

Horney, Karen. "The Dread of Women." *International Journal of Psychoanalysis* 13 (1932): 348–50.

Hunter, William. *Anatomy of the Human Gravid Uterus* (1772).

Huxley, Aldous. *Brave New World.* New York: Perennial Library, 1989.

——. *Music at Night.* London: Chatto & Windus, 1931.

——. *The Perennial Philosophy.* New York: Harper & Bros., 1945.

Irigaray, Luce. *Speculum of the Other Woman,* trans. Gillian C. Gill. Ithaca: Cornell University Press, 1985.

——. *This Sex Which Is Not One,* trans. Catherine Porter. Ithaca: Cornell University Press, 1985.

Jacobus, Mary; Evelyn Fox Keller; and Sally Shuttleworth, eds. *Body/Politics: Women and the Discourses of Science.* New York: Routledge, 1990.

Janov, Arthur. *Imprints: The Lifelong Effects of the Birth Experience.* New York: Coward-McCann, 1983.

Jones, Libby Falk, and Sarah Webster Goodwin, eds. *Feminism, Utopia, and Narrative.* Knoxville: University of Tennessee Press, 1990.

Jordinova, Ludmilla. "Gender, Generation, and Science: William Hunter's Obstetrical Atlas." In *William Hunter and the Eighteenth-Century Medical World,* ed. W. F. Bynum and Roy Porter. London: Cambridge University Press, 1985.

——. *Sexual Visions: Images of Gender in Science and Medicine between the Eighteenth and Twentieth Centuries.* Madison: University of Wisconsin Press, 1989.

Kaback, Michael M., and Carlo Valenti, eds. *Intrauterine Fetal Visualization: A Multidisciplinary Approach.* New York: American Elsevier Publishing, 1974.

Kanter, Rosabeth Moss. "Family Organization and Sex Roles in American Communes." *Communes: Creating and Managing the Creative Life.* New York: Harper & Row, 1973.

Kevles, Daniel. *In the Name of Eugenics: Genetics and the Uses of Human Heredity.* Berkeley: University of California Press, 1985.

Kristeva, Julia. *Desire in Language,* trans. Leon Roudiez, Thomas Gora, and Alice Jardine. New York: Columbia University Press, 1980.

——. *The Kristeva Reader,* ed. Toril Moi. Oxford: Basil Blackwell, 1986.

——. *Revolution in Poetic Language,* trans. Margaret Waller. New York: Columbia University Press, 1986.

Kuhn, Annette, and AnnMarie Wolpe, eds. *Feminism and Materialism: Women and Modes of Production.* Boston: Routledge & Kegan Paul, 1978.

Lacan, Jacques. *Écrits: A Selection,* trans. Alan Sheridan. New York: W. W. Norton & Co., 1977.

Lawrence, Christopher. "Alexander Munro *Primus* and the Edinburgh Manner of Anatomy." *Bulletin of the History of Medicine* 62.2 (1988): 193–214.

Leavitt, Judith. *Brought to Bed: Childbearing in America, 1750–1950.* New York: Oxford University Press, 1986.

Leboyer, Frederick. *Birth without Violence.* New York: Alfred A. Knopf, 1975.

Lederer, Wolfgang. *The Fear of Women.* New York: Grune & Stratton, 1968.

Lessing, Doris. *A Proper Marriage.* London: Women's Press, 1983.

Le Sueur, Meridel. *The Girl.* Minneapolis: West End Press, 1978.

Lindsey, Karen. *Friends as Family.* Boston: Beacon Press, 1981.

Loudon, I. S. L. "Deaths in Childbed from the Eighteenth Century to 1935." *Medical History* 30 (1986): 1–41.

Lygre, David. *Life Manipulation.* New York: Walker and Co., 1979.

Mann, Susan. "Women's Access to Abortion and Day Care." *Family, Economy, and State: The Social Reproduction Process under Capitalism.* London: Croom Helm, 1986.

Martin, Emily. *The Woman in the Body: A Cultural Analysis of Reproduction.* Boston: Beacon Press, 1987.

Mitchell, Juliet. *Psychoanalysis and Feminism.* Harmondsworth: Penguin, 1974.

——. *Women: The Longest Revolution.* London: Virago Press, 1984.

Moi, Toril. *Sexual/Textual Politics.* New York: Methuen, 1985.

Moraga, Cherríe, and Gloria Ansaldúa, eds. *This Bridge Called My Back: Writings by Radical Women of Color.* New York: Kitchen Table–Women of Color Press, 1981.

Morrison, Toni. *Sula.* New York: New American Library, 1973.

Muller, H. J. *Out of the Night: A Biologist's View of the Future.* New York: Vanguard Press, 1935.

Muller, John P., and William J. Richardson. *Lacan and Language.* New York: International Universities Press, 1982.

Neumann, Erich. *The Great Mother: An Analysis of the Archetype.* Princeton: Princeton University Press, 1974.

Nilsson, Lennart. *A Child Is Born.* 2d ed. New York: Bantam, 1990.

Nin, Anaïs. *Under a Glass Bell.* Chicago: Swallow Press, 1948.

Nye, Andrea. "Woman Clothed with the Sun: Julia Kristeva and the Escape from/to Language." *Signs* 12.4 (1987): 664–86.

O'Brien, Mary. *The Politics of Reproduction.* London: Routledge & Kegan Paul, 1981.

O'Driscoll, Kieran, and Declan Meagher. *Active Management of Labour.* 2d ed. London: Ballière Tindall, 1986.

Pachter, Henry M. *Paracelsus.* New York: Henry Schuman, 1951.

Petchesky, Rosalind. "Fetal Images: The Power of Visual Culture in the Politics of Reproduction." *Feminist Studies* 13.2 (Summer 1987).

Piercy, Marge. "Active in Time and History." In *Paths of Resistance.* Boston: Houghton Mifflin, 1989.

———. *Woman on the Edge of Time.* New York: Fawcett Crest, 1976.

Plath, Sylvia. *The Bell Jar.* New York: Harper & Row, 1971.

Pratt, Linda Ray. "Woman Writer in the CP: The Case of Meridel Le Sueur." *Women's Studies* 14.3 (1988): 247–64.

Ramsey, Paul. *Fabricated Man.* New Haven: Yale University Press, 1970.

Rich, Adrienne. *Of Woman Born: Motherhood as Experience and Institution* New York: W. W. Norton, 1976.

Rocker, I., ed. *Fetoscopy.* New York: Elsevier, 1981.

Rorvik, David. *In His Image: The Cloning of a Man.* New York: J. B. Lippincott, 1978.

Rossi, A. S. "A Biosocial Perspective on Parenting." *Daedalus* 106.2 (1977): 1–31.

Rothman, Barbara Katz. *In Labor: Women and Power in the Birthplace.* New York: W. W. Norton, 1982.

Russ, Joanna. *The Female Man.* Boston: Gregg Press, 1975.

———. *We Who Are About To . . .* London: Women's Press, 1975.

Scully, Diana. *Men Who Control Women's Health: The Miseducation of Obstetrician-Gynecologists.* Boston: Houghton Mifflin, 1980.

Singer, Peter, and Deanne Wells. *Making Babies: The New Science and Ethics of Conception.* New York: Charles Scribner's Sons, 1985.

Spallone, Patricia. *Beyond Conception: The New Politics of Reproduction.* London: MacMillan Education, 1989.

Spector, Judith A. "Science Fiction and the Sex War: A Womb of One's Own." *Literature and Psychology* 31.1 (1981): 21–32.

Speert, Harold. *Obstetrics and Gynecology in America: A History.* Baltimore: Waverly Press, 1980.

Stack, Carol. *All Our Kin.* New York: Harper & Row, 1970.

Suleiman, Susan Rubin. "Writing and Motherhood." In *The (M)other Tongue: Essays in Feminist Psychoanalytic Interpretation,* ed. Claire Kahane, Shirley Nelson Garner, and Madelon Sprengnether. Ithaca: Cornell University Press, 1985.

Tiptree, James, Jr. [Alice Sheldon]. "Houston, Houston Do You Read?" In

Nebula Winners Twelve, ed. Gordon Dickson. New York: Harper & Row, 1976.

Trebilcot, Joyce. *Mothering: Essays in Feminist Theory.* Totowa, N.J.: Rowman & Allanheld, 1984.

Volpe, E. Peter. *The Patient in the Womb.* Macon, Ga.: Mercer, 1984.

Wilhelm, Kate. *Where Late the Sweet Birds Sang.* New York: Harper & Row, 1976.

Williams, William Carlos. *The Doctor Stories.* New York: New Directions Books, 1984.

Wolfe, Gary. *Science Fiction Dialogues.* Chicago: Academy Chicago, 1982.

Young, Bruce K., ed. *The Patient within the Patient.* New York: Liss, 1985.

Zaretsky, Eli. *Capitalism, the Family, and Personal Life.* New York: Harper Colophon Books, 1976.

Index

259